IN OUR INFANCY

Other books by Helen Corke

The Class Books of World History, Oxford University Press, 1927–30
A Book of Ancient Peoples, The Clarendon Press, 1931
A Book of Modern Peoples, The Clarendon Press, 1933
Lawrence and 'Apocalypse', Heinemann, 1933
Neutral Ground (novel), Arthur Barker, 1933
Towards Economic Freedom, Methuen, 1937
D. H. Lawrence's 'Princess': A Memoir of Jessie Chambers, The Merle Press, 1951
Songs of Autumn (poems), Texas University Press, 1960
D. H. Lawrence: the Croydon Years, Texas University Press, 1964
The Light of Common Day: An Autobiography Part II (in preparation)

TELEVISION: In July 1967, Helen Corke was interviewed by Malcolm Muggeridge (whom she once taught) for the BBC-2 colour television programme, *D. H. Lawrence and The Dreaming Woman*, produced by Don Taylor. The programme – which also included a dramatised excerpt from *The Trespasser*, filmed in the Isle of Wight, and readings of several of Lawrence's 'Helen' poems – was first shown in June 1968 and was repeated in July 1969 and August 1973; the script appeared in *The Listener* in July 1968.

IN OUR INFANCY

An Autobiography
Part I: 1882–1912

HELEN CORKE

CAMBRIDGE UNIVERSITY PRESS

CAMBRIDGE

LONDON · NEW YORK · MELBOURNE

Published by the Syndics of the Cambridge University Press
The Pitt Building, Trumpington Street, Cambridge CB2 1RP
Bentley House, 200 Euston Road, London NW1 2DB
32 East 57th Street, New York, N.Y.10022, USA
296 Beaconsfield Parade, Middle Park, Melbourne 3206, Australia

Library of Congress Catalogue Card Number: 74-31799

ISBN: 0 521 20797 5

First published 1975

Printed in Great Britain
at the University Printing House, Cambridge
(Euan Phillips, University Printer)

CONTENTS

PLATES

PREFACE

That life should produce some clear evidence of sanity, purpose, intention – it is the ultimate human demand. Perhaps this was never more obvious than during the autumn of the year 1939. Those of us who had, during the First World War, learned to discount the false heroics that ushered it in, faced the coming of a Second World War without illusions.

September 1939 found me in the neighbourhood of the old Suffolk town, Bury St Edmunds, and, like it, disposed rather to look back into the past than to contemplate a dubious future. The ancient borough drowsed in sunshine these calm autumn days, re-living its memories – so would I... Beyond my window the East Anglian slopes carried a gently waving harvest of Suffolk wheat...I looked down through the harvest of my own half-century and found its major impressions clear and sharp, even retaining their original emotional atmosphere. Was I wasting my time, or might the record induce readers to recall half-forgotten but still significant knowledge of their own childhood and youth? Mothers and teachers tend to accept what passes as 'child-study' at second hand, from professional psychiatrists' primers and lectures. Or they treat children as dwarf adults, and dress their minds, as in former centuries their bodies, in clothing of adult design, unsuited to the new identity. Put aside on my recall to school organisation during the war, the autobiography was resumed during the '50s and the first writing finished in '68. Incidental revision has taken place since. The present volume covers the first half of the story, dealing with the period 1882–1912.

I found it fascinating to trace, in the being that was myself in the teens and twenties, the interplay of heredity and environment. How fully might a new, strong influence, personal or eventual, defeat or subdue the legacy of my fore-fathers? What part of my birth-right persisted within the ultimate, adult Me? Biographers tend to present their subject as a unique creation, owing little or nothing to the myriad influences, exerted both by human contacts and the movement of events, throughout the formative years.

In my own case, from birth to the seventh year, the direct personal influence of my parents was unchallenged, and the quiet, ordered monotony of my days varied only by those attacks of childish illness – bronchitis, whooping cough, chicken-pox – then regarded as the normal experience of children. Influence exerted by book-images began with the Bible, and these remained paramount throughout early childhood, though illustrated toy books, featuring animals, were not lacking...From my father I inherited a love of poetry and literature of marked rhythm, from my mother some sense of drama. My father kept, regularly, a personal diary, but I am not aware that any other member of his family wrote, either as a hobby or professionally. I began to write stories for children in my ninth year, but these were shown to no one, and the last, a long story of school life, set in a romantic old castle, was discounted and destroyed in my early teens. During subsequent years until the end of teacher training, my pen was harnessed to the required syllabus. The entry of David Herbert Lawrence into my world gave a new impetus to my urge to write. He came to Croydon as qualified teacher in the autumn of 1908.

It may be interesting to compare the conditions of D.H.L.'s infancy with my own. He was born in 1885, three years later than me – his age being that of the elder of my two brothers. The conditions of his childhood in the small mining town of Eastwood, Nottinghamshire, were remote from mine. The relations between his father and mother were unhappy to a degree – a stormy household expressed its affections and antagonisms freely. There was no assurance of peace, since the mother marshalled the feelings of the children against the father. But outside the home there were similarities between D.H.L.'s early influences and my own. In both cases religious teaching stemmed from the nonconformity of a Congregational chapel and Sunday School – its moral code based on the Jewish Ten Commandments and the Christian Sermon on the Mount. To that code both our communities did lip service. Similarly, we absorbed and loved the rich symbolism of the Bible in its Authorised Version.

Jessie Chambers, in her *Personal Record*, lists books – mostly obtained from local public libraries – which Lawrence had absorbed and wished her to read. Many of them were favourites of mine, to be classed among early influences. They included Longfellow's poems, Tennyson's *Maud* and *Morte d'Arthur*, *Locksley Hall* and *The Lady of Shalott*, Scott's novels, Rider Haggard's *She*, and Dickens – especially *Oliver Twist* and *David Copperfield*. American writers on both our lists began with Louisa M. Alcott and Fenimore Cooper. Two writers whose influence on me was deep and lasting, Olive Schreiner and George MacDonald, seem to have had no place during Lawrence's formative years. Roughly, the lists apply to our more influential reading between the ages of seven and seventeen. There is one further coincidence – for each of us a performance of *Hamlet* provided the entry to the study of tragedy.

But if we consider the immediate influence of local environment upon awakening minds we may expect to find a marked difference between D.H.L.'s development and my own. For him in childhood the life of a small mining community within which the coal industry was replacing farm and woodland by a broken countryside, its personnel the dependent servants of an underworld. For me the warmer, non-industrial, easier-going South of wealthy land-owners served by obsequious Trade. Does one, it has been asked, grow grapes from thorns or figs from thistles? Or, one might enquire, can the soil in which the pine-cone germinates nourish also the palm?

Yet, despite differences, and on account of common sympathies, David Lawrence and I walked together for the three years 1909–12.

This autobiography is not a collection of interesting or amusing episodes and anecdotes. It is a record, as faithful as memory can render it, of the awakening of an individual consciousness, and its subsequent expansion through a long life. It is an attempt to indicate the supreme miracle – the mystery of being and becoming, of perceiving and knowing, repeated with infinite variations in every generation. For those who remain blind to the wonder of this miracle the record can have no interest, and for the professional psychologist accustomed only to the measuring rod of the classic theories it will perhaps prove disappointing. The writer offers it, in all humility, to the reader who is content to explore, as impersonally and patiently as the geologist his rock levels, a small tract within the vast field of human sensory and extra-sensory awareness.

H.C.

February 1975

ACKNOWLEDGMENTS

The author and publisher would like to thank the following for giving their permission to use copyright material: Laurence Pollinger Ltd and the Estate of the late Mrs Frieda Lawrence for letters by D. H. Lawrence in extract or entirety not previously published; Laurence Pollinger Ltd, the Estate of the late Mrs Frieda Lawrence and William Heinemann Ltd for extracts from letters in *The Collected Letters of D. H. Lawrence*, edited by Harry T. Moore (1962); these same extracts from *The Collected Letters of D. H. Lawrence*, edited by Harry T. Moore, Copyright © 1962 by Angelo Ravagli and C. M. Weekley, Executors of the Estate of Frieda Lawrence Ravagli. All rights reserved. Reprinted by permission of the Viking Press Inc.; Mrs V. Wood for extracts from letters by Jessie Chambers previously published in Helen Corke's *D. H. Lawrence's 'Princess': A Memoir of Jessie Chambers* (The Merle Press, 1951), and for the photograph of Jessie Chambers; David Garnett for the photograph of D. H. Lawrence.

FOREWORD

My paternal grandfather was a Kentishman; his ancestors, according to the record of the tombstones in St Nicholas's churchyard, Sevenoaks, had lived in that parish for at least two centuries. The family was prolific, church-going, and strongly Liberal. It provided the town with several generations of tradesmen and minor professionals, more or less closely interested in the affairs of the great house Knole, seat of the Sackville West family. Its prevailing respectability was varied by a strain of vagabondage which appeared in Great-uncle Ben, cattle driver, and Uncle Gambier, whose inherent distaste for work no privation could overcome. Another variant was my Great-uncle Silas, who in the 1850s entertained the local lecture societies with experiments illustrating the possibilities of electric power.

At the date of his marriage my grandfather was a salesman in the local drapery store. But he discovered a vocation for religious ministry, and in his thirties became a London City missioner, and struggled through lean years on less than a curate's stipend. Ultimately he came back to Sevenoaks and the drapery; my little grandmother, whose brown eyes, netted ringlets and gentle voice disguised her strength of character, probably decreed his return in the interests of her five sons.

My father, Alfred, born 1851, was the second son. From boyhood he was a book-lover with a placid imagination. He respected his father and accepted, with certain private reservations, the ruling of his mother; his conformity hid a questing spirit, with a measure of independence. It enabled him, as a young man, to escape from his mother's dominance. The other sons all remained unmarried; three

1

of them lived in the home of their parents until the death of my grandmother at the age of eighty.

During his City mission years my grandfather and his family lived in Southgate, where the sons attended a private school. It enjoyed considerable endowments, and must have been an exceptionally good school for its period and kind; my father spoke of it always with enthusiasm. He owed to it his fine, firm, copper-plate handwriting, his introduction to English literature, and his imaginative appreciation of history and geography. It opened a door to the newly popularised wonders of invention, and stressed the opportunities of youth. It awarded prizes generously, and as his 'leaving prize' Alfred received a heavy volume in cloth gilt entitled *The Steady Aim*, containing biographies of successful and famous men, all of whom had begun life at the bottom of Fortune's ladder. He read and re-read the book and kept it to the end of his life. I believe it fixed upon his mind the impression received at school – the road might be hard and the journey long, but integrity and determination led ultimately to fame and competence. Those who failed must recognise in themselves the cause of failure, some personal weakness or lack of driving power.

When the family returned to Sevenoaks, Alfred was ready for apprenticeship. His mother was well satisfied that he should begin work in the old-established country business to which my grandfather had reverted. But Alfred preferred the grocery department – his undisclosed reason being that it was agreeable to contemplate and dispense food; meals at home left the growing lad hungry. Apprenticeship over, he entered as salesman a similar store in the village of Seal, where he lodged in his employer's house. At that time he was a solitary youth, who loved the natural beauty of the Kentish countryside, and all that territory of romance opened to him by the English poets. His employer, a strict Baptist, forbade the reading within his house of any book but the Bible, with which Alfred was already very familiar, so most of the young man's reading was done out of doors. While on his routine order and delivery rounds he absorbed the whole of Scott's novels; the old horse, ambling along the lanes he knew so well, needed no direction, and the driver could safely pursue his book. A local chess club was the resort of many winter evenings... Probably the most exciting event of the period was, for him, the invention of the 'bone-shaker'; Alfred managed to acquire one of these primitive cycles, and gained a temporary notoriety by riding it on the high road where this descended steep River Hill.

My mother, born in 1849 at Hastings, was descended from a family of fishermen, who had beached their tough little boats upon its shingle generations before the first row of holiday-makers' boarding houses faced the sea. Adopted in infancy by a childless aunt and uncle living in Newhaven, she remained with them until her marriage at the age of twenty-nine. Her uncle's position as harbour-master was locally important, and established her as belonging to the well-to-do of the townlet. Except for an occasional shopping excursion to Lewes or Brighton its boundaries marked the limit of her orbit for the twenty-eight years. It provided her with ample scope for emotional satisfactions; she had a single-minded interest in the lives of her relations and friends, and these included the majority of the Newhaven people. Drama, and indeed melodrama, for which she had a strong instinct, she found in plenty; it was her absorption. She had no intellectual preoccupations, and accepted without question the religion, logic, social values and moral standards of her circle. Her school was the private establishment of Ma'am Brown, which specialised in sloping, Victorian hand-writing, ornate cross-stitch samplers, and the use of the back-board for the correction of round shoulders; she left school at the age of twelve, and was thereafter thoroughly tutored in household management by her aunt. My great-aunt Harriet was tiny and frail, but of exceeding tenacity. Her demands upon her niece increased with the years, but this my mother did not resent; the feeling that she was indispensable added, indeed, to her *amour propre*. Louisa's aunt played a prominent part on that stage where Louisa saw herself moving, a desired and necessary presence, a dominant influence, among the lives of her friends.

She was good-looking, with a white skin and smooth dark hair, parted on the crown of her head and drawn back from an oval face. She had large grey eyes and well-shaped nose and chin. She dressed in current fashion – her dress allowance being generous – and Sundays saw her at chapel in ribboned and frilled silks and satins of chaste grey or mauve, with fine kid lavender gloves carefully pressed and scented. She never missed a wedding, a funeral, or any other social function, and her unfailing interest in the jots and tittles of their lives endeared her to the women of the neighbourhood. The small-town life of the sixties and seventies was probably less narrow than it seems to us with our greater radius: it provided both opportunity and depth lacking today. If my mother needed anything essential to a full and satisfying existence she was unaware of it. A Puritan self-sufficiency permeated place and period. Familiarity with the literal text of the Bible was literary education enough; in comparison with the profundities of the Book, history, geography and the arts were ornamental frippery. Louisa's geographical range did not exceed a dozen miles, but she had only to step into the street to lift her eyes to the hills, 'from whence cometh my help', and to remember 'my help cometh from the Lord which hath made heaven and earth'. Standing by the window of her bedroom at the top of the tall house in Meeching Road she watched with fascination 'this great and wide sea, wherein are things creeping innumerable, both small and great beasts' – but she took no pleasure in the sight, associating it rather with those tragic family tales of seafaring misadventure common in the local records.

From early childhood she attended regularly the morning and evening services of the ugly Congregational chapel, without a suspicion of its ugliness. She was there, singing in the choir when a young Kentishman, recently installed at Bannister's general store, first saw her, and fell romantically in love. It happened when Louisa, at the age of twenty-seven, was concerned with a difficult decision. Suitors had not been lacking, but they were not welcomed by Aunt Harriet, whose will was set to keep her adopted daughter. Louisa was none the less determined not to be stigmatised as 'old maid', and at this point was seriously considering the proposal of a distant cousin with banking employment in Paris. She was not in love with John, and did not want to go to Paris, but the marriage would be a good match, and her age was beginning to worry her. This dilemma made my father's wooing easier; he was not only an eligible and desirable young man with whom she readily fell in love – he was also a way of escape from the frightening possibility of going abroad. They could marry and settle in Newhaven.

But the shy suitor with the grey–blue eyes that were difficult to meet, revealed, on better knowledge, other intentions. Alfred was easy-going on the surface, and generally acceded to Louisa's wishes, but on one point the steadiness of his aim was unquestionable – he meant to be his own master. He would have a shop of his own, and soon. To open one in Newhaven, in opposition to Bannister's, would be courting failure. He saved, he sought; he even, when the chance to buy came, borrowed a small sum from the harbour-master, who liked him. In 1879 he married Louisa and took her to the Sussex village of West Hoathley, where he had bought the goodwill of an old-established general store from its retiring owner. At the moment the village had an inflated population; Irish navvies were laying a railway line to connect Horsham and Lewes, and lived in huts there. The men spent freely at the store, and within a year Alfred had repaid his debt.

Louisa enjoyed the excitement of her wedding (which her aunt refused to attend) and the seven-mile drive from

Lewes to her new home. The month was June, the weather perfect, and the little old house picturesque. But before the end of the autumn she was moping like a plant transferred to unsuitable soil. Small-town society had provided the spring and zest of her life; she pined for the give and take, the gossip, and the sense of 'belonging' which had always been hers, at home in Newhaven. West Hoathley was foreign, and its few, scattered inhabitants strangers. They did not want her or she them. Most West Hoathley folk were church-goers; the minority who attended the little chapel looked upon Louisa's Sunday dresses with patent disapproval. The small, low-ceilinged house was dim and depressing. She was accustomed to spending most of her days indoors; the Sunday constitutional to the sea-front or up the Brighton road had sufficed her and her friends for exercise. Neither reading nor sewing gave her any pleasure. After her first conception she clung to her husband pathetically; he seemed so resourceful, so cheerful, so strong. He did his best to help and divert her; lured her out for short walks, tried to interest her in the flower-garden – she knew nothing of flower cultivation – and read aloud to her from his shelf of classics, trying Dickens, Scott, Shakespeare and Milton. (The volume of Milton was indeed her own – he had given it to her in their courtship days, when impressed by the facility with which she quoted dramatic passages from the Bible, learned through years of Sunday repetition. She never read Milton herself.) Alfred even, though reluctantly, permitted her to serve behind the counter of the shop, since she brightened after chat with customers. He looked forward to the child's birth with mixed hope and dread. It was born in the autumn of 1880, and lived only a few hours.

An easy-going cousin, bringing the small-town atmosphere, came to stay, and probably saved my mother's reason; but she was still white-faced, with eyes 'like two burnt holes in a blanket' when the great snowfall of January 1881 descended upon Sussex. West Hoathley was literally buried, and my father dug his way out of the cottage with great difficulty. When the road to Lewes was cleared sufficiently to permit transport of food and mails, a wall of snow ten feet high stood on either side of the single track. Louisa was terrified, and this experience completed her revulsion against the place; she declared she should die if they did not leave it. Alfred, unused to hysteria, felt that the matter was serious, and promised to lose no time in finding another home.

They were living in Hastings when I was born, in January 1882. My conjecture is that Louisa's homing instinct, her longing for the friendly, communal life, was the decisive factor in taking them there. Hastings was not Newhaven; the former was, indeed, a strange town to my mother, whose link with it had been broken in infancy. But relations, near and distant, lived there, and in particular one cousin widowed under tragic circumstances, left to support a young family; to her story Louisa responded with her usual affinity for drama. Louisa and Cousin Helen became intimate friends, and after Cousin Helen I was named.

I think my father made the move to Hastings against his better judgment and in denial of his own wishes. The shop available was one of a row of cheap new shops, built with a view to catching the custom of the increasing number of summer holiday visitors. Its trade was of the predatory, competitive kind. Hitherto competition had entered little into his business dealings; his experience had been gained in stores of the old, firmly established country type, where a regular turnover ensured a moderate unfluctuating profit average over the years. Such a business he had hoped to maintain in West Hoathley. But my mother's happiness came first. Then, and thereafter until the end of his life, he would place her interests before his own.

Three years of married life were more than enough to convince him that the woman to whom he had called did not exist. He had dressed Louisa in the stuff of his romantic imagination. The real woman who had answered his call should never suffer on that account. It was no fault of hers, he felt, that she did not share his deeper experiences, or his tastes, and could not follow the ways of his mind. Henceforward he accepted her limitations and made no further attempts to extend her range. His early tendency to inhibit his thoughts and feelings became a fixed habit; all that was foreign to his wife's mind was denied expression.

During the winter of 1882, while maternity absorbed my mother, my father sat by his desk in the empty shop, reading Gibbon, whom he had discovered in the local library. *The Decline and Fall of the Roman Empire* diverted his mind from the declining condition of his fortunes. He read attentively, with little interruption from customers. Against the great stage of the decaying Empire his own affairs shrank to manageable proportions, and he was able to make a decision. He must leave Hastings as soon as the summer trade had temporarily fortified his small savings...The decision held, though, when it had to be communicated to Louisa, the proportions of the matter expanded to fill earth and heaven. She cried bitterly, and her mouth set in tight and tragic lines. Nevertheless, when she realised that the compulsion was one of income, her practical sense accepted the situation. Hence, at the age of eighteen months, I was taken to live in Tunbridge Wells, and the impressions registered in my mind for the first eight years of my life (with the single exception of the earliest recorded) are connected with that town and Newhaven.

INFANCY

An inexperienced, exasperated mother; an unsatisfied, fretful, wailing infant. Born in January, the first three months of my life were spent almost wholly indoors. The later introduction to an out-of-door world may have had its terrors. 'You screamed when I took you out', observed my mother in after years. 'Yes, I wanted to leave you on somebody's doorstep and run away.'

Mercifully we forget the sensations of our first year.

On a June day in 1883, Albert Edward, Prince of Wales, with his wife the Princess Alexandra, came to Hastings for the purpose of opening the public park thereafter known by the Princess's name. My earliest clear recollection is associated with this event. The blank sheet of memory suddenly records a picture of coloured bunting fluttering overhead against a blue sky, and the motion of my perambulator as I am wheeled along a street. Nothing so sharp succeeds this impression until I am in my third year.

An infant's perception relates partly to its inherited background of shadowy, racial images, potent but confused, and its instant apprehension of a momentary experience, pleasant, painful or terrifying. Having no conception of past or future, no power of comparison or scale of values, it is completely engulfed in the sensation of the moment...My second recollection is of my mother's dangling ear-rings, which attract my attention as I sit on her lap. I reach up and grasp one; she cries out and slaps my hand smartly. My world dissolves, and I am lost in a vortex of pain, fear and confusion.

A swing hangs from the kitchen ceiling – my parents' solution to the problem of a ubiquitous toddler. Its painted wooden bars enclose a cushioned seat. Penned into

9

the swing I spend the mornings, and wet-weather afternoons, gently swaying between my heaven and earth, the
ceiling and floor of the kitchen. Behind me there is a door;
those who enter give the swing a little push. Immediately
after breakfast I am lifted into the swing, together with my
rag doll Molly, a toy rubber cat, and a picture book. The
rhymes in the book have been read to me often; I know
them by heart, but my interest is sustained; I turn the pages
slowly, note the pictures of well-beloved farm animals, and
recite the appropriate rhyme for each page. At the end of
this ritual the book is dropped on the floor, and my senses
begin to register the familiar scene and sounds. In the
ceiling I trace, as if with my fingers, the curves of the big
black hooks and rings from which the swing hangs. Before
me is a large window, its lower panes covered with netting,
but the upper ones framing a picture of the sky, blue or
cloudy, into which I gaze with a curious pleasure...The
warmth of the kitchen comes from my right side, where the
fire glows and the boiler bubbles and the kettle steams on
the hob. If I glance over my right shoulder I may see
Mamma by the white-topped table, ironing, or making
pastry, or laying a meal. Much of the morning, while
Mamma is busy in bedrooms, I am alone, but not lonely;
when people are absent the little voices of friendly Things
greet me – purr of kettle, crackle of fire, creak of door and
of the ropes of my swing, and other tiny sounds I cannot
identify, pricking out of the silence. I am afraid of the voice
of Wind, but he is shut outside the house.

Up to three years of age

(By the age of three there was considerable fixation of my
impressions, and some classification. Those below were
definite.)
    Sky and earth. Above and below; upper and under.
    Day and night. Light and darkness; waking and sleep.

Day associated with a wide range of forms, colours, sounds; night with a shadowy bedroom, the candle flame staring from its shelf; bed, and dreams.

Pain. That which compels me to identify myself with my body.

Pleasure. The feeling associated with eating or drinking nice things; with warmth; with the touch of the cat's fur; with being in the open air.

Fear. The immediate reaction to everything strange. Aroused especially by the sound of high wind or heavy rain at night, strangely shaped shadows, odd noises.

My general classification of experiences and things – nice or nasty; with the corresponding but less precise variant – good or bad.

Impressions: four to seven years of age (1886–9)

Family. Mamma, Papa, small brother Arthur, baby Frank, the maid Emily. Grandparents, aunts, uncles; occasionally one or more of these may come to the house, stay a day or two, and depart into the unknown. With my mother's cousin, known to me as Aunt Bec, comes my third cousin, Evelyn; she is taller than me, and a year older. All other people are strangers, and I gather that strangers, on the whole, are not to be trusted; some particularly bad ones, called gipsies, steal children.

People are grown-ups and children; the distinction is not merely one of size and age; the grown-ups are in some undefined way different from *me*. I may play with stranger children only on my birthday, when Mamma gives a party, and I am placed at the end of the tea-table to pour out tea for guests from a small china tea-pot; after tea there are noisy games in which the grown-ups lead. It is so unfamiliar that I am glad when the party is over.

Satisfactions. Nice things to eat; pictures of animals in books; the smooth completeness of a big, shining red rubber ball – *mine*; sunlight and warmth; running with my hoop. Also the feeling when I do something which Papa and Mamma approve.

Illness. A dark tide of discomfort, submerging known things; bed in day-time. The obvious impotence of Mamma and Papa to change these conditions. The ceiling, and a flat grey sky pressing against the window. Fear of the strange man they call 'doctor'.

Reading. At four years I am encouraged to spell out words from a primer. '*Now get up. It is six. Is it six? Yes it is, and the dew is off.*' This conversation is accompanied by an illustration showing a mother standing by a child's cot, pointing to a spiky rising sun. The thought of being able to get up at six is most alluring, but the presence of the mother by the child's bedside makes the incident incredible. Eight o'clock is getting-up time, and I must not move from my bed until Emily comes to dress me. I form an impression that the early morning hours, when the sun can be expected to shine as it seldom does on me, hold something of wonder and magic that I am denied.

There are week-day books and Sunday books. I know by heart the rhymes and pictures of the week-day books. Mamma reads to me the Sunday books, until at six years I can read them for myself. They comprise three story books, described on their title pages as *The Earliest Religious Teaching the Infant Mind is Capable of Receiving.* From these I learn that inside me I have a Soul. The suggestion is vague, and unpleasant. What is it like? How can it live shut up in the dark? My little dog, the book continues, has no soul, and will turn to dust when it dies. I have no little dog, but visualise the family cat changing to a small dust heap such as road-sweepers leave about...The books have pictures; the green-covered third primer tells the story of Jesus, shown as a long-haired, long-frocked being, walking ahead of some half-dozen other frocked men with shorter hair and rounder faces. The text reiterates phrases about how kind is Jesus, and how I ought to love him! I cannot feel that I do; at most I *like* him, as shown in the picture presenting him with a child seated on his lap. It seems that he lived on the earth long ago, and then went to heaven, which is above the sky. A later chapter of the book tells me that Jesus may come down again at any time, surrounded by winged women angels, who will blow trumpets. Awful things will then happen – the sun will turn black and the moon blood-red, and the stars fall and set the world on fire.

Mamma does not read to me the passages telling of these horrors, but when I am six and read the book for myself they fascinate and terrify me. The prospect is far too appalling to mention to anyone. I try to forget it. But the moon, rising red–gold out of the mist, becomes a dreadful portent. When I see it, through the eastern window, like a red-lined face peeping between the trees, my throat contracts and my heart thumps; I sit down on my stool in the kitchen, averting my face from the window, and gabble over nursery rhymes. Try to think of Goosey Gander, or Mary Quite Contrary in her garden with the silver bells. When bed-time comes, and I must pass the uncurtained landing window, I shut my eyes – yet blink through the lashes to see if the moonlight is blood-red on the stairs. Immense relief – the pallid, ordinary gleam is lying like water on the carpet.

Papa will sometimes read to me from one of his own books. I learn to chant the old rhythm of the Northern peoples used by Longfellow in his *Hiawatha*.

> In his lodge beside a river,
> Close beside a frozen river,
> Sat an old man, sad and lonely,
> White his hair was as the snow-drift,
> Dull and low his fire was burning,
> And the old man shook and trembled
> Folded in his Waubewyon,
> In his tattered white-skin wrapper,
> Hearing nothing but the tempest
> As it roared along the forest,
> Seeing nothing but the snowstorm,
> As it whirled and hissed and drifted.

I pore over the accompanying illustration. It is all there – the wigwam under the gaunt, wind-torn tree, looming through the snowfall, the old man stretching thin hands towards his little fire. Papa, reading of the old Indian, becomes queerly identified with him, and the story itself with something of mine partaking of feeling and memory, but beyond the consciousness of both. The small, thick volume of Longfellow, with ornate cover design and shining gilt edges takes a higher place in my scale of book values than the toy and story books, though these have larger print and coloured pictures.

Imagination. Everything in my world puts on personality when I contemplate it. The chair can think and feel, the ball wants or does not want to run away. The dolls, Amy, Molly, Sylvia; my hoop Strong-troller and hoop-stick Stick-switcher are my companions – better company than the small, stolid brother with whom I must play simple games that I find very dull. Hoop and stick talk to each other, and I to them – and yet, when I *think* about it, I am fully aware that all the talking and feeling that seems to be theirs really goes on inside *me*. The dolls are good, but Amy is stupid. Strong-troller is sometimes a bad hoop, and runs away from me. I tell Stick-switcher to beat him nearly to death when he is caught; Stick-switcher beats until Strong-troller cries for mercy.

The human personnel of my sixth year. Mamma, dominant, always at hand; Papa, not so omnipresent, less insistent, beneficent and wise; the ultimate authority. Three-year-old Arthur, with clumsy, stout legs, and fat, pink, pouched cheeks. The maid, Emily, whose *tightness* impresses me unpleasantly; her hair sticks tightly to her head on either side of a white parting, and its ends are twisted into a tight little bob behind; she is buttoned tightly into her black dress. Other members of the family make occasional appearances – a thin, black-clothed, white-haired grandfather, two grandmothers with wrinkled faces, the one having brown eyes, and small brown curls dipping on either side of her face from beneath a black net cap, the other with grey hair smoothed under a white stiff lace cap, and having a small mole, out of which grows a single hair, beside her mouth. Gold watch-chains dangle from both grandmothers, and rings are on their fingers; these are features of Mamma also, on Sundays. Of the incidental aunts and uncles who make rare appearances, Aunt Bec, the mother of my cousin Evelyn, is predominant. I like Aunt Bec, whose presence makes one feel safe and quiet, much more so than that of Mamma. Of all my world, my cousin Evelyn is nearest me in the sense of mutual understanding, except that she cries frequently, and without shame – this is strange to me. She has golden-brown ringlets and large grey eyes; is a year older than me, and writes me tiny, carefully pencilled notes on midget sweet-scented notepaper, which come enclosed in Aunt Bec's letters to Mamma.

We have a tall house on a hillside. It is built over a shop; the shop door opening on to the street. The kitchen is behind the shop; the sitting-room above it, and there are two stories of bedrooms. I sleep in a gabled room on the third floor. Bed-time is horrid; one shivers on leaving the warm kitchen, where one has been bathed by the fire, to travel up the flights of steep, dark stairs, preceded by Emily carrying a candle. On the opposite side of the top landing is the store-room, where sacks of peas and beans, and tall sugar loaves in blue wrappings are kept till wanted in the shop. There is an empty iron bedstead, and a bicycle with one big and one little wheel. The bicycle is Papa's, but Mamma does not like him to ride it, and it seldom goes out. In the day-time Arthur and I may play in this room – or we sit on the bean sacks by the window, feeling high up, looking over the tree-tops in the wood beyond a disused sand-pit. But at night the room is always dark, pitch-dark, and I, lying awake among the shadows of my own room (the pea-point of a tiny lamp flame burns on the wash-stand) hear rustling and movement, mysterious, coming from behind its closed door...I seldom sleep at once. Out in the night the trains puff along up the High Brooms gradient. My ears strain to the first puff and rumble, my heart beats to the acceleration of sound...louder...louder...not quite so loud ...passing away. I *will* go to sleep before the next train comes...One Sunday evening Papa and Grandpa talk of a recent earthquake in the news – I carry the idea of a new terror to bed. Earthquake is some great dreadful thing that has killed people – might a train bring it? I fancy the sound of the wheels getting louder, louder than usual. Surely it is making my bed shake! I cower under the clothes – will the walls of the house fall like those of Jericho when the priests blew with the trumpets (this is pictured in the Sunday book)! I hear, suddenly, the knocking of my heart; the train rumble recedes.

One may go into the shop when there are no customers on the far side of the red-brown counter; should a customer enter, one sits down under the counter on a sack of dried peas, close to the fruit and sugar drawers. One drawer holds lump cubes, representing the final stage of the tall sugar loaves that stand in the store-room – the sugar-chopper waits at one end of the counter. Another drawer has soft, sandy-brown sugar, a third raisins, a fourth currants. Behind the counter rise the shining black and silver tea canisters on their out-of-reach shelves; under them small drawers containing queer things – black, strong-smelling stuff, cinnamon in broken sticks. All this territory is intimate; that beyond the counter is alien land, reached only when the counter flap is raised and its spring door opened. Cold it is beyond the counter, and unprotected; the outer door of the shop is open to strangers, their dogs, and the wind that rushes down the hillside. Sacks of potatoes stand by the door, strings of pegs and onions dangle from the ceiling; on the shelf by the counter are boxes of hard, chalky, pink and white sweets I am told not to eat. Up and down the length of boarded floor, always rather dirty, one may run for exercise on wet days when the shop is empty. The top window shelf bears a row of mineral water bottles, which make one feel happy when the light shines through them, amber, rose, and deep green, late on a winter afternoon.

Certain other things evoke a haunting happiness – dripping water, saffron piles of cloud floating in blue heaven, a bell ringing in the distance, shop-window lights gleaming on wet pavements...It is by their atmosphere that these things are perceived, sensitively, not with any intellectual grasp of their properties and characteristics. By keen, direct, sensuous reaction, of which adult memory holds but a vague suggestion, I am aware of the external world. Things attract or repel with greater or lesser intensity. Of the vanished apprehensions belonging to early childhood I can dimly recall one only in later life – a strange excitement evoked by the first hoar frosts of autumn, by the glitter of frost upon fallen leaves in my path and the nip of frosty morning air.

Pity awakens during my sixth year. For tiny, thin-legged birds, bright-eyed and fearful, that hop to the window-sill, hoping for crumbs. For little brown mouse, quivering behind bars of trap, mouse panting in an ecstasy of fear, brought down from the store-room in the trap. Mamma says she is glad it is caught, and it will be given to the cat. Cats were made to catch mice. She will not let me take it into the yard and set it free. The small, lonely mouse, all alone to itself and its fear! I offer it some crumbs, but dare not rescue it, and choke down the lump in my throat, hating my mother's power and my own helplessness.

Two boys live in the neighbouring house. I see them often, playing in their garden. One day they call to me, 'Come and see the execution!' I run to the fence. They have a frog, tied by its legs, stretched on the palings; it struggles, feebly waving its queer little hands. I beg them to let it go, but one boy takes his pen-knife and slits the frog's belly. I rush indoors, sobbing wildly, and ignoring Mamma, burst into the shop, demanding that Papa shall kill those boys. Mamma follows, and both parents try to soothe me – yes, the boys were cruel, and Papa will speak to their father about it, but I must *not* make that dreadful noise! I repeat my demand and continue repeating it until through the paroxysm of pity I am able to sense the extreme annoyance of Mamma, and the shocked face of Papa. Then comes the realisation, slow but abiding, that to them my loss of self-control is a worse matter than the cruelty of the boys.

I see morning sunshine only through the window of the sitting-room or the shop; but on fine afternoons we go out with Emily, Arthur in his 'pram' and I with a hand on its handlebars. The longest walk is to the Common, where I may bowl my hoop. The Common is a vast place of grassy hollows, tree-crowned hills, and grey rocks standing in soft, loose sand. Other children dig in the sand with wooden spades, making sand pies in their pails. We are forbidden to touch the sand, which Mamma says is dirty; we linger on the grass edge, envying, but feeling superior. More attractive to me are the rock slabs, with the slippery little paths running up and over them. I should love to climb, slowly and carefully, to the top. The Common stretches away to the rim of the sky, all ups and downs, dark patches, light patches; distant hills and trees lean against heaven. One hill – which, I wonder – we sing about in chapel:

> There is a green hill far away,
> Without a city wall.

(But why should the hymn remark thus upon the absence of a city wall?)

More often our walk is only a dawdle along shopping streets. On afternoons in winter Emily will make a detour to a particular town square not otherwise visited, for the purpose of showing us 'the 'lectric light'. On a high mast a rare globe of brilliant white light swings, making a little sizzling noise. A marvellous light, seen nowhere else in the town. It is Tunbridge Wells's first experiment in electric lighting. We all three stare at it with fascination.

From the background of my sixth and seventh years, memory seizes upon a jumble of unrelated data. But happenings and impressions are not recalled by a simple intellectual process; they return each with its proper clothing of emotional atmosphere, the composition of which is dominated by fear, the subconscious and irrational dread of the Unknown. These years are illumined only by passing gleams of sunshine, and steadied by a transitory and unstable confidence. Yet Arthur and I were ostensibly happy children. Why not? According to the standards of the time we were amply and suitably fed and clothed, our home was comfortable, our parents duly affectionate towards each other and to us. There was not even (at this period) any financial worry to trouble the domestic scene; the Tunbridge Wells trade was increasing and my father had opened a branch shop in Tonbridge. If we were quiet, 'good' children, playing the serious games my imagination prompted, that was how it should be! Arthur's 'good' moods alternated with fits of temper, when he would stamp his feet and roar an incoherent challenge to the arbiters of his being, but I was fully under the influence of my father's long practised and now habitual principle of inhibition.

Jubilee Day (1887) is initiated by the presentation to us, at breakfast, of white and gilt mugs, bearing a coloured portrait of Queen Victoria, who looks like a stouter edition of my maternal grandmother. The closed shop indicates a sort of Sunday; not so the appearance of the Common, where we all repair after mid-day dinner. Its slope facing the town is transformed into the 'fair' of my nursery books.

A great tent, many small tents, stalls displaying bright china and glittering jewellery, boat-like swings, and a roundabout. We walk from stall to stall, Mamma, unusually gay, leading, Papa following patiently, but we buy nothing, and Mamma explains to me that these attractive stalls sell nothing but rubbish. Papa places coppers on a table and bowls a hard ball at cokernuts placed on sticks set in the ground; presently I have a queer, hairy cokernut to carry. No, I may *not* go on the swings, *nor* on the roundabouts; Mamma is very definite about this. It is hot and noisy among the stalls, and the cokernut is heavy, so I propose to take it to Arthur, left in the pram with Emily in charge, on the near-by path. Picking my way among the tent-pegs I think suddenly of Abram, to whom came the three angels as he sat at his tent door 'in the heat of the day'. It would be a fine white tent, that of Abram, but most of these are dirty-looking. Higher up the slope a white tent stands out plainly in the sunlight, and involuntarily I turn in that direction, half expecting to see a patriarch with a long white beard sitting on a camp stool at its entrance. But there is no Abram, only a swarthy, bright-eyed woman who stares at me; she does not suggest Sarah, and I feel sure she is a gipsy. And with a flash of panic I realise that I am lost. Papa, Mamma and Emily with the pram are all out of sight, and I am alone in a wicked gipsy world. The panic overwhelms me; I turn and run blindly away from the white tent, run until I fall headlong, my foot caught in a looped rope. Kindly people hurry to help me up, all trying to assure me that Mamma will be here directly – and indeed it cannot be more than ten minutes before she and Papa appear, and the scolding begins. Mamma also has been frightened – which is why she scolds so hard – but Papa smiles, ties his handkerchief round my scratched knee and carries me to the pram. Musing over this experience I feel that Mamma was justified in calling my conduct wrong and silly, though she need not have repeated this so many times. I did the wrong thing because I was afraid. (This was the first of many experiences leading ultimately to the conclusion 'there is nothing to be afraid of except fear'.)

Christmas Day 1887. Grandpa and Grandma Corke, from Sevenoaks, are staying with us. Grandpa is black but for his white hair and stiff white collar, the corners of which turn up where those of Papa turn down. He wears a long, black shiny cloth coat that reaches his knees. He is very kind, and likes reading to me; also he lets the cat lie on his lap, and now and then strokes its fur with a thin, white hand. Grandma is small and round. Her special peculiarity is the black silk net worn on her head; it keeps in place two dark brown ringlets on either side of her forehead. She has a very soft voice (except when Grandpa drops his handkerchief or forgets something, when she says, sharply, 'Now! now! father!'). Mamma seems to keep the grandparents in the sitting-room which is used by the family only on Sundays; they sit in armchairs on either side of the fire.

It is nearly tea-time on this long Christmas Day. Emily has just placed the lamp on the centre of the big, round table which at two o'clock held the turkey and plum pudding, and now carries a substantial tea, with Mamma's Christmas cake and special oswego biscuits. Papa has drawn the heavy, dark-red curtains over the window, and shut out the blue twilight and a yellow star that might be the Star of Bethlehem. Mamma, in her Sunday dress and jet bracelets, gold watch-chain and ear-rings, moves round adjusting plates and giving directions to Emily, who, in *her* Sunday dress, looks her tightest and shiniest. Arthur and I sit on stools by the fire, and I read to him from the new book that at dawn this morning was discovered hanging beside my Santa Claus stocking by the bed-rail. It is a picture book with verses beside each picture. I look at a snow-covered church on a hill, towards which people are making their way through a village street. Reading the verses I arrive at the lines:

21

> The apples are roasting brown,
> The pealing swells of the merry bells
> Sound sweet o'er the little town.

Considering this, and with my attention centred on the roasting apples, I decide that there is something wrong with the wording. I revise, aloud:

> The apples are roasting brown,
> The peeling smells, and the merry bells – etc.

The family (Arthur excepted) seems enormously amused, and puts me right with unction. 'The peeling smells' becomes a perennial family joke.

During the dreary weeks of later winter, my hours, day and night, are punctuated by tearing, choking fits of whooping cough. Arthur has it too, in milder form. No doctor is called. Mamma has little respect for people who 'fly to the doctor for a cold in the head', and is quite certain that she knows how to treat whooping cough. Papa is equally unwilling to consult a doctor, having prejudices against the medical profession similar to those of Mr George Bernard Shaw. These have been strengthened by the unfortunate effect of vaccination upon Arthur – his arm carrying an open sore for months after injection...We are also delivered by Papa's intervention from the traditional weekly dose of brimstone and treacle, or senna tea. Mamma's faith in the small green bottles of homeopathic pillules remains unchallenged.

The cat is also ill, and Mamma says it must be drowned. She says this in a tone of finality, to Papa...I look at Tabs, stretched on the kitchen hearth-rug, eyes closed, dejected head dropped between front paws. Pity tightens my throat. Tabs, one of the family – I cannot remember a time when there was no Tabs. Lonely Tabs, so small, so different from us big people, but always, until a few days ago, when she began to be ill, the clean, contented, friendly little cat. But Mamma, who has been so patient with me during the weeks of whooping cough – never too busy to help when the fit was bad and frightening – is looking at Tabs without pity, even with dislike. When I stroke the cat's head she tells me sharply to keep away from her. Papa, glancing at Tabs, says nothing. He is fond of her; it is he who prepares her breakfast saucer of bread and milk every morning before he leaves the table, and she sits on his knee while he is reading in his fireside chair at night...(It comes to me later that Mamma likes only *funny* animals – such as the dog they had at home when she was a little girl – who would sit up and howl when Uncle Stevens said grace before meals.)

Tabs's breakfast saucer is again untouched next morning. After mid-day dinner I am told to take Arthur up to the store-room to play; it is too wet for our usual walk. The store-room window is open a few inches at the top; suddenly I hear from the yard below the clanking of pails and the sound of running water. Immediately I know that Papa is going to drown Tabs. He is going to drown her because Mamma wants him to do it. I climb on the window-sill, but the window is too high up for me to see into the yard...*What* can I do? What *can* I do to save Tabs? Into my mind flash the words THOU SHALT NOT KILL, as I have seen them among the Ten Commandments on the chapel wall behind the pulpit. It is a *Commandment*. Perhaps, if I should run downstairs and say this loudly to Papa, like one of the old prophets in the *Line Upon Line* books – perhaps – but he might think me just silly! My feet feel fastened to the floor, my forehead is pressed hard to the window. Inside me I say, endlessly, *Tabs! poor Tabs!* as if that could help. When we are called down to the kitchen for tea I glance, furtively, at the hearth-rug. There is no Tabs. I sit at the table in a maze of grief and anger – anger, chiefly, at my own cowardly inaction!

On a sunny afternoon, Emily, pushing Arthur's perambulator, turns in a new direction. We are soon facing a wonderful gate; it has spirals and circles patterned in bright

23

metal, and on the top golden knobs. Looking through it I
see glittering water at the end of a flower-bordered path,
water moving in small light-flecked waves. The gate is half
open, and I run forward, but Emily calls me back and gives
me precise instructions. I am to walk beside the perambulator, and promise to keep my hand on its handle all the
time we are in the Garden. If I forget my promise, we shall
never be brought here again! I make the promise; it hardly
lessens my excitement and delight. Emily examines the
strap securing Arthur to his seat; then we advance, and
slowly promenade round the enchanting lake. I have a
background impression of trees that wave pink or yellow
blossom against blue sky, but my attention is held by the
dancing surface of the shining lake, and the myriad tiny
hills and valleys that rise and sink and rise again con-
tinuously. This, I think, must be 'living water', of the kind
mentioned in a familiar hymn. Toy boats dance upon it –
some are being dragged round its margin at the end of a
string. For those I feel sorry, but one, quite free, with white
sails set, is swiftly and steadily making her independent way
across the lake. I wish I were that beautiful, clever little ship,
whose owner is not afraid to let it go free.

Presently Arthur, who has been staring at the scene with
his usual frown and stolid intent gaze, suddenly demands to
be lifted from the pram. Refused, he stiffens himself and
prepares to yell and kick. Emily hastens to turn away from
the water, and wheels the pram along a narrow path
between flowering bushes; it leads to a cool grotto,
shadowy but flecked with sunlight, where water is dripping from roof to floor of a little cave. We watch round
drops gather on its ceiling, catch the sunbeams, become for
a moment pendant diamonds, fall tinkling into the pool
on the dark, moss-greened floor. A lovely place! But Arthur
is not to be diverted; his mind is now fixed upon the
attractions of the lake, and Emily says we must go. By the
shining gate I turn and gaze back longingly, remembering,
'The Lord God planted a garden eastward in Eden.' It

is good to be able to approve an action of the Lord God.

The daily paper is carefully kept out of my way, and no hint of the Jack the Ripper murders reaches me at home. But the boys next door are well advised of them. Since the incident of the tortured frog my play in the yard has been restricted to the periods of their school hours, but the possible joy of making a silly girl cry presents itself to them occasionally. Standing by the open back door I give ear to a low call, peremptory and important. The tormentors have their story ready.

'There's a man in a leather apron coming soon, to kill all the little girls in Tunbridge Wells. It's in the paper.'

He stands before me, vividly enough, that man with the leathern apron and the uplifted, blood-stained knife. I have not forgotten the Bible story of King Herod's order to kill all the babies of Bethlehem. I scarcely ask myself if the boys are lying. It was true 'in the days of Herod the king' – and what happened once can happen again. I delight the boys by running indoors screaming, begging Papa to take me away at once from Tunbridge Wells; nor is my confidence fully restored when Papa and Mamma both insist that the story is silly nonsense, made up to frighten me...Mamma and Papa, though generally right, can be mistaken... There was that unforgettable matter of the wasp. While Papa was explaining that wasps only sting if people hurt or irritate them, the creature flew down from the window-pane and stung me on the knee. So now, though I tell myself that Papa is wiser than the boys, the penumbra of terror lingers.

Papa has a branch shop in Tonbridge. On a sunny June day he takes me with him when visiting its manager. On leaving the railway station we walk across a bridge from which I look down on my first river, its bright current gliding steadily between green banks. The water looks deep, mysterious and fascinating; the sun shines a little way into it and I can see gently waving water-weed beneath the surface. There are rowing boats moored to the bank close to the bridge. I want to go down to the river's edge, but Papa says we must visit the shop at once, and we hurry on. The shop is smaller than ours at home; Papa's name, in large gilt lettering above door and window, gives it importance. The manager shakes hands with me as if I am grown-up and then I am sent outside to walk up and down while Papa and he talk business. This waiting time is long. I wish I had brought Strong-troller and Stick-switcher with me. Strange people pass me, but I never look directly at them, and feel uncomfortable if they seem to be looking at me... When the business is finished I am called into the shop to receive a packet of sweets; then we return to the riverside, where Papa leads the way to a seat and produces sandwiches from his pocket. It is very pleasant here, but I want to dip my hands in the water, and Papa is contemplating the rowing boats; presently I am being helped into one of these and sit on a soft, bright red cushion in the back seat, nearer the green ripples than I had hoped to be. Papa takes the oars and pushes out into mid-stream.

The river is called Medway. Even without its name it would have been a personality. I catch my breath in fear and delight, the earlier emotion merging into the latter. I trail my hand alongside the moving boat, and shake off the shining drops so lightly, so easily, yet feel that in its depths the water is solid, a live, moving thing strong enough to carry Papa and me in our boat. I am given the steering rope and shown how to steer, and feel proud of my power to control our direction – proud, too, of Papa's strength as he pulls upstream. He has taken off his hat and coat and rolled up his shirtsleeves; he is a younger, happier Papa than usual. We are both enjoying ourselves, like the swans swimming near the river bank. But presently Papa swings the boat round, we drift downstream and all too soon are back at the landing stage.

A Sunday evening in the autumn of the same year. Papa asks if I should like to go with him to chapel. It is always exciting to walk at night, treading in and out of shadows; and as our chapel-going is a Sunday morning routine, Papa's suggestion is novel. We take the well-known route to the Congregational chapel, up Grosvenor Road and into Hanover Square, but here, to my surprise, Papa turns into the porch of the Roman Catholic church. The inner door stands open, and through it comes a strong, queer, pleasant scent. Beyond the darkened nave the further end of the church is ablaze with the light of the biggest candles I have seen. A man in a black gown shows us into a pew where there are just two empty seats. In the half-darkness I can dimly see images standing in niches against the walls, touches of gilt upon them visible in the light of small candles burning below. The sight of these images is disturbing; on the wall of *our* chapel I read, every Sunday, THOU SHALT NOT MAKE UNTO THEE ANY GRAVEN IMAGE...

The warm air is heavily scented with the curious, unknown scent...Suddenly there is organ music; the congregation begins to sing, but no hymn I have heard before, nor words I can understand. The music is rather like the voice of the wind on a stormy night when I cannot sleep, when it tries to get in, but, baffled, sighs and moans its way back to High Brooms wood. The music loudens and softens, to throb in my ears or to fall away almost to silence. The people kneel, the strange singing goes on...The man in the black gown is bringing lighted candles and giving them, one by one, to the kneeling man or woman at the end of each pew. Papa receives a candle. I think he would rather not hold it, but does not like to refuse. The stool on which I am kneeling is very hard, and I am glad when we all stand up again. The music seems to continue endlessly, but at last the organ stops playing as suddenly as it began, and the people sink back into their seats. Papa's candle is taken from him by the man who brought it; and I see, between the flames of the large candles ahead, a strangely dressed minister walking towards a high pulpit. He is going to preach a sermon – but at this moment Papa rises, and I follow him down the aisle and out of the church.

Outside I stare back at the lighted windows, trying to cope with this strange experience. Papa calls to me and we walk silently home. Even if I could express the many questions I should like to ask, Papa's silence would discourage. But when we reach the house, Mamma meets us at the door of the sitting-room, her questions ready. Why are we home so soon – the evening service is not over yet. Have *I* done something wrong, or been ill? Papa gives the right answers, briefly. We have not been to evening service at chapel – he thought it was time for me to see the inside of another place of worship. '*But*' – Mamma almost screams, 'the *Roman Catholic* church!' She has flushed cheeks and bright eyes. She scolds Papa – how, *how* could he take me to such a place? Her words pour out, but Papa is very quiet.

In the August of this year I go to stay with Evelyn and Aunt Bec. We ride in the train, my doll Amy and I, having a compartment to ourselves. The guard of the train, at Mamma's request, has locked the door, and comes along, red-faced and smiling, to see us when a stop is made. At Newhaven station Evelyn and Aunt Bec meet us; we walk away over a bridge under which deep green water flows; on the right are green hills, on the left wharves and sailing ships and a dark-blue line which I know must be the sea. At home I have heard much about the sea; it is somehow importantly connected with this visit of mine; I understand that it is wide, wide water, and that Mamma lived within sight of it before she married Papa...There is a strange scent, new and exciting. Aunt Bec and Evelyn ask many questions about the journey; when we arrive at Gran's house, the same sort of questions are put by Gran and Gran'ma, and it presently occurs to me that by travelling alone I have done something unusual.

This house has large rooms; it smells of nice polish and Gran's tobacco smoke; it is warm all over. Gran, who is Evelyn's grandfather but not really mine, smokes a long white pipe, sitting in a big armchair in the breakfast room. When he is going to smoke he puts on a black velvet cap with a wreath of flowers worked round it in silk – Evelyn points this out to me as being her last Christmas present to him. Gran'ma is tall; her face is wrinkled; she looks at me with kind scrutinising grey eyes. Gran'ma and Aunt Bec both wear black silk dresses, and Gran'ma a black silk apron and a brooch bigger than any I have seen – a picture brooch of a man on horseback, gold-rimmed. Aunt Bec wears rings and bracelets; her bedroom and everything about her have a very pleasant scent.

Evelyn often reminds me that she is a year older than I – hence she must always choose what we will do. We are sent to play in Gran'ma's large front bedroom, dominated, but by no means filled, by a great four-poster bed. The floor space at its foot is covered by a grey drugget, and here we bring our dolls and Evelyn's wealth of toys. Afternoon sunshine pours in on us through an ample bay window, beside which I like to stand and watch a line of black telegraph poles marching along by the white thread of the turnpike road over the green hills...With Aunt Bec we take short walks up this road, always turning back at the point where stands the stone cottage they call Turnpike. More frequently Aunt Bec's walks take the form of visits to other aunts and uncles. Aunt Stevens lives in a tall house; it is here that Mamma once dwelt. All the rooms of this house are hung with pictures of ships, pictures in large gilt frames, many-sailed ships on brightly painted blue seas, or ships worked in coloured wools. There are models of ships, under glass shades. Uncle Stevens is dead, but the little room at the top of the first flight of stairs is still called his study – its walls are covered with smooth yellowish charts on rollers. Aunt Stevens receives us in the 'living-room', dimly-lit, its windows open to a glass-roofed courtyard, where among plants and ferns, white-painted figure-heads of departed ships have found resting-place. Aunt Stevens is small, frail, grey; she sits in a tall straight-backed chair, her withered little hands resting on its arms. To look at her gives me a queer, half-scared feeling...She has nice nutty biscuits for Evelyn and me...Her great four-poster canopied bed stands in her bedroom on the first floor; here green venetian blinds are kept half drawn over the wide bay window – very high up, it seems to me, this window of the straight tall house on the hillside above the harbour.

'Aunt' Sarah lives in Chapel Street, low down – a low, narrow old street of the little town. She keeps a sweet-shop; it has a window with small square panes, a counter spread with sweet boxes, and under the counter an ice-cream can. She is fat, and in mentioning this one must say 'very stout'. She sits in the small room with prickly horse-hair stuffed chairs behind the shop. Evelyn and I may buy sweets here, but Aunt Sarah will let us have only a half-pennyworth at a time, either of sweets or ice-cream, and altogether forbids many interesting varieties of the former...Aunt Ada is Uncle Ben's mother, and has corkscrew curls, partly grey, emerging from a large cap and resting on either temple. I hate being taken to see her and one-armed Aunt Clara, because the way to the house is through Uncle Ben's butcher's shop, where the sawdust on the floor, thick as a carpet, is spotted with drops of blood dripped from the hanging carcases of beasts. The crimson spots lie on the white sawdust like red coins.

The Sea – it is far off – blue, flat, with many little white tongues and a rustling voice. But one day Aunt Bec packs a basket with sandwiches and cake, and we go to the steep pebbled beaches of the bay, beyond the harbour. The great waves boom and crash and stream broken up the beaches in a world of sunlight and dazzling foam. I stand barefoot on the hard smooth pebbles, Evelyn's hand holding mine fast, and the foam bubbles froth very softly about my feet. So hard and slippery the pebbles, so infinitely soft the foam, so cold the water welling between the pebbles! Shuddering but delighted I cling to Evelyn's hand; we move a step forward as the wave recedes. Aunt Bec calls sharply from behind – we are to stand *still, quite still* – or our socks will be put on at once. But joy! a kind wave runs a foot higher, and tosses small shingle over our feet...My ears are full of the roar, the tearing roar of the exultant sea, my eyes sense sunlight and foam, not for the hour, but all night long.

I am acutely conscious of scents, pleasant or unpleasant. Within and around Gran's house all the scents are subtle, and mingle pleasantly. The small front garden breathes of mignonette and roses. Within, the smoke of Gran's light tobacco hovers perpetually, blending with the scent from Aunt Bec's pot-pourri bowls, and that of the scarlet geraniums on the window-sills. Odours of meals past or meals to come are confined strictly to the kitchen and to baking days, twice a week. All the people of the house are steeped in its pervading perfume, and I am happy to be near them. No one hurries, no one scolds; the atmosphere is one of peace, of quiet contentment. Out of doors I have a more vivacious happiness. A month passes, but I have no wish to return home. Mamma and Papa – how nice it would be to see them *here*...One morning Aunt Bec calls me. She has a letter in her hand, and is smiling. Taller Gran'ma just behind her is also smiling down on me with a kind of expectancy. The doctor has brought me a new baby brother, says Aunt Bec...My reception of this news disappoints them. No, I do not want another brother – one is enough. The doctor should have brought a baby girl!

A Sunday morning in my seventh year. I am taken to chapel, between Mamma and Papa. We pass down the aisle as the first hymn is being sung...I enjoy singing hymns; my voice seems to separate itself from the heavy voice of the congregation and the boom of the organ, and soars away above them, rising up like the bubbles from the bottom of the lemonade bottles when the marbles are pushed from their necks into the grooves below...When the minister walks up the steps of the pulpit and opens the big Bible for the second time I follow the reading in my own copy of the New Testament, given to me last year as a prize for stumbling through the tenth chapter of St John – my favourite chapter, about the sheep. The minister, however, frequently changes the words without changing the meaning – I, being uninformed as to the use of the Revised Version, think this extremely clever of him. His sermons are long, and often incomprehensible, but this morning's echoes a dreadful theme from the green Sunday book and records itself deeply upon my memory. The text, announced slowly and with the solemnity of a doom is: *Then shall the end come.*

I carry from chapel on this occasion the weight of a knowledge, now fully confirmed, that makes the sunshine a mockery, and the talk of the dispersing congregation a silly chatter of stupid people who cannot have understood what has been told them from the pulpit. They, and everything I see, houses, gardens, the great trees, the sun in heaven itself, are of no more account to God than a heap of dead leaves for His bonfire! My mind, in self-preservation, turns to its charms – weak charms, temporary palliatives. I repeat, inwardly, with determination:

> The Lord is my shepherd, I shall not want,
> He maketh me to lie down in green pastures,
> He leadeth me beside the still waters.

Desperately I try to substitute my placid mental picture of the Good Shepherd, watching his sheep by the quiet river, 'gathering the lambs with his arm', for the terrifying conception of a destroyer god and a burning world. Outside the chapel, while the organ is still playing, Papa and Mamma exchange greetings with other people emerging from the porch – I walk slowly on. When they overtake me I glance at their faces. Mamma is not thinking of the sermon; she is smiling and looking happier than usual. Papa's face is undisturbed. No! I cannot remind them of what they have heard, or ask them any questions about it. They are not frightened; and somehow I feel that my questions might frighten them. *That* I could not bear.

SCHOOLING

Seven to ten years (1889–92)

A new family topic – school. Mamma talks of her school-
days – of Ma'am Brown and the 'back-board'. School is a
place where one sits, and sits up straight, by effort or
compulsion. Papa talks of a play-ground, swings and a
roundabout, of a school treat in a great park; his school is
more attractive, but perhaps it is only for boys. Evelyn in
Newhaven goes to a private school, Miss Stone's, and talks
of 'secrets' with other girls. And presently I find myself at
a small day-school in a 'front room' where a dozen
children sit on forms working addition and subtraction
sums on slates. The class also learns to recite 'We Are
Seven'. I go home at mid-day but some of the pupils remain
to lunch. Once there is an unpleasant afternoon succeeding a riotous lunch hour; forms have been used to make a
slide and ink in quantity spilt. Arriving before authority has
discovered these misdeeds I am implicated, and punished
by 'keeping in' and an extra sum. It is my introduction to
injustice of a personal kind.

Eva, Sidney and Claude are the 'rich' pupils. They must
be rich because they all wear velvet, the boys having
Fauntleroy suits with broad lace collars. Rich people have
large houses, long gardens, and their children ride on
ponies. Eva talks of her pony – I never see it. Papa and
Mamma are not rich; a pony, and a dolls' pram with rubber
tyres are only dreams for me; I have long since ceased to ask
for toys seen in shop windows, knowing that Mamma's
answer – 'When my ship comes home', signifies an end to
expectation. But if we are not rich, neither are we poor.
Poor people live in 'hovels' or 'slums' (the meaning of these

words is vague). They grind organs, sell flowers in the
street, or sweep crossings. It is kind to throw them
pennies.

Papa brings me books. One is a long story called *The Wide
Wide World*, probably chosen because of its agreeably
suggestive geographical title. It fascinates but repels me.
The heroine is a little girl named Ellen, unattractive
because habitually in floods of tears, but fortunate because
she is sent to live in mythical America, country of the
whip-poor-will, described in my *Book of American Birds*.
She has an unkind aunt, but this lady is to be preferred,
in my secret mind, to the saintly Alice and her brother,
the moral dictator John, who rescue her from the aunt's
guardianship. Alice dies, and Ellen listens to the bell
tolling out her twenty-three years of life, after which the
weeping one settles down to John's company and dictator-
ship in a manner quite abhorrent to me.

The theme of saintly death occurs *ad nauseam* in the
majority of tales reaching me at this period. Arthur and I
look eagerly for the monthly magazine *The Prize*, because
its front page is printed in high colour – most pictures are
only in grey print. An illustrated serial tale runs through
this journal. The hero is a little boy who is in consumption,
and whose conduct and piety advance towards perfection as
his disease progresses. He dies, and the last instalment of
the story leaves his brothers planting violets and snowdrops on his grave. Rex Victorius has 'gone to be with
Jesus'. I feel very strongly that I do not want to follow Rex,
and it would seem prudent, in view of his case, not to be *too*
good. On the other hand, if I steal a sweet from the shop
(which I do occasionally) or tell a lie, I am in danger of going
to hell. Heaven would seem preferable – yet the vague New
Jerusalem of the golden pavements, where is no sunshine,
but only 'the glory of God' must be avoided as long as
possible. Moreover, it is merely that part of me called my
'soul' which can go to either place, and a soul is perhaps a

horrid thing one would not wish to see exposed. In my Natural History book there is a picture of a wasps' nest – an egg-shaped thing half concealed by leaves, with wasps buzzing about it – the word 'soul' oddly suggests this picture. My body would be buried if I were to die, unless – single alternative – it were eaten by a lion. I conclude that it will be best to live in the long present, and retire in old age to a country where there are lions.

An important book is *Pilgrim's Progress*. Important because it is Papa's book, a small volume closely printed, and containing queer illustrations. I read it for its story, skipping most of the long conversations. The title page says it is 'delivered under the Similitude of a Dream'. The stuff of dreams is familiar to me, and if this is a dream story it need not be taken as seriously as the Bible, although its language is similar. I am quite ready to leave the City of Destruction with Christian, but reserve a private opinion as to that pilgrim's conduct in deserting his wife and children. Thereafter that entrancing Journey, with all its glooms and glories, its conquests and defeats, is mine for the travelling, as a whole or by chosen stages, throughout my remaining childhood.

The June of my eighth year…a sultry day and a darkening sky. Distant thunder, and then the overhead attack of the storm, with hail, hail shooting down from the dark sky white and hard, icy marbles in millions bounding up from road and pavement. I remember the plagues of Egypt, 'thunder and hail, and fire ran along the ground'. The darkness, the cut of the lightning, and the noise are frightening, and my heart beats hard, but so far there is no 'sound of a trumpet'. I try to put the idea of the Last Day out of my mind. I take *Pilgrim's Progress* and lie down on the sofa in the sitting-room, face turned to the wall…Christian in the House Beautiful will be a good part to read: 'And the pilgrim they laid in a fair chamber whose windows opened to the sun-rising; and the name of the chamber was Peace.' (But will the sun rise any more after today?)...It is very hot; Mamma has shut all the windows; she is going from room to room covering the mirrors with towels, and scolding Emily, who is crying with fright...Mamma returns, and stands by the window, watching the pounding hail; suddenly she exclaims, 'Oh! there's a runaway horse!' I run to see, but the horse has dragged its van into the sand-pit at the turn of the road just above our house; I see only a man who comes rushing down the hill, the hail beating on his bare head. Papa is standing by the shop door – I hear the man call to him desperately: 'Is the horse safe? Is the horse safe?' My fear is forgotten in admiration for this driver. How good, how right of him to rush through the storm caring for the safety of his horse! If only I could see what is happening in the sand-pit! But presently, as the storm passes, the driver, his head bandaged, leads the horse down the hill; I watch them go in gratitude and joy – I have seen a hero!

A Sunday morning this same June. Papa has a headache, and we are not going to chapel. He and I sit out of doors, in big and little chairs, with our books. The sky is blue and radiant, the sun shines warm on my face and arms, picks out bright flakes in the tawny sand of the yard, softens and whitens the tar bubbles on the black fence. I look up at the sun with closed eyes, and see scarlet patterns in my eyelids, then lift the eyelids ever so little and am lost in a dazzling white wave. This must be the 'eternal light' of a hymn which fascinates me.

ETERNAL LIGHT! ETERNAL LIGHT!
How pure the soul must be
When, placed within thy searching sight
It shrinks not, but with calm delight
Can live, and look on Thee.

The spirits that surround Thy throne
May bear the burning bliss,
But that is surely theirs alone,
Since they have never, never known
A fallen world like this.

My father's quiet voice, like a brown shadow, enters and dispels the dazzling trance. He is warning me not to look at the sun – it will blind me. My hand goes over my eyes involuntarily and for a moment all is darkness; then my vision slowly adjusts itself, identifying dim shapes of near things, and presently that of *Pilgrim's Progress*, on my lap. I return to the not greatly admired Christian, by now, in my reading, approaching the Land of Beulah, which country takes shape in my mind as the South Downs about Newhaven, where under mellow August sunshine ripe corn bends to the passing of the sea-breeze.

Mamma talks over the shop counter to Mrs Vernall. Laura Vernall stands beside her mother. Mrs Vernall is tall, big, with heavy dark hair; Laura, a head taller and a year older than I, has short tawny hair and a white face with golden-brown eyes...Because Mamma likes Mrs Vernall, I may play with Laura. This is something new; never before have I been allowed to associate with a neighbour's child, or to enter a neighbour's house.

The Vernalls live near, in a tall, bay-windowed house with a long garden. Laura has brothers – Sonny, red-haired, and small, dark, mischievous Eddy. Occasionally, during the evenings of this summer, I am permitted to go alone to the Vernalls; we play in the garden, where a swing hangs under the elms; or if wet, in the dining-room, where the noise made is no less than in the garden. I learn 'catching' games, shouting games – all strange and exciting. 'Play quietly!' is ever the rule at home. One makes up games to keep Arthur quiet – he must be a child in an orphanage or hospital, and I the kind visitor, bringing toys.

Every evening, after the shop is closed, Papa goes for a walk, Sometimes he says afterwards that he has been to a lecture. One morning, over breakfast, he tells us of something called a phonograph, operated at last night's lecture. My voice, he explains, can make a needle scratch marks on a wax-covered plate. When this plate is revolved inside the phonograph, my words can be heard coming out through a funnel. There is also a new thing called a telephone, which has two parts joined by a wire. Papa, standing at the back of the lecture hall, listening through an ear-trumpet, could hear even a whisper spoken by the operator on the platform, and words unheard by the audience.

Large coloured placards announce the visit to Tunbridge Wells of Poole's Panorama. Very excited, and half afraid, Arthur and I are taken at night to see this show. In a big hall, where the lights are lowered, pictures move across an illuminated screen; the show ends with the representation of a fire – a street of houses and a church realistically burning. This is terrifying, but only pleasantly so, because I know that it is not really happening. In and near Tunbridge Wells several houses have been burnt; from our windows I have seen the fire-glow on the sky. I do not know why they were burnt, but seeing a notice board announcing To Be Let in the foreground of an empty house I wonder whether its turn comes next. The last word of the notice may have been spelt wrong.

A new school – Vale Towers – by the edge of the Common. A big house, with lofty rooms and high, oblong windows, the lower ones thickly frosted. This school is nearly two miles from home; we carry dinner bags, Laura and I, and two other girls from Grosvenor Road, Mildred and Edith. We impose upon ourselves a code of rules governing the walk to school; some parts must be walked, some run, some hopped or skipped. A road must only be crossed at a certain fixed point. Penalties for transgression include pinches on the arm and stinging the hands with nettles that grow on the edge of the Common. Treading on joins between flagstones will ensure some secret, mysterious misfortune. There are imaginary danger spots, and one that we really fear, and would avoid if that were possible. At the point where Grosvenor Road leads into Hanover Square stands the Roman Catholic church, and beside it the school that Mamma refers to as the Ragged School. In the late afternoon, generally just as we pass, its doors fly open and out rushes a rabble of dirty, ill-clad children who surround us and march alongside with shouts and songs. We, as instructed, remain aloof and silent, a little afraid of them, but superior; they counter our superiority with insolence.

I can read and spell – I can answer all Miss Kent's questions. Only sums are difficult; one works at them very seriously. They have no relation to anything else in life; they are just *sums*, incomprehensibly important rows of figures, to be manipulated according to rule. That abstract but desirable position 'the top of the class' depends on correct manipulation. In our classroom are four long desks, seating seven pupils each, and two locker desks, standing apart, remote and superior, occupied always by the two pupils gaining highest marks for the previous week's work. Soon I have one of the locker desks – how I want to keep it throughout the term!

The 'dinner-girls' eat their sandwiches in the 'drill-hall', a large, first-floor front room that should, but for the frosted panes of its high windows, give a wide prospect of the Common. Sitting on the broad window seat two of us try spying through pin-holes in the frosting. We scratch at the pin-holes and enlarge them; we can now see out quite well; but the prefect of the room notices, comes and discovers the scratched window-pane. We are placed in ward, and presently marched down to our classroom, where Miss Kent is told of our offence. Questions are asked. My companion denies nothing, and stands sulkily, in disgrace, by the teacher's desk. It is my turn. Why did I scratch the glass? Did I not know it was wrong? (Yes, presumably it *was* wrong, though just now it seemed a fine, daring thing to do...) How escape the sense of self-condemnation shaming me? 'I did not start the hole – it was there.' 'Yes, but you scratched and made it bigger?' comes the suggestion. 'I began to scratch, but when I found the frosting coming away, I stopped.' (That is true – I *did*!) '*At once?*' (Oh, why must she ask that – there is no possible answer but yes or no!)

'Yes!'

'Very well – go back to your seat!'

Did she know I was lying? I kept my locker desk; the other child bore the obvious disgrace for the day – I carried the memory of the lie then and thereafter.

Laura...Her skin is like the petals of a cream rose, but with a little golden freckle here and there. Her short bright hair has a ruddy gleam, redder in firelight. This winter one is sometimes permitted to spend tea-time and the hour after tea at the Vernalls' house; we gather round the dining-room fire and ask riddles. Laura will make toffee; her mother says nothing to forbid her from taking a saucepan, butter and sugar, and anything else she likes to add to the mixture, and boiling the toffee over the dining-room fire. Even when the toffee sticks and the saucepan burns there is no scolding – only a laughing protest...We do our home-lessons together, the boys making a noise all the while, shouting the multiplication table, adding aloud. But Laura's brow wrinkles when she does sums. It is queer that she finds them so difficult and gets them wrong so often – but somehow I am glad of this. She is taller, much taller than I, and in a class above me; she is a year older. I want her to be near me, I want us to share things; and this single disadvantage of hers helps to draw us together. I can help her with the sums. Yet it is not only because I am useful that she likes me – I don't know why...There is a kind of warmth inside me when I think of her which increases when I look at her...a new and pleasant feeling.

Leaving school one afternoon I notice two little girls with their mother, walking just ahead. The little girls bowl hoops along the path. Arriving at a side street opening the mother pauses, the elder girl stops her hoop, because a van is driving out into the main street. The younger girl cannot stop her hoop; it runs across in front of the van; she is frightened and rushes after it. The driver pulls up his horse sharply, the mother screams, the hoop rolls on and falls on the opposite curb, the little girl narrowly escapes the hoofs of the rearing horses. When the van has drawn out, the mother hurries forward, seizes the child and shakes her violently, and then – horrible! picks up the hoop, leans heavily on it, breaks it in two. The bulging of the poor hoop – the snap of the wood – the wail of the little girl! I have seen a murder committed!

At the close of the autumn term there is a breaking-up party at Vale Towers. It is a great occasion. I wear my best dress, a new soft dove-grey cashmere, most uncomfortable, with a tight sateen lining and a red plush collar with underfrill of lace, high and choky. Laura, Mildred and I drive to the party in a hired cab. The cab calls for me first, and I step in, to be assisted to the back seat; we rumble and shake down Queen's Road hill to pick up Laura, dressed in blue, with a fleecy white shawl over her short hair. Mildred's long dun-coloured hair is rippled, freed from recent plaits. Pleasantly exciting it is, leaning back in the dark of the cab, feeling the roll and jolt of the wheels, listening to the horse's trot, watching moving shadows flung by bare, swaying trees when street lamps are passed. Importantly we are driven up to the main entrance of the school, used only by the mistresses on ordinary days. Above it the gas-light flickers in its big white globe. We mount the high steps. Opposite looms the black gulf of the Common, where night is full of mystery; we pass in to warmth and the babel of excited voices, to the games and the gaiety, and forget the encompassing dark, except as, between the games, we happen to glance up at the tall, uncurtained windows. Then we avert our eyes, lest Something should be staring in.

A walk with Mamma will frequently take us to the Parade. It is a shop street, different from all the others, and useful on wet days, because the upper stories of the houses are built out on pillars, and one can run from end to end of the row of small dark shops without going into the rain. Tiny, lovely little things are sold in these shops: boxes, cabinets, thimble-cases, pincushions, all made or cased in woodwork formed of minute squares and oblongs of scented wood. Exquisite and expensive things. Before the houses a wide flag-stoned pavement is bordered by tall elms; and at one end of the street a wide flight of stone steps descends to the Wells. The Wells are fascinating; one looks down over an iron railing into an oblong pit divided by a stone parapet; in one half is a big iron basin very brown with rust, having an iron cup beside, chained, and kept bright for people's free use; in the other half a fountain bubbles into a small basin, and an old woman sits there beside it, polishing a row of glasses, and handing out the water for a penny a glass. Once only, on a hot day, Arthur and I ask to buy a glass; Mamma and the old woman laugh when we screw up our faces at its bitter taste.

The trade of Papa's shop declines; Papa has business headaches. I hear that the branch at Tonbridge has been given up. Now, in the spring, we are to move into the country. Papa is selling what he calls the 'goodwill' of the Tunbridge Wells business.

On an April morning we all travel by train to Horley. I am very eager to go to 'the country'. My books have assured me of pretty cottages and cottage gardens always full of flowers; of meadows where cows stand knee-deep in buttercups; of scented haystacks and farm dairies rich with butter and cream; of clear brooks and almost perpetual sunshine. Our walks will be taken between blossoming hedges instead of between rows of grey-walled houses ... There is no immediate disappointment. We arrive at a little station having an openwork iron bridge on which one may stand in a thrilling cloud of warm steam watching the trains rushing away beneath. We are taken for a meal in a country eating-house, sit at table in a funny back parlour, and eat a queer novelty of a pie which has a thick pad of currants and treacle sandwiched between thin paste. Then we go to the new home.

It is the single shop in a long street of semi-detached cottages – certainly not pretty cottages, but standing in long gardens. There is a wide gate beside the shop, and I see with joy that our house also has a long garden. Only a child whose sole territory has been a sandy yard enclosed by a high tarred fence can feel my delight. A rough lawn, a space of recently dug soil, a lower grass plot, a green bank and boundary hedge. *Lawn*, *bank* and *hedge* are all *good* words; *lawn* expresses a magic of vivid green, on a *bank* one finds wild strawberries and thyme, wild roses and hawthorn grow in *hedges*.

I am to have a bedroom facing east; through the window the early morning sun of the 'real country' will wake me. A 'chamber open to the sun-rising', like Christian. Two shelves are fixed on the wall for my books. An illustrated *Aesop's Fables* with large print and a broken binding; *The Wide Wide World* – I know both nearly by heart...the Sunday books...my poetry book, distinguished by its footnotes and very small print. *Pilgrim's Progress*, next to Dr Smith's English History. A picture book about American birds. Two little meditation books by F. R. Havergal, containing a text and the meditation thereon for each night and morning per month; the evening portion Mamma generally reads to me before saying goodnight. Bound volumes of *The Prize* and *Chatterbox*; Susan Coolidge's *What Katy Did*...The last is a great favourite – the only *storybook* that does not feature religion.

Near the end of the street is a red-brick school building surmounted by a wooden belfry holding a cracked bell. Arthur and I must attend this school, to Mamma's extreme dissatisfaction. It is a Board School, which she regards as being but a degree superior to a Ragged School. No other school is available in Horley. Mamma does not hide her prejudice, and I despise this one from the day of entry. The head mistress admits me without examination, placing me with children of my own age. Follow six months of school boredom; the children in the class cannot read or spell; I have to stand, holding a primer (often torn and dirty) pretending to learn, compelled to keep my finger on one word at a time, forbidden to turn the page until all have read it. School-time is *endless* – one writhes and fidgets while Dinah Tizard stumbles through a sentence of single-syllable words. The teacher is tall, thin, scared-looking; worrying over Dinah and the rest, especially when the head mistress, called 'Gov'ness', comes into the room. 'Gov'ness' is fat, grey-haired, rosy-faced, and has a brisk manner. Prison of a school-room! How fine is the yellow sunshine outside, and how the free bushes at the end of the play-ground wave in the wind! How the clock hands crawl. At mid-morning we rush out for ten minutes play-time, and I learn to play skipping. That at least is new to me. At Vale Towers there was no 'play-time' – only musical drill in the drill-hall.

At the street corner stand the small red Baptist Chapel and manse, in the midst of the flower-garden which is the minister's hobby. Failing the existence of a Congregational chapel Papa and Mamma decide to 'attend' here. On Sunday mornings we sit in a straight-backed pew; Mamma wearing her best black silk skirt and grey silk blouse, Arthur in the blue sailor suit which is the object of my envy, three-year-old Frank in black velveteen frock with short, lace-frilled sleeves, myself in white embroidered frock with silk sash. Papa's cloth suit is just part of Papa, always, as Emily's black dress is the greater visible portion of Emily ...The sunlight shining through the pinkish diamond-shaped panes of the chapel window casts pink stains on my frock; fancy transfers to them the frequent references to 'stains of sin' made in the hymns. The preacher is an ugly man; at first sight I prepare to dislike him, but his voice is attractive and winning; from the pulpit he says nothing that terrifies, but brings to the confines of religion suggestions of the beauty that hides in phrases. That queer beauty, which I am able to recognise but cannot define, he can charm. I listen to the cadence of his voice, waiting for the charm to take effect. '*Thine eyes shall behold the King in His beauty; thou shalt see the land which is very far off*' (there are Christian and Hopeful in the land of Beulah). '*I am come that they might have life, and that they might have it more abundantly.*' '*In the beginning was the Word, and the Word was with God, and the Word was God.*' Reading such phrases the voice fills the chapel with echoes – rich echoes arising from some private darkness of my own.

Before the school closes for its summer holidays comes a momentous occasion – the annual Government Inspection. During the preceding week strenuous preparations are made; Dinah Tizard and her kind scratch sums on slates and spell out words from the soiled primers during play-time as well as in school hours. On the morning of the inspection, classes assemble in excited silence; 'Gov'ness', usually, at this hour, stationary at her big desk, seems to be everywhere at once, her round pink cheeks pinker, her mouth set in a straight line. Our teacher is more scared-looking than ever. Men's loud voices are suddenly heard from the porch; the inspectors enter, demand 'Gov'ness', and are taken to the upper classes; we of Standard One must sit and wait, arms folded behind, before each of us a clean slate, a new pencil and a closed primer. Our forms have no backs; it is tiring; but the greatness of the occasion keeps the most fidgety child 'good'. Miss Collins tries to tell us a story, but unsuccessfully; she is too nervous to sit on her stool, and every few minutes goes to peep through the glass door communicating with the main room. After the passing of an hour shoes begin to scrape the floor, girls to giggle, Miss Collins, anguished, implores silence; at last the door-handle rattles, and there is 'Gov'ness', the Inspectors behind her. The room fills with a new authority; Miss Collins seems to shrink to insignificance. Primers are opened, reading begins. The Chief Inspector sits with pen in hand, and blue mark sheet before him; each girl, called by name, reads a single paragraph (how can they *help* knowing the primer by heart?) and is marked 'Pass' or 'Fail'. The procedure has been explained to us. I rise to my name with alacrity, welcoming the minute's release from inaction, happy to note that my paragraph is one of the longer ones – but the Inspector bids me sit down after my second sentence. Reading over, addition and subtraction sums are dictated; we have each a letter A or B, with different sums, lest we should 'copy'; sums being worked, an Inspector passes along chalking the number right on each slate. Then names are called from the mark sheet, we announce our number in turn, and see the fateful figure put down...I am vaguely reminded of the Last Judgment ...Only the head mistress appreciates the fact of a School Government Grant, determined by the numerical total of the P's or F's on the Inspector's sheet.

The inspection serves to advance me in the school; during the next term I study with necessary concentration long division sums and rules of English grammar. My teacher is Miss Rose Chamberlain, whom I admire. She is graceful, with fine dark hair, loosely waved; she has large dark-brown eyes; her voice is low and appealing – never raised to the nagging tone used by the other teachers. She will sometimes wear on Monday a beautiful embroidered dress that obviously belongs to Sunday. And she openly flatters me, encouraging a pleasant sense of superiority. I begin to be content, even happy, at school. It provides a way of escape from a consciousness too aware of the pressure of the eternal. Unknown and unknowable this encompasses, darkly, the small circle of sensuous and conscious life, reducing me to nullity, losing me in its immensity. School problems are exacting enough to compel my attention, but finite, having known solutions. I gain in myself by solving their puzzles, and the puzzles themselves acquire a value for me when I have solved them.

Lily H., a schoolfellow, comes to the back door of the house and asks permission, in a slow, broad, country drawl, for me to come out to play. The H.'s are builders, and attend chapel, so Mamma concedes it. Lily's mode of invitation to me begins, 'Don't you dare...?' Always she suggests, in no spirit of high adventure, but rather as if it were a tiresome duty, the climbing of walls, crossing of ditches, scrambling through hedges – bringing forward her suggestions in a manner so challenging that one's pride compels one to accept, until convinced, by observation, that acceptance is not really pleasing to Lily, since it obliges her to find some further and more unnecessary proposition ...Lily has a grown-up sister Mabel, who writes poems in a note-book, as I do. This great discovery I make on a Sunday evening when the two are invited to tea...Mabel, to my chagrin, picks up a note-book I keep very secret, glances through it, then takes a pencil and writes three lines of verse in grown-up hand-writing. 'There's the beginning of another one!' she says, and passes me the book.

> The lamp on the table was burning bright,
> The fire was throwing its ruddy light,
> Over the kitchen so clean...

Thus I know Mabel to be distinguished. No one but Papa loves poems – poems in books. Not even Papa can write them.

Winter evenings are always spent indoors, except on those rare occasions when a 'magic lantern' lecture is given in the chapel. The boys play table games; I read. Exercise during the day has been limited to the ten minutes play-time and the five minutes walk to and from school. Nine o'clock bed-time finds me with hot head, cold feet, excited brain. The images evoked by my reading accompany me to bed. Scott's poems; Ainsworth's *Lancashire Witches*, and a collection of Scotch and English ballads stand in memory as belonging to this ninth winter. Of the poems, especially *The Erl King* and *William and Helen. The Erl King* is illustrated by a sharp print in black and white of the ride through the forest – there is a black background of forest with sheeting of white rain and hideous goblin faces and fingers:

> Sore trembled the father, he spurred through the wild,
> Clasping close to his bosom his shuddering child.

None the less vivid, though unpictured, is the legend of Helen's defiance of heaven, and her ride on the demon horse to the open grave of her dead lover:

> The furious barb snorts fire and foam, and with a
> sudden bound
> Dissolves at once in empty air, and leaves her on
> the ground.

The sedatives of Miss Havergal's *Little Pillows* have small effect after such stimulants. Through the lashes of hot eyelids I blink at queer shadows, and listen to the ticking of the death-watch beetle working in the old wood of the bed. Sometimes I lie till sleep comes in the small hours; sometimes, desperate, creep into my parents' room and confess I cannot sleep.

One night a different kind of vision keeps me wakeful. The jobbing gardener has found a hard conglomerate beneath the top soil in what is to be vegetable garden, has pick-axed it out and stacked it in lump piles at the end. The rough piles suggest to me a picture I have seen of a crofter's hut; the desire to build one seizes me. In waking dreams I construct and furnish a hut, placing it on the lower grass plot. It shall have a latticed window...There are difficulties, but surely they can be overcome...the chimney would

be awkward to build, but the fire should burn on the hearth
– we could do without a stove. Tiny glass lamps are sold in
the shop for sixpence, and I know odds and ends of
furniture that may be spared from the house...I see that
utterly desirable hut complete, its curtains waving at its
open window; a border of golden marigolds growing
before its front wall...

Next day the plan is confided to Arthur and three school
friends; the latter are to enter the garden singly, by the side
gate, the same evening – the month is late May. We will
begin to build. I feel sure that to discuss matters at this stage
with grown-ups will be to invite prohibitions – but if we can
confront them with a half-built hut they may approve
initiative and help us. We lay a two-course oblong of the
conglomerate blocks, plastering the spaces between with
mud for mortar, an evening's work, without interference.
The next evening we proceed with the third course, but
before it is finished Papa strolls down the path and briefly
directs us to return the stones to the stack. I can make no
appeal; he clearly thinks the idea just *silly*. It is humiliating; my cheeks burn. I tell myself hard that he is wrong –
the plan was not silly. We *could* have found out, by trying,
how to build the hut!

Laura Vernall and her family have removed to London. A
letter comes asking that I may spend the after-Christmas
holidays at their London home. This prospect is very
exciting. There it is, in the distance; and can be used as
a high background against which more immediate 'dis-
agreeables' – a forthcoming interview with the dentist for
example – may be seen in reduced proportion. Powder and
jam is a detestable mixture, but jam *after* powder a point of
philosophy...Impressions of London have come to me, so
far, by way of *The Ballads of Mrs Sewell* and the city waif
tales of R.T.S. publications.

The yellow fog lay thick and dim
O'er London city, far and wide,

It filled the spacious parks and squares
Where noble lords and ladies ride;
It filled the streets – the shops were dark –
The gas was burning through the day,
The Monument was blotted out,
And lost in gloom the river lay –

But thicker still and darker far
That noisome smoke-cloud dimly fell
Among the narrow courts and lanes
Where toiling people poorly dwell;
Down seven steep and broken stairs
Its chill, unwelcome way it found,
And darkened with a deeper gloom
A low, damp chamber underground.

This description does not depress me; there is even something stimulating, satisfying, in its huge glooms and contrasts. When the time comes for the London visit, Mrs Sewell is fully justified. Christmas brings hard frost; my bedroom ceiling glitters with frost crystals when the lamp is lighted. On Christmas Day I pick up a frozen robin and take it into the kitchen, where it struggles back to life. The frost continues; the countryside is hoary on the day when, buttoned into my reefer coat, I board the London train. The fog yellows as the city nears; I see London first as an immensity of tall, shadowy buildings in deep yellowish twilight, sprayed luminous in the circles about the street lamps.

The Vernalls' house is one of a terrace, basemented, four-storied, narrow, with many stairs. The frost has put the gas meter out of action, and to the joy of the children, coloured candles light the house. Taps are also frozen, and it is necessary to fetch water from a main tap at the corner of the square. My Mamma's sympathy seems uncalled for – all the Vernalls clearly enjoy these novel conditions. Perhaps it is a good thing Mamma has to go home the following day, before the candle-light party which has been arranged in my honour. Do I like the rough and tumble of the party, or only think I *ought* to like it? The kissing games are nasty, and I hate being called Sonny's sweetheart. Laura is my friend, not Sonny, but the grown-ups insist that I hold Sonny's hand in the ring games...Laura is so tall, and the boys, except at the party, go and play by themselves. Somehow they are not the Vernalls I thought I knew... Mrs Vernall takes Laura and me to see St Paul's. The frost has broken, and we push our way through mud and slush, among crowds of hurrying people, most of whom, to judge from their clothes, are poor. I see a crossing sweeper with his broom, but nobody who looks like a lord or a lady. The noise of the street traffic is so loud that only by shouting can we talk as we go. Then we enter St Paul's, where it is quiet and dim, where there is only a sound like the sea talking to itself a way off. I look up into the immensity of the dome; a gilded gallery gleams against the soft, higher darkness. It is very good to be in St Paul's...On the way home we cross London Bridge. The river Thames is a muddy, swirling stream carrying down a jumble of ice-blocks, some no bigger than bricks, some large enough for two people to stand on.

At home our books are supplemented by those from the Sunday School library. With disturbing insistence these stories present to me pious young people monotonously inclined to some form of picturesque, wasting disease, which proves the means of 'taking Alice home to God', or 'leaving Ernest safe in the arms of Jesus'. These euphemisms fail to disguise for me the actuality of death, and it is with a feeling of horror that I suddenly observe how thin are my own hands. Alarming also is an intermittent pain in my side...All the books stress the efficacy of prayer for the sick, but make evident the unpleasant fact that God usually, either of intention or misconception, answers such prayers in a manner unsatisfactory (as I see it) to the patient. I therefore state my petition in the plainest possible terms, explaining in words too precise for possible misunderstanding what I mean in asking to be made better...But my hands remain thin, and it is often painful to draw a deep breath.

1a Louise and Alfred Corke
on their wedding day,
17 June 1879

1b Helen Corke in 1887

11 The 'Siegmund' of D. H. Lawrence's *Saga c.* 1905

Is prayer of any use? The next School Inspection Day provides the opportunity for a test. Needlework is a subject listed for inspection, and my class is required to show a knowledge of three processes, one of which is the sewing of a flannel patch. I cannot do this, having been absent from school when the process was taught. I pray God, the night before Inspection Day, and inwardly whenever the apprehension of 'failing' seizes me, to help in the matter...The hour of the test arrives; distinguishing letters, A, B and C, are allotted to the pupils – mine is C. A blackboard, hitherto lying face downward, is raised, announcing the 'specimen' to be worked by each group. Letter C indicates the flannel patch!

Suddenly the Inspector decides, for reasons best known to God and me, that Class IV's singing test must take place in our classroom. We stand, and file out, changing position with Class IV; in the new room the letters are re-allotted, and this time mine is A. I am much comforted and reassured by this evidence of Divine intervention, but it is not confirmed by the result of later experiment.

This spring I first notice, consciously, the budding and blossoming of daffodils, and the rising tide of buttercup gold in the meadows. Each sunny morning I wake earlier. It is an adventure to dress in the strange, new sunlight that strikes the wall of my room when the sun-globe lifts into the rose-coloured east, burnishing to an unbearable radiance the cloud-bars confining him...There is a rare freedom to win – a world for my own if I can succeed in getting away from the house without waking anyone. Every stair must be tested with the lightest pressure lest a creaking board betray me. Can I move the bolts of the door?

Patience and the utmost care bring their reward; I stand outside on the garden path, glance back at the closed blinds of the house, and am free of the May morning. '*Behold, I make all things new!*' says God, a God most utterly different from Him to whom my carefully worded prayers are addressed. His world of the sunrise and keen morning air contains no people, no prohibitions, no suggestion of suffering or sin. Bright quick birds flit about, intent on their purposes. I visit the primrose clumps in my own strip of ground, but this is still too near the house for safety. There is a gap in the hedge at the end of the garden, a great buttercup meadow beyond, larks fluttering above. I wander in the meadow, picking a large buttercup here and there, till hunger suggests breakfast. Mamma, in the usual hurry of morning preparation, receives the flowers coldly, saying that I shall be dead tired before the day is out. How stuffy and dim the house! The brilliant morning clouds before school-time; yet something of the radiance remains inside me.

A religious 'mission' is held in the village. The big tent is set in a meadow close to the school, and the missioners hold meetings every night of a June week. 'Missions' play a large part in the Sunday School library-book tales, being generally the means of heroes' and heroines' 'conversions'. I do not want to go, and shrink from seeing the religious demonstrations of which I have read, yet the tent has a sort of fascination for me, and Lily H. urges...Evening is warm, calm, the air full of hay-scent; the sun setting in rose and gold, the eastern sky a forget-me-not blue; inside the tent the light is grey and dim, yellowed a little at the end, where candles already burn on a raised table. People sit on rows of benches in hunched positions, grey-faced in the dim light. There is a heavy, throat-irritating scent of crushed grass, damp canvas, and candle-smoke. Hymns are sung – chorus hymns – I hate their drawled repetitions. A missioner begins to pray – it is as if he is grovelling before God, and then as if God goes away, not wanting to listen, and he raises his voice begging Him to return, to have 'mercy on the souls before Him'. Then the other missioner, standing between the flickering candles, begins to preach. I have a 'captured' feeling – a longing to get outside, to be alone, to

breathe deeply in pure air – but I cannot bring myself to stir
from my place. If I move, if I am seen going out, the man
may address me personally. I sit tense, while the loud voice
gets louder. I try not to listen, try to confuse his words, to
mix them up so that I shall not recognise any meaning, for
he is saying things I shall have to remember against my will.
He is spoiling the June world of mellow sunset, of quiet
cows dreaming in dusky meadows, of stars that are
night-lamps lit by God to reassure a child – he is spoiling
it with lurid suggestions of another god who required
the death of his own son as a sacrifice. Follows the old,
well-known stuff of the Sunday books – one must pray to be
saved from hell and then believe one *is* saved, and there is
no time to lose, because the end of the world is fast
approaching. The old fear, latterly subdued, is back again,
with the old command to love an unlovable god.

Twice during my childhood I 'feel' that I am 'saved'. The
first occasion is my sixth birthday. Preparations for the
party are proceeding; I am wearing my best frock, and am
told to read in the sitting-room till the guests arrive.
Excitement will not let me read; I walk about the room,
humming, softly, a tune the Salvation Army band plays at
the corner of the road on Sundays. I remember how the
band begins the tune, and then the uniformed men and
women take it up and sing the words – these presently come
to my mind. I sing them:

> Hallelujah, 'tis da-un,
> I believe on the Sa-un,
> I am saved by the blood of the crucified one.

When the triplet is finished there is nothing to do but begin
it again; I sing it over and over with rising exultation,
presently shouting it – stamping its rhythm, until Papa,
from his desk in the shop below, is disturbed, and calls to
me, with an unusual sternness, to desist.

The second occasion is the Easter of my tenth year, an
Easter of sudden spring after long winter. The festival of

55

the Passion, that supreme triumph of religious art, has been stressed in school Bible lessons of the previous week. There is no service in our chapel on Good Friday, but the hot cross buns for breakfast, the closed shop, and the morning walk with Papa mark the day as something between a Sunday and a holiday. We pass the parish church quietly, aware of some long, mysterious celebration proceeding therein – happy that we are 'chapel' and on that account free to stay out in the sunshine. And then, on Sunday, Easter Sunday, it is no privation to go to chapel, for we have seen pots and pots of daffodils going in from the minister's garden on Saturday, and people with heaps of primroses. In that flower-scented chapel a cross of daffodils hangs before the pulpit, and behind it on the wall glows a text in bright immortelles: THE LORD IS RISEN INDEED. Everyone seems happy, and as we stand singing the Easter hymn I feel I have never been so happy...'The strife is o'er, the battle done...' Who could help loving Christ, now that He is arisen...? Why has it seemed so difficult before...it is now an ecstasy to love Him...The exalted mood lasts through the day, and there is an echo of hallelujahs in my dreams; but the cold rain of Easter Monday washes out the vision.

Papa's bicycle, with the big wheel under the saddle and the little wheel behind, did not travel to 'the country'; it figures only in Mamma's stories of Papa's wonderful rides. Mamma tells the stories with pride, but even in retrospect she views with misgiving a thirty-mile ride to London on a *Sunday*, although the journey had been made to hear a celebrated preacher. We hear how worried Mamma was every time Papa *would* cycle. 'Thankful am I', says she, 'that at last I persuaded him to give it up.' But now safety bicycles are coming into use; one sees large numbers of them pedalling down the main road on Bank Holidays. One morning my Uncle Charles arrives unexpectedly, on a new 'safety'. Papa, showing an excitement strange to him, leaves Mamma and Uncle to attend in the shop if they will, and, not even waiting to remove his apron, rides round the village on the bicycle with the twin wheels.

But Papa does not buy a safety bicycle...A piano arrives – a highly polished piano, smelling strongly of new wood and varnish. Amazing to me, the arrival of this piano. I have long classed pianos with ponies, model dolls' prams, and all such objects of desire as remain beyond reasonable ex- pectation – evidences of wealth which is no part of my heritage. Yet here it stands; and Mamma plays a 'battle piece' she learned when a girl. I creep downstairs early next morning to assure myself it is not a dream; smell its varnish with exultation, push up two venetian blind shutters, letting in light enough to see its form. I long to play it; never have I wanted to learn anything so much! An instruction book soon appears, but no teacher.

Papa also wants to play the piano. Before it came he used to play little tunes on his flute in the evenings after closing the shop, but now he practises piano scales instead. He touches the keys very gently, sometimes too gently to make them sound, so that he has to tap a second time. I wish he would not play at night when I am in bed; thin, fright- ened, scale notes follow one another nervously; each seems to rise in the air like a little smoke spiral, spreading, diffusing into a darkness. To me, who must listen, the near, familiar things shrink; my consciousness must follow the little spirals into the boundless – it is like a disintegra- tion...Still more desolating is the wail of the postman's fiddle from a nearby cottage...

Time – the seven days, marching visibly from Sunday to Sunday; the seasons; the past years of my life, recalled by memory as the sequence of experience. I make no picture of the future, unless it be the near future promising something pleasant. From the remoter future one shrinks: better not think of it. Mamma's hymn, 'A Few More Years Shall Roll', is discouraging. I cannot understand why this hymn is a favourite with Mamma. She will choose it to sing on Sunday evenings, after chapel, when friends come in and we sing hymns to the piano. I wish I could shut my ears to its drawly tune, and avoid seeing in fancy the row of tombstones its first verse brings to my mind. Putting the hymn aside, and also the prospect of Judgment Day, there is the possibility of being grown up. I do not find it attractive. Grown-ups must wear long frocks, and cannot run. There is also to be faced the grave question of what one shall *be*.

Sunday is always marked off from the other days by clean underclothing and best frock, and by the prohibition of games, toys and running. Songs must not be sung, nor must one learn anything but the text and verse for the day. I like Sunday morning for its leisurely breakfast; I like the chapel service and the voice of the minister reading the lessons. Afternoon Sunday School is noisy, and the room very stuffy when the classes are penned off by the sliding partitions. Miss Harris, whose father is landlord of the Chequers Inn, is my teacher; she wears a tight new dress, with chain and bracelets. She hears the dozen of us in her pen read the chapter for the day, then expands it a little – always ending by urging us to 'lead good lives'...Sunday evenings in winter are oppressive. The shadowy chapel at evening service, the solemn tunes, the high depths of the star-pierced sky, combine to set one's mind adrift on the infinite. One reads, thinks, feels, but does nothing, physically active, and goes to bed dreading the sleepless hours. In summer there is a walk after chapel through lanes, field-paths and woods; and on two occasions Papa takes me with him to Fernhill, a village three miles distant. At Fernhill the chapel is a tiny one with latticed windows and honeysuckle growing over its porch; Papa reads the lessons to a congregation of about twenty people. I love the walk home from Fernhill in the long dusk after sunset. Papa recites Gray's 'Elegy' as we walk along, and talks of the stars, showing me the Pleiades and the Great Bear.

Monday morning is flat and dull. One goes mechanically

to school, taking one's school fee. Fees are collected each
Monday morning, a register is called and each pupil in
turn pays her fee at the desk or confesses, with head bent,
that she has not brought the money. Poor children pay
twopence or threepence; my fee is sixpence. 'Gov'ness'
scolds those who do not pay, and this scolding seems to take
a long time. I feel tired, and my hair-ribbon, tied too
tightly, makes my head throb during arithmetic lesson
...The day shambles away...the afternoon session ends
with a singing lesson from a tonic sol-fa chart, and songs.
The first song tells a story of a little beggar girl who came to
the gate of a rich man's garden, where a cripple boy gave
her a flower; eventually

> that high-born child and the beggar
> passed Homeward side by side,
> for the ways of men are narrow,
> but the gates of Heaven are wide.

The second song is about a blind organ-grinder girl, who
finds her way to Heaven through 'gates of the west'; the
third the soliloquy of a prisoner who anticipates changing
prison for Heaven (by way of execution) the following day.
These songs are 'Gov'ness's' choice.

From Tuesday to Saturday I am more concerned with the
things of this life. Most important, from the school-day
viewpoint, are spelling, parsing and analysis, and arithmetic. I learn no verse except a maudlin poem called 'Little
Jim', presented as 'scripture lesson'.

No daily newspaper appears at home. The *British Weekly*,
always folded very precisely, comes regularly by post from
my grandfather. Papa brings in an occasional *Titbits*, or
Answers or more rarely a *Pearson's Weekly*...Some copies
of the *Strand Magazine* appear about this time. They
contain the Sherlock Holmes tales, extracts from the
Journal of Marie Bashkirtseff, and a series of portraits of
celebrities, showing each one as a child, and at varying
stages of adult life. Mamma, who seldom reads, takes

Horner's *Penny Stories*, because she has a personal interest in one of the authors of this series. He, a Liverpool street waif, went to sea, joining the navy, and being weak-stomached and unadaptable, suffered considerably. He deserted, was caught and imprisoned. Into the stories he put his experiences, making much of his subsequent 'conversion' (the series being of the religious tract variety). Mamma met 'Howard Wilson' before her marriage, at the chapel in Newhaven, and she has seen him sometimes since. He is now a successful missioner and a prosperous author, she says...I like the tales for their sea adventures, and miss out as completely as possible the religious parts.

Mamma has a copy of Milton's Poems – a birthday present from Papa many years ago. I read the *Paradise Lost*, liking most particularly the Garden of Eden part, feeling the rhythm soothing and satisfying...Two only of the books in the house are forbidden to me, Eugene Sue's *Mysteries of Paris* and Olive Schreiner's *The Story of an African Farm*. There is a copy of the latter in the drawer of a chiffonier I have to dust weekly. Opening the book first at random, I happen upon the account of the team-driver's cruelty to his ox – a vivid, terrible incident which cannot be isolated from the rest of the story. When Papa notices I have the book, he tells me to put it away; this prohibition is in itself so unusual that my curiosity is aroused, and the chiffonier drawer exerts a fascination I cannot always resist. Very real becomes the boy Waldo – I understand how he feels and thinks – many of his thoughts are mine. And the writer of the book *knows* how confusing is religion, and how impossible it is to believe the incredible and love the unlovable. The badly printed, pirated American copy of *The Story of an African Farm* becomes the hiding place of intimate friends. Only one other book holds a rival position in my affection and admiration, Lew Wallace's *Ben Hur* – a Sunday School prize. Without realising it, I am grateful to Lew Wallace not only for opening up Syria to my imagination, but for placing the figure of Christ in such relationship to the characters of his drama that I can see him as a real personality.

Conversations between Mamma and Miss Chamberlain centre round the question of my future and possibilities. Miss Chamberlain is always flattering to me, not with a motive, but because the bookish nature of my upbringing has set a difference between my schoolmates and myself which she sees in terms of real superiority. I like being so obviously approved, but shun the references to the future, knowing too many texts of the 'Boast not thyself of the morrow' type to want to think of it. That one will presently be an adult, wearing long dresses and pinned-up hair, looking ridiculous if one runs, is so remote a consideration that it can be postponed indefinitely. I am going to be an author, but that is my own secret, and somehow quite unconnected with growing up.

Papa has a good memory, stored with poems, and Mamma is proud that he can recite the whole of *The Pied Piper of Hamelin*. We listen on winter evenings, sitting round the fire, and learn to chant much of its rhythm ourselves. I like it better than Mamma's more dramatic selections. Mamma knows two long pieces; *The Death of King Henry the Third*, and *King Alfred and the Cakes* – the latter is our favourite. The note of tragedy, in Mamma's voice, makes me shudder with discomfort. (I might have appreciated a similar rendering given impersonally by a stranger, but could not bear that Mamma should strike any deep note.) Innumerable proverbs Mamma knows also, and quotes them on every possible opportunity...The boys and I are encouraged to learn texts, hymns and verses. The texts and hymns are Sunday School preparation; the poems figure in chapel recitation contests, for which there is sometimes a book prize.

One Saturday morning Lily H., with her usual secrecy and more than her usual portentousness, comes to tell me that the bank is broken. What this means neither she nor I know, so we slip away quickly to the main street, and see small groups of people, talking excitedly, gathered outside the closed door of the bank building. There is a notice pinned on the door. The faces of the people are grave; some of them are crying. A sobbing woman walks up and hammers on the door with her fists, but no one opens. 'All my savings gone – all my money!' she cries, and rushes away. I ask Lily if her father has lost all his money – she says not all, but some of it; and I hurry home to find out whether Papa has lost *his*. Mamma reassures me; Papa's money was not in that bank. But Lily's father builds no more new houses in Horley, and soon the family leaves the district. (Anon the bank opens its doors again and the public gloats over the prison sentences awarded to the scapegoats of the Liberator scandals, but this does not prevent a slump in Horley's retail trade.)

We lived at Horley only two years, but the ninth and tenth years of a child's life are very long ones. The days and nights were filled with new impressions, and of a duration apprehended emotionally, not by mathematical time sense. In the foreground a panorama of familiar things, small matters, to which adults appeared to attach strangely heavy values – as if, living on a small island, they were unaware of the sea lapping their beaches...Beyond the range of one's immediate perception the more or less constant awareness of undefined and infinite possibility. The commonplace, the blatantly visible, had rather the aspect of mirage, only becoming convincing and significant when some personality, with a sort of magic, gave it reality. This condition remained true throughout childhood and adolescence.

My memory leaps lightly enough over the time-space dividing the being I was in 1890–2 from the being I am in 1953. I feel glad that it links today so indubitably with the last decade of the Victorian era, and that I belong indisputably to both nineteenth and twentieth centuries.

The world of my childhood, existing for the majority of living writers only in the pages of history, is as real and vivid to me as the world of the present; indeed, the present is merely its extension in time.

There had been no heaven lying about my infancy – nor, I fear, except in Wordsworth's imagination, is this felicity the common experience of babes. My infant consciousness caught, at best, but an occasional glimpse of blue sky and scudding cloud through a dusty window, and wound its uncertain way through a veritable valley of the shadow during its early years. By the twelfth year primal terrors and confusions were past, if not yet forgotten. Law and order had entered my world; its great rhythms were constant. 'While the earth remaineth seedtime and harvest and cold and heat and summer and winter and day and night shall not cease.'

Ten to fourteen years (1892–6)

We leave Horley in the May of my eleventh year. This spring Papa looks worried; Mamma, greatly confiding in me, says that the trade of the shop, never very prosperous, continues to decline, and that he is looking for one nearer London. His choice is a corner shop in a southern suburb, in a neighbourhood of the sort described by builders as 'ripe for development'.

Mamma and I are sorry to leave Horley; Mamma because she has made a little circle of friends connected with the chapel, I because we are going to live in the town. Papa says he will be glad to see hills again – Horley is flat country; the boys are merely excited by the idea of change. We are told that we shall live within sight of the Crystal Palace towers. This may be a compensation for the loss of garden and meadows – it is advanced as such. Mamma has a crystal, a beautiful prism, through which light is seen as a rainbow; the prism rises from a bed of snowy sparkling stone. A palace built of such crystal must be very fine to see from one's windows. And a place called *Norwood* surely cannot be all streets of houses!

We arrive at the new home in Clifton Road, South Norwood, on a hot May evening. Opposite the house is a large brick-yard where two great pyres of baking bricks smoke steadily. The tops of the ugly Crystal Palace towers, visible from the front attic, are not consoling, but the rockets of its fireworks lighten the depression of our incoming. The drawn blinds of a still empty shop, the heaviness of my father's mood, the nervous irritability of my mother's, the acrid smoke overhanging the brickfield and adjacent rows of ugly little villas, and penetrating into the house in spite of closed windows – these conditions mark the beginning of our new phase.

This year I have no sense of spring or summer. There is a sun-glare on yellowish bricks and asphalt pavements, a sultry gloom upon life – this gloom has a visible presence in the smoke of the brick kilns. There is a heaviness of the air which is not even dispelled by the series of June thunderstorms. One of these, breaking out on a hot evening, continues with but short intervals until the next louring morning is well advanced. There is always a tense feeling in the house. Papa does not smile, and talks only of things to be done or arranged. In the autumn I am to go to school, but now, Mamma says, I can be useful at home. So I help to keep the boys amused, and to polish and arrange the furniture; and Mamma tells me, as we work, how worried Papa is, and how we *must* make this new shop pay, or she does not know what will happen to us. Sometimes she cannot bear the sound of the milk separator in the dairy next door; two or three times a day it begins, very softly – *rum-rum-rum-rum-rum-rum* – and gradually loudens till one must raise one's voice to be heard speaking.

Papa has to go out himself for orders – he has no assistant as in the other shops. When he is out I sit in the little room behind the shop and call Mamma if the shop bell rings. Sitting there I read *The Last Days of Pompeii* – the book is my escape from all-pervading gloom – Lytton's Pompeii and the gay, flower-crowned lives of Glaucus and his love Ione. I finish the story but to begin it again, and pass from the brilliant sunshine of Pompeiian streets and the warm, scented repose of houses where slaves run noiselessly on bare feet and only the tinkle of the fountains accompanies conversation, up to the cave of the Egyptian on the mountain side – the wise woman who reads in the stars the destinies of such as Glaucus and Ione. And then to the Circus, with Pompeii's populace thronging its galleries – to the excitement, the heat, the shouting, under the high-stretched awning – Pompeii all unaware that over its gaiety and cruelty, up in the blue sky, the smoke-cone from the long-sleeping crater is rising like a gigantic tree under whose branches the city shall sleep in death...The whole experience of that night of wondrous doom, until dawn breaks over the Bay of Naples and the ship that is carrying the lovers to safety...With *The Last Days of Pompeii* I take the curtain of romance and draw it deliberately across the window of my mind to shut out undesirable reality.

But at night I cannot sleep; the Pompeiian images persist, the beetle ticks in the old wood of the bed-frame. One night in July Mamma discovers me feverish, convulsed. A doctor comes – there is much consultation...I am to go to the seaside at once.

So it is Newhaven again, where August is lapped in sea-breeze and sunlight, and bright clouds cast gliding shadows over the slopes of the rounded hills, over waves of green vetch and golden corn. It is the cool, quiet, pleasantly scented house of Gran, with its kindly, leisurely routine and peaceful atmosphere. My cousin Evelyn has school holidays, and she and I are together all day, playing, wrangling, paying little visits to the many 'aunts', lingering on the breakwater to watch the ships sail in and out of the harbour. Dolls, woolly caterpillars caught in the garden and kept in cardboard boxes with abundance of their chosen food, jack-avils from the beach brought home in pails of sea-water, table games – these provide important and absorbing occupations. If I am wakeful at night, almost lured from this comprehensible world by the long pendulum of the grandfather clock slowly, deliberately voicing time, and by the sound of distant surf whispering of infinite space, I push my face among the warm curls of sleeping Evelyn, and presently slip into dreamless sleep myself.

The ships fascinate me. Most of them are sailing vessels, little brigs and schooners that in harbour huddle together along the lower western wharves. The higher, eastern wharf is the landing stage for the cross-channel steamers. We are forbidden to go on the eastern wharf where the great iron hooks of cranes dangle and swing, so we must watch from the opposite side of the harbour the landing of the 'foreign' passengers, strange people from a vague, only half-realised France. When one sees the white-capped waves lifting away and away to the sky-line I feel that the sea is infinite, without bound or further shore. The dim idea of France takes indefinite shape when I pass the Old Inn and read on its wall the inn's great boast – that here King Louis Philippe slept on the night of his flight from a nation which had disowned and expelled him. 'France' becomes a crowd of foreign-looking people waving weapons and running after a fleeing king.

The little brigs and schooners, with naked masts and decks white with chalk, black with coaldust, or yellow with sand, lean by their lower wharf, insignificant in comparison with the lordly cross-channel steamers. But each one of them puts on dignity and consequence when, at the harbour mouth, it drops the tug's towing rope, unfurls billowing sails, and stands out to sea, the equal, perhaps the superior, of steam craft coming in. It is the sailing ship and not the steamer whose picture adorns the parlour walls of the aunts, and the finest picture of them all hangs in Aunt

Bec's parlour – a painting of Uncle Will's tea-clipper the *Omba*, with all sails set, swinging over a deep blue sea. In the same room is a large photograph of the *Omba*'s crew, Uncle Will surrounded by his men. The loss of the *Omba* is one of Mamma's stories – a brief one. Nothing is known of the ship after she left Canton on her last voyage; a chest, bearing her name, was washed up on an Indian shore. Evelyn does not remember her papa; but he looks down on us, with a merry smile, from a portrait above the piano when Evelyn plays and we sing songs together – 'White Wings' and the rest.

In Aunt Bec's parlour there are curious things brought home by Uncle Will – delicate, fragile sea-plants like trumpets, tiny foreign birds perching on branches in a glass case, a Chinese junk carved in ivory, the helmsman standing high on the prow, the rowers at their oars. And though Evelyn and I play table games here, and sing songs to the old, highly polished piano with the red silk-pleated front, there is always a feeling of Sunday – the good sort of Sunday – in this pleasantly scented room. While we play, Aunt Bec sits in her chair by the window, sometimes with embroidery-work in her hands, sometimes just gazing at nothing.

Scarlet-coated soldiers are met occasionally in the streets of Newhaven. They come from the fort on the right of the harbour. They have very white belts and shining brass buttons, and walk stiffly. It surprises me that they can look so smart, seeing that they live underground – the doors of the fort are set in the side of the hill. One can see no windows, but only bits of wall and roof sticking up here and there from the hillside. When the guns fire from the Fort across the bay the people in Fort Road must keep their windows open lest these be cracked. Once the firing starts when we are picnicking on the beach of the Bay, and we watch the shells burst about the target, sending high fountains of spray to the sky. The boom of the guns is horrid in one's ears, but there is nothing to be afraid of, I know. The soldiers at the Fort are only playing at war nowadays. Real war was long ago – it belongs to history books.

Evelyn keeps silkworms. When first I see these great maggots lying on mulberry leaves in a shallow box they fill me with loathing. But Evelyn speaks of them with affection, and shows me a book-marker of yellow silk spun last year by their antecedents; she hopes to get much more silk from this boxful. Twice a day we give them fresh mulberry leaves; they at once desert the old ones, and start sawing industriously at the new. Evelyn is excited when she sees a worm waving its fore-legs, looks for the thinnest thread of silk to come from its mouth, and drops it into a paper spill. Before a week of my holiday has passed all the silk-worms are in spills, and the spills pinned in rows on the wall of our bedroom...A day comes when Aunt Bec says we may wind the silk, and the spills are taken down – there are no fat maggots in them, but silken spools, pointed at the ends: we put them into warm water, and presently I am shown how to unwind one...at the centre of the silken spool a brown skin case, closely wrapping a folded creature, alive, for one end of the cases moves...All the creatures are put into a box of warmed bran...

Moths! Moths with short, silly little wings and thick, velvety bodies. What, I ask, shall we bring them to eat? Evelyn says they never eat, and bids me watch them. I do. I see them struggle from their cases, buzz excitedly round, female seeking male; I see her link herself with him, and movement cease but for a faint quivering of wings; so linked they remain.

The next day the larger moth moves away from the smaller, and begins to drop rows of yellow eggs on the clean paper in the box-lid where Evelyn places her. The smaller moth's body and wings seem to crumple – soon he is dead, but his mate lays hundreds of eggs before she dies.

It is my first study of life stages. I feel that the male moth is to be pitied. To struggle out of the cocoon with wings, but never to rise in the air...to be grasped and held by the female until strength is spent and wings are useless!

But I carry home with me a hundred yellow eggs which are to be kept safe until next spring...

Thus, being at Newhaven, I miss the happenings of the week when the bailiffs while away their time of occupation in the shop parlour at home, and the day when Mamma hears the hammer of the auctioneer knocking down to strangers her cherished possessions. The house, on my return, is queerly empty. The beds remain, indeed, and a chair in each bedroom, and washstands, and Mamma's chest of drawers; the kitchen, where we have meals, remains much as before. The shop parlour, the sitting-room and the attics are without furniture. This curious state of things at first excites me not unpleasantly, especially when I am told that the piano is not sold, but merely returned to the piano store for the time being. Mamma explains everything when Papa is out of the way, crying, sometimes, as she talks. How Papa had not the money to pay the wholesale grocers for goods supplied at Horley; how Papa would have paid them everything if they would have agreed to wait until he had worked up the trade of this shop – how they refused to wait, preferring to 'sell him up'. Even the stock of the shop now belongs to them, and Papa is only their manager for a few months, until it is sold off retail. How nothing at all would have been left to us if my uncle James had not come to the sale and bought for our use the remaining furniture.

The boys and I are allowed to take possession of the empty attics, and they undergo various transformations. We start a family journal and they become editorial offices. We form, with the Conninghams, Marion and her brothers, who live near, a secret society, after the manner of the children in *What Katy Did*. Marion is a year younger than me, small, neat, with a little round, rosy, delicate face, brown eyes and short, golden-brown ringlets. I never feel intimate with Marion, but admire her small, compact prettiness, her soft, musical voice. She has two brothers, who prefer their own games to ours, though a wet Saturday afternoon will bring them to our attics...The connection with the Vernalls is dropped. Mamma cannot overlook Mrs Vernall's 'gross carelessness' in not advising her, in time for her to cancel a prearranged day's visit, that Eddy was ill at home with scarlet fever.

Arthur and I are sent to a large new Board School in the neighbourhood – there is no money for private school fees. The segregation of the sexes is complete, so we never meet in school. Bare walls of painted brick, long varnished desks, a large varnished cupboard and teacher's desk before each block, high, square-paned windows and asphalted playgrounds characterise this school. The head mistress of the girls' department, Miss Smythe, is of solid and commanding personality. The word *ample* well describes her. She has large features, a large, firm mouth, benevolent brown eyes, a ready smile always well under control, which could not conceivably degenerate into a grin. Her plentiful, wavy grey hair is smoothly plaited and coiled on the crown of her head. She wears a sort of individual uniform, a dress of black or plum-coloured serge whose pattern never varies; it has a full, high-necked bodice frilled at the neck with narrow white lace, a broad waistband edged with braid, puffed bishop sleeves frilled at the wrists, a long, full skirt gathered into the waistband. All her movements have a heavy benevolent dignity. To the pupils she is kind, generous; her authority is complete and unquestioned, her personality unchallenged by any member of the staff. The senior classes receive Bible lessons from her every morning – for the space of these lessons she leaves her official desk and sits perched on a high chair, like an infant's table chair, but without arms. I am always surprised at the alacrity with which she mounts into this chair, and wonder that her weight does not tip it forward when she steps on to its footrest. Her lessons are full of precise information and graphic description; she brings scripture history to life; under her guidance the jumble of familiar Bible narrative begins to fall into sequence. My class teacher has hollowed brown eyes in a thin white face framed with fine soft black hair, and seems so grateful for carefully written exercises that carelessness appears inexcusable.

During the winter of this year we leave the Norwood shop and move into a miserable six-celled box of a cottage in a mean street. Its dirt and surroundings nearly drive Mamma frantic. It is, however, only a makeshift, and in six weeks we are again in a house with a shop-front, situated in Portland Road, South Norwood. This is a queer house. Originally a small wooden cottage standing in a garden, it has been enlarged by extensions back and front, so that the old outer walls and windows are enclosed. The shop, linked up in a line with others, occupies the one-time garden space. A glass partition has replaced the old cottage parlour window, and the parlour, like the room above it, gets only the light that filters through from shop and front bedroom respectively. Dark stairs lead from the kitchen to the upper floor, and my enclosed bedroom, which opens to Mamma's, is lighted only by the glass panes in either door...Mamma is to keep this shop, where sweets only are sold. Papa has now an insurance agency and is out most of the day.

On my eleventh birthday Papa gives me a copy of Dickens' *Nicholas Nickleby* and takes me to the Crystal Palace. I have long since discovered that the Crystal Palace is not built of crystal; but on fine days the huge glass roof shines in the distance, and I am eager to see the inside. Seen nearby the glass panes are dirty, and the iron framework wants paint, but when we have passed the turnstile and walked up the long corridor to the main building these defects are forgotten. Inside the Palace there is a magic of strange scents, of organ music, of palm-trees lifting high the great splay leaves seen in picture books, of marble basins where goldfish swim between the stems of water-lilies. There are coloured lights over glittering stalls in dark corners; there are tiers and tiers of choir benches rising to the great organ loft, where now, a small black figure under the shaded keyboard lamps, the organist is enthroned, creating waves of wondrous sound, a magician controlling storms. 'A day in thy courts is better than a thousand' – the text comes to my mind. But surely if one came a thousand times there would still remain something to explore, something overlooked of wonder, some corner mystery of crimson and gold, and an infinity of music…The statue population is a little awesome – everywhere are statues of cold, yellowish, occasionally cracked plaster, standing and sitting in stiff attitudes, and yet, if one studies the faces, with more meaning and significance than one sees in the faces of the aimlessly strolling, staring people. The statue folk – it is as though, like Lot's wife, they had looked behind, and a curse had petrified them. I fancy them released at night, walking about the Palace after all the living have left it. With a sense of shock I read Voltaire's name. Voltaire and Tom Paine were the Atheists. Mamma has told me that an atheist is a person who does not believe in God – the very worst kind of man. I look with awed fascination at the small, bent figure in the armchair, slender fingers resting upon its arm, thin, sunken face and sharp nose, fixed, smiling mouth, eyes that see – see – what is it that he can see? I catch my breath, leave Voltaire, and find, to my joy, a Pompeiian house, with a tiny fountain in a marble bowl, and a plaster fawn in its courtyard.

Papa signs public library ticket vouchers for me, asking me to promise him that I will choose alternately fiction and books of some other category. Reluctantly I promise; the reading of fiction projects me into a world of romance which provides an easy escape from the dullness and limitation of daily life. Travel and verse are acceptable alternatives to novels. Beside the counter of South Norwood public library I study the red and blue numbers shown on the indicator – red if one's choice is available – blue if not. What exciting chance lies in a title! In general, my demands in my thirteenth year are magic, music and mystery.

Daily life supplies none of these qualities. Poverty governs life, and worry is poverty's companion. Half-consciously I notice the set, driven expression which poverty has ironed upon my parents' faces. Shabbiness and monotony are the dominant features of our environment. I think that the parents try to console themselves with the reflection that in the mean streets around us the majority of inhabitants are poorer than we – but to me this fact is no consolation. I have sensed another plane of existence, one in which there is no poverty, but an ample sufficiency of desirable things – good clothes, books, music, travel, happy people who spend their lives in writing books and plays, painting pictures, enjoying each other's company...I can, and will, write. The *Christian Commonwealth* (children's column) pays me half-a-crown for a story (not to exceed 300 words).

The boys attend a nearby school, in Birchanger Road, South Norwood; an old, inconvenient building, but one in which modern methods of teaching are tried out. Frank is taught to read by the new phonetic method, and to the amusement of the family spells 'fox' *fer-or-gooza*...I have a long walk to school; at Miss Smythe's suggestion I remain at Whitehorse Road, making, each day, a privileged late arrival which pleases my vanity. School life is not without attractions. Standard V is taught by 'Peggy' – the most vital and fascinating of the class-mistresses – in the best class-room of the school. All the matter of the course, from 'fractions' and 'practice' sums to the geography of the British Empire, is new to me. I understand that the arithmetic, which must have some hidden use, is to 'train you to think'. The British Empire is that part of the world which really matters. Literature is taught by the head mistress, who has chosen passages from *Paradise Lost* for our study. I memorise and declaim with secret exultation the speeches of the fallen angels in the great language of Milton. Great Milton, great Beelzebub, thus to defy the God of the terrors, the God of blazing stars and burning worlds! The exultation is yet half fearful – the menace of the Last Day is not yet out-lived; and though my universe has a better appearance of stability and assurance than it had in early childhood, my confidence in it can be shaken from time to time by Latter Day Adventist pamphlets pushed through the letter box or passed round in school.

Every day there is a Bible lesson, or a set of questions to answer in preparation for the annual scripture exam. But there is much in the Bible which does not enter into exam syllabuses. Curious things, fascinating, horrible things – verses that girls point out and pass along the rows of desks in silent study time. Half-understood, revolting sugges- tions, at which the girls excitedly giggle…I glance hastily at the passage and shut the Bible, but when I am alone find the page again and study it curiously.

There are school periods when the subject is 'composition'. These may be sheer enjoyment. Complete silence in the room but for the scratching of pens, and this I soon forget, in the pleasure of my own writing. The story or essay grows quickly, the right word comes when I call it. Sometimes the class adjoining ours is singing songs. One of the songs is about summer – I catch the line 'and the glow of lilies rare' – and no more; but the tune as a whole stays with me, giving a kind of atmosphere to my thought. (Years later I discover that it was a melody from one of Handel's oratorios.)

The R.S.P.C.A. offers the school a prize for an essay on a subject relating to animal welfare. In preparation we receive lessons inspired by the literature of the Society, and I read with horror of the cruelties associated with the provision of flesh foods and with the manufacture of kid gloves. I determine to eat no more meat and never to wear kid gloves. Mamma has strenuous objections to the first of these resolves, but ultimately compromises by doubling the quantity of my daily milk ration. Very readily she agrees to accompany me to the Crystal Palace for the purpose of receiving the prize at the hands of the Duchess of York. But this function is disappointing. Heaven knows what glory I had expected; I find myself one of an unending line of prize-winners trailing past a table where a bored lady hands each a small book of animal stories resembling the books of my early childhood.

The long needlework periods at school are boring, except during the term when the class-mistress introduces George Macdonald's fairy-tale *The Princess and the Goblin*, which is read aloud to us as we sew. How welcome is the sight of its fine Blackie edition, the silver design on its green cloth cover, and its oliveen edges. The fairy-tales of the Brothers Grimm I have at home, but they seem to be just fantastic stories without application to anything in my experience. *The Princess and the Goblin* is more than an entrancing story, and I am now of age to appreciate a parable. The immortal being envisaged by Macdonald as 'the old princess' provides me with a new conception of divinity. It is a red-letter day for me when the book's sequel, *The Princess and Curdie* finds its way into the tiny school library. The reading of these two books enables me to dismiss for ever the horrific image of the Almighty impressed upon my mind by 'the Earliest Form of Religion the Infant Mind is Capable of Receiving'. It also prepares me, two years later, for that presentation of the Buddhist philosophy to be found in Sir Edwin Arnold's *The Light of Asia*. And it inaugurates a period of years during which my imagination seizes only too avidly upon the fascinating creations of novelist and poet, and turns from the observation of life at first hand. At the moment I am being taught that all creation moves upward or downward along a scale ranging between absolute evil and supreme good. Virtue is the way upward, towards beauty, sin the way downward, towards ugliness. All is well if desire tends upward. I have no doubt that I may climb the tower stairway with the Princess Irene, and find, not a wizened old woman in a bare attic, but the glorious being in whom age is a diviner youth. I shall scarcely fear to sink into that silver bath of hers, in whose depths the stars glimmer, or to thrust, like Curdie, soiled hands into her fire of burning roses for cleansing. The Princess Irene's 'grandmother' is my first fully visualised symbol of the ever-living, the human–divine that comprehends life as one, linking youth to age in unity, significance and strength. But I confuse *symbols* with *things* as do all primitive people.

Out of my fervid desire to meet both on the same plane I make an experiment, half-credulously – an attempt to find a fairy world with a door opening into daily life. A school-fellow shows me a tiny bright key, set with an amber stone – probably a watch key – but she tells me it is a fairy key and will fit any lock. She will lend it to me; I must put it under my pillow and stay awake till the clock strikes midnight – then, if I fit the key into my bedroom door-lock it will admit me into a marvellous fairy garden. Well, perhaps! Hopeful in *Pilgrim's Progress* found the key called Promise, but that, of course, was an allegory. Macdonald's story *might* be true or partly true; the Princess Irene was much more real than Christian or Hopeful, and she walked straight from her nursery up an actual staircase and found wonders of which no one else in the house dreamed! I take the key, dubiously, not unaware that my school-mate may be romancing, and will think me silly for believing what she says, yet with a faint hope that the marvel may be realised. Staying awake till midnight is easy; hope and excitement increase with the passing of the half-hours. Midnight strikes – I rise, shivering, and immediately feel heavy with doubt. The tiny key is inserted; a tiny key it remains! My disappointment is more than equalled by shame that I have allowed myself to be fooled.

Mamma's shop does not pay. It is no minor tragedy when, accidentally, I knock one of the heavy sweet bottles from the top window shelf down into the window, smashing a large pane of plate glass. In less than a year we move again, this time into rooms behind a greengrocer's shop. The greengrocer is a curly-haired young man who lounges about collarless, with hands in the pockets of his wide knickers. His sister, several years older than he, does his accounts and appears to be there to keep him in order. She has a coiffure of much waved, bright yellow hair set cone-shaped on the top of her head; she talks fast and often to Mamma about her troubles.

Mamma attends the Baptist church – a rather pretentious new building, blank-walled down one side, awaiting the raising of funds whereby it may be finished according to plan. Arthur and I are sent to its Sunday School, where the pupils' obviously new clothes make me feel consciously shabby. I hate the pew beside the overbearing high blank wall. Papa does not attend this church. He is tired on Sunday mornings and seldom goes out, but always dresses in his best suit for mid-day dinner, and after tea attends one of a variety of churches in the neighbourhood. If he has had what he calls 'a good week' he will perhaps go to a church in London…a Greek or French or Russian church, dividing the journey between a long walk and a tram ride.

I make two friends, Gertrude and Eva Davey. Seeing them first wheeling their dolls' pram up and down the street path, I imagine them twin sisters, but find Gertrude to be my age and Eva a year younger. They are dark-skinned, with brown eyes, Gertrude's very placid, Eva's laughing. Gertrude's hair is long, slightly waved, Eva has heavy dark curls, which I admire. They wear pretty frocks of apple-green crêpe with silk sashes.

In former days Mamma would have been horrified to know her children playing in the street with those of neighbours. But here there is not even a yard into which she can pen us, the yard being full of the greengrocer's fruit and vegetable crates. My dolls therefore make the acquaintance of the Davey dolls.

Doll-play took no small place from babyhood to my thirteenth year. It was serious play; the dolls were my real children, whose day's routine must coincide with my own. Functions such as eating and walking had to be pretended, but such obvious pretence was seldom exercised. Imagination supplied each doll with a definite personality; relationships between them were of more or less friendly kind. Much of the time spent with my cousin Evelyn, and most of my association with the Davey children, was connected with doll-play – the continuous serial of the domestic drama we wove around our doll-children. I was always the mother of my dolls when the play was social – yet when day-dreaming or inventing situations alone, or in dreams at night, my part was that of the husband and father.

Gertrude and Eva attend weekly Band of Hope meetings, organised in connection with South Norwood Congregational church Sunday School. Mamma is contemptuous, but does not forbid, so I accompany them. There are ugly, chorussy hymns and boring addresses, but also recitation competitions in which I can take part. Not the prize, but the consciousness of achievement is the recompense for those moments of excruciating nervous tension as one waits to mount the platform.

In my thirteenth year we move again, from South Norwood to Selhurst. This time it is to a cottage – one of a row of dingy cottages on the extreme limit of Mamma's conception of respectability. It is but a stone's throw from 'the slums'. The slums, I understand, are unclean places where two or more families share one small cottage, where cheap lodging-houses provide sleeping room for a few pence a night, where people are physically dirty, and wear ragged clothing without shame.

My mother declares, before we have spent a week in this cottage, that she cannot endure it. The walls are infested with bugs; they make their appearance under the edges of the new wall-paper; nightfall is horror. My father wearily recommences search for a possible dwelling, very cheap, but clean; he has no success. The rooms, meanwhile, are one by one sealed and disinfected with burning sulphur. The pest is conquered; we stay.

Papa's commission as an industrial insurance agent is just sufficient to keep us, with cheese-paring economy on Mamma's part, and odd contributions of half-worn clothing from relatives. I dislike wearing these second-hand garments, but they at least are of good material and cut. We have no boy cousins, so the suits worn by Arthur and Frank are necessarily the cheapest that can be bought, with knickers ill-cut, too long in the leg, bagging at the knee. Arthur is thickset, but Frank has a slim, shapely body and limbs, and I do wish I could buy him suits like those shown on the models in the clothiers' windows. Our stockings are darned and darned; Papa puts patches on our boots; but we never go hungry. Nor do any more debts accumulate; our parents have learned in one lesson to 'cut their coat according to their cloth', and in later years develop even a perverse satisfaction in its scantness, making a virtue of necessity. During our eight years in this cottage, my mother's eye-sockets hollow until her eyes seem each to gleam from the back of a little cave; my father's body becomes a bony framework on which his clothes hang limply, and his carefully brushed, once thick fair hair, crosses the crown of his head in scanty, lifeless strands.

One school morning a new pupil is admitted to my class, a fair-haired little girl in a short golden-brown velveteen frock, edged at the neck with broad, pointed lace. She has an oval face, clear-complexioned, each cheek pink-flushed, and light brown eyes. Her mass of pale golden wavy hair, loosely caught back with golden brown ribbon, reaches her waist in a shower of small, perfect ringlets. Behind the new pupil enters a miniature woman with a tight-skinned, colourless face dead white between her plain tight black dress and crêpe bonnet. Rose R. is the child's name; the class-mistress enters it in the register. There is some quite ordinary conversation between mistresss and mother, and the latter is about to leave, when she turns to the class and announces, clearly – 'Rosie is a child of the King, as I hope all her school companions may be!'

The girls are too astonished even to giggle. I guess that the woman is giving a religious significance to her words, and feel instantly sorry for the pretty child. How embarrassing to have so conspicuous a mother! Rose R.'s eyes are downcast, and her blush has deepened. When the classroom door has closed, 'Peggy' calls me forward and gives Rose into my charge...At morning interval the girls gather round, shy ones admiring silently, one or two of the bolder venturing to stroke her hair...She accepts our admiration with smiling, downcast eyes. Only when suddenly the eyes are raised I feel disappointed – they are rather like a doll's – not glassy, but lacking depth. I look away from the eyes to the rose-petal cheeks, the beautiful hair...Her coming is a joy.

Rose invites me to her home. The widow is a laundress. On Mondays and Tuesdays the kitchen living-room is steamy with wet linen, on Wednesdays and Thursdays full of the scorchy smell of linen freshly ironed. On Friday linen baskets are packed, and mother and daughter carry them home. On Saturdays the widow cooks and cleans, and in the evening lies back on the old sofa to darn and mend, while Rose reads to her, always from the Bible. On Sundays she rests, as she tells us, 'in the porch of the King's house'. On Sunday evenings, having put away the black silk bonnet and mantle worn only to the chapel of the Plymouth Brethren, she again lies on the sofa, her bony, shiny little hands

folded, her eyes bright. 'Rosie knows', I once hear her say
from the sofa, 'it doesn't matter what rough box she has me
put into when I'm gone.' With a beaming smile she says it,
making my flesh creep...She is a good laundress, and
people readily employ her; she works eleven hours a day
rather than refuse proffered work – it is all for Rosie –
Rosie who must be dressed in velvet because its dark
richness sets off the fine silken ringlets of her dancing hair.

She begs me to help Rosie with her lessons, offers me tea,
and suggests that I may like to practise on the organ. In
the parlour is a big American organ, which Rose plays,
employing its swells to their utmost, so that ornaments on
the shelf rattle, and I have a buzzing in my ears. When
Evelyn plays the piano I love watching her racing fingers;
but Rose's fingers slither slyly over the keys, showing her
queer, flattened, bitten nails. I think a marble would lie
without rolling off upon each indented finger nail. I wish
Rose would not play.

Rose invites me to go to her Sunday School – she says she
is 'converted', and doubts whether I am. One summer
Sunday afternoon I accompany her to the Plymouth
Brethren's hall. Daintily dressed, her bright curls bobbing,
she walks with assurance up the aisle, perhaps knowing, as
I do, that the poorly dressed children who fill the seats
watch and envy her. Religiously she joins in the singing, and
closes her eyes during the prayer. The address given from
the platform is of the mission sermon sort, about one's sins,
and the need for conversion, and the nearness of the Last
Day. The children, at first fidgety, become half-frightened
and quiet as the preacher's voice arises to threat and
entreaty. I glance at Rose; apparently she is not listening;
her eyes are wandering indifferently round the hall. As
soon as we leave she begins to talk laughingly about some
boys who were there – she looks behind to see if they are
following her. Suddenly I feel angry with her and with
myself...I want a friend with whom I can share my
thoughts and something hidden beyond them which the

people around me drive back into the dark – and Rose is not that friend...Rose is like a brightly coloured flower without scent.

Papa sometimes takes the boys and me to London. We walk to the horse-tram terminus at Streatham, and ride on the tram to one of the bridges. Then there will be a visit to the Tower and the surrounding streets, or a long tramp through Nine Elms and Vauxhall, ending with the Embankment and the new picture gallery built on the foundations of old Millbank prison. Papa is very interested in old places, and I think likes showing us how slum people live. The spacious halls of the Tate Gallery, the huge pictures of Watts, Turner, Titian and the rest are the more impressive because we come to them out of the squalor of Nine Elms. I enjoy the gorgeous colouring of the incomprehensible pictures, and stand absorbed before the painted dreams of tropic seas, ships frozen into the ice, the Pool of London seen with the painter's eye – its 'toil, glitter, grime and wealth on a flowing tide'. The infinite variety of life makes its first conscious appeal to me.

One day Papa invites us to come and see a procession on the London–Brighton road. The Act of Parliament requiring all locomotives proceeding along the highway to move behind a pedestrian carrying a red flag has just been repealed. Engine-driven cars may henceforth travel freely on the public roads, and to celebrate the occasion a motorist's club has organised a run from London to Brighton. We watch a hundred or more cars pass – not really in procession, but jerking down the road at intervals, puffing, clanking, spurting fumes of petroleum. Papa tells us we have witnessed an historic event, and that in time horse-driven vehicles will give place to such cars. A tract, thrust through our letter box, declares the cars to be a sign of the End of the World. The cars, it states, are mentioned in the Bible, 'Many shall run to and fro, and knowledge shall be greatly increased.' But my study of the Bible is advanced far enough to secure me against the ancient fear. The dread twenty-fifth chapter of St Matthew contains its own disproof. 'This generation shall not pass', it records as the words of Christ, 'till all these things be done. Heaven and earth shall pass away, but my word shall not pass away.' Jesus must have been wrong. Generations after generations – all the centuries of English history – have passed away since He spoke, and the earth endures. If Christ could be mistaken it is impossible to accept the Bible as true in every verse and word. This, I know, would be a dreadful thing to say aloud, but it is a comforting secret.

Mamma forms a connection with a Baptist mission chapel near home, where she makes a circle of friends. The boys attend the Sunday School of the parent church, and most of their social life is centred there. Presently I am pursuing much the same desultory round of church-going as Papa. In my fourteenth year our paths coincide for perhaps six months; we attend at even-song on Sundays in St James's church, Sydenham Road, attracted by a preacher of personality and oratorical power, who increases his attraction by providing chamber-music recitals after the service. There are Sunday evenings with sunset glow lingering in the stained glass of the west window; night advancing to organ music and accompanied by the stately flame-rank of tall altar candles. I join in the singing of the hymn:

> We thank thee that thy Church, unsleeping
> as day rolls onward into night,
> her constant watch is ever keeping...

Easy and pleasant to picture this world-wide peace, this Sunday evening concentration of the world's family upon the All-Father.

> As o'er each continent and island
> the dawn leads on another day
> the voice of prayer is never silent...

I see grey waves flecked with the rose of dawn – palm-trees standing stark against the sunrise. But I can rise above them, high enough to see the continents moving with the spin of the earth – and then I do not hear that voice of prayer. It is too thin, too petty, too futile a voice. In the heaven there is a music great enough to drown it utterly – the music Shakespeare knew:

> There's not the smallest orb that thou beholdest
> But in his motion like an angel sings,
> Still quiring to the young-eyed cherubims.

With 'cherubims' I return to the choir, to the soft shine of candle-light upon gilt mouldings, to the string quartet now moving to its seats in the chancel. I listen to violin music that leaps and flickers like broken sunlight on rippled sea, while a 'cello booms from the depths...A woman soloist in white glides among the candles and sings of Sunday on a ship at sea. In conclusion the Reverend Clement Bendish, so obviously 'the stoléd minister', pronounces the ancient Hebrew benediction, standing in commanding outline before the illuminated altar, while all the people kneel. When the quiet voice of the organ intimates that *it* is rising from its knees we pass out into the dim street. There is a whoop from a released choirboy and the clank of a tramcar...all spells are broken...Tomorrow will be Monday.

(Life within me is moving faster upward from the subconscious, where experience is unclassified, to the conscious, where everything claims to be placed in order of its relative value. It is as if the two boxes labelled *Good* and *Bad*, provided for my primitive efforts in classification, must now be emptied and their contents re-examined. Not only do I find it necessary to make transfers from one box to the other, but I discover a perplexing number of matters which seem wrongly placed in either box. If Good be white and Bad black, what of the many tones of grey? Henceforward I become increasingly aware of the blending of good and evil in human conduct, and sometimes

III Jessie Chambers *c.* 1908

IV D. H. Lawrence *c.* 1908

even find it necessary to reverse values which people about me appear to hold, and which instruction has emphasised.

If I have less difficulty in defining the difference between beauty and ugliness it is because the standards of others have been little imposed upon me in such matters. My appreciation of beauty is either directly sensuous, being of sight, sound and scent, or is controlled by perceptions and emotions beyond my present power of analysis.

The trappings of home and school are ugly: ugly with a uniformity of cheap, shoddy material and blatant design. The rows of yellow brick houses joined in long terraces, all alike, are monotonously ugly. Through streets of these terraces I walk daily to school. Yet beauty appears, as a surprise, casually and unexpectedly – in a gleam from a red sunset deepening a chimney pot to a rich orange, in a point of starlight pricking the dusky blue over three bell towers of a school block...My memory of the Sussex Downs about Newhaven suggests a more constant beauty, whether they lie in a clarity of green and gold against a fair sky or are glimpsed through driving cloud.

I perceive little of beauty in people as yet. But my cousin Evelyn's presence, her step, voice, and the dance of her golden-brown curls, arouse in me a keen pleasure. I admire the dexterity of her fingers as they race through her pianoforte studies, and sadly envy her the music lessons I have missed. With all her superior advantages Evelyn does not patronise me. She knows, of course, that she is a year older and half a head taller, and expects this to be recognised. But our differences interest her – if she can play, I can write, and she frankly admires my stories and poems. To no one but Evelyn can I show them.

In my fourteenth year there is a happy after-Christmas holiday at Newhaven. A rare snowfall covers the Downs, and low-lying, flooded lands by the Ouse are frozen. We go skating with Evelyn's friends, some of whom are boys. Secret friendships with boys become exciting only because Evelyn is involved; at school I have no interest in the

85

popular game of passing forbidden notes into the Boys Department. But Evelyn associates ideas of love, marriage and babies with her boy friends. Love, as I imagine it, belongs to romance – to the fine, remote lovers of the book world; a world that I hardly dare hope to see in reality. Marriage seems a state to avoid. Evelyn herself has told me how babies are born, and other things about the lot of married women. I do not want babies, or a husband I must promise to obey, or a life of continual housework. This I say outright, before Aunt Bec, Gran'ma and Evelyn. Gran'ma raises her eye-brows very high, stares at me and says nothing. Aunt Bec smiles and says, 'Wait and see!' Evelyn laughs and calls me queer.

I am now in the 7th standard at school – one of the half-dozen pupils not withdrawn before reaching the limit of elementary school life. There are no possible scholarships to higher schools and grammar school fees are prohibitive. The day of the public secondary school is yet far off in time. But the education authority – now Croydon Borough Council – holds a yearly examination of senior pupils. It is called the Pass and Honour Exam, and four ornate certificates, testifying to my abilities, hang on my bedroom walls. The certificates are worth just as much as they cost to produce – no more.

I have acquired a facility in the use of the written word that has brought me easy prizes, and an easy and undue sense of superiority. The written word is the key to appraisal in school. Information may be scanty, observation superficial, the tongue clumsy, the hands untrained – but if the well-turned phrase goes down on paper, all is well! I can parse and analyse sentences according to the rules of English grammar; I have learned something of the geography of the British Empire, also of the history of Roman Britain and Saxon England; I have studied the Pentateuch, the gospels of St Matthew and St Mark, and the Book of the Acts of the Apostles; I have memorised several

Psalms and other Biblical passages, some Milton, and a long poem by E. Nesbit...I can work various types of sums, including Simple Interest and a mystery called Stocks and Shares. I have practised hemming, sewing, patching and darning (on scraps of material). From a primer I have gathered some idea of elementary hygiene.

My parents and teachers have assumed that at the age of fourteen I shall become a pupil-teacher. Hitherto I have concurred, but now I am in revolt. It is not that any other means of earning a living presents more attractions. I know that as a teacher I may expect a greater measure of free time and a better salary than if I take work in shop or office. I do not dislike the prospect of work in school. But the immediacy of school-leaving suggests a prospect of freedom – not freedom from study, which interests and absorbs me – but freedom from the suburban life I have grown to hate. I want wide spaces, fresh wind blowing over green country, an idealised village life, the Downs, the sea! The bond of apprenticeship will compel me to four more years of suburban existence. Perhaps a post in the country may be possible, or – vain dream – an editor may accept one of my stories and be the means of discovering a patron ready to guarantee opportunities of education...This vision is inspired by Evelyn's initiative; she shows her mother my verses written at Newhaven on the occasion of a shipping disaster – Aunt Bec sends them to a local paper, which prints them, giving my name and age. (An even worse effort would, under the circumstance, have awakened local interest.) Evelyn, delighted, posts me a copy of the paper. 'The captain of the *Lyon*', she writes, 'is going about saying something ought to be done for that little girl.'

I build some castles in Spain.

4-2

ADOLESCENCE

Adolescence (1896–1903)

The survival of man, says biology, is due to his capacity for adapting himself to changing conditions. Sociology perceives a threat to his further development in the working of this same capacity. Depress the standard of living, limit opportunity, reduce the range of possible experience, and the majority of people will, unconsciously, and in longer or shorter time, shrink to the measure of their narrowed environment.

My mother, when first confronted with life on the verge of the slum, hugged her middle-class traditions and sense of superiority, avoided her neighbours (except when she might step down from her pedestal to *help* them) and cherished the pose of an exile. By the end of five years she had become assimilated to our degree of poverty. The sanctions of her religion had assisted the process. Misfortune, seen as the will of God, called for resignation. A nearby mission hall welcomed her, and contact with its missioners resulted in her membership of its parent church. Within this community she rooted, taking with her my younger brother Frank. My father stood aloof. He attributed his misfortunes not to the will of God but to his own incapacity. He had failed in business through sheer lack of judgment – his own stern Liberalism, and the philosophy of The Steady Aim condemned him. He felt himself lacking in the qualities that make for success, and this conviction crushed his initiative. As an employee of the insurance company, miserably paid and treated, he could still admire the financial success of its organisation. He told himself that he was yet, in all essentials, his own master. He could arrange his collecting rounds as he pleased, canvass in any area he liked, and the sky was his ceiling. The city reading room gave him the world's news, and its library many more books than he could read. Once a week the collection of a few insurance premiums took him out of the town, to the hill villages of Shirley and Addington – on this day he walked twelve miles and ate his mid-day banana sandwiches among the Shirley heather.

My parents accept, with fatalism, my decision against apprenticeship as pupil-teacher. I leave school, and for the next eighteen months carry on a desultory search for the end of the rainbow and the pot of gold. Housework is expected of me in the mornings, but my mother is no fanatic in respect of cleaning, nor does she make me responsible for any special domestic duty. She is slow, thorough, exacting in detail, and her precise instructions, so often repeated, are irritating. (Only in later life did I realise how well she taught me the things she understood.) My father offers to give me shorthand lessons; he has made the subject a hobby, and can use several systems with speed; I accept – but my interest is temporary. Secretly I continue to write children's stories. The romances written earlier were, I know now, silly; one cannot write convincingly of things one has not experienced. In secret I send the stories to magazines, paying return postage from my weekly shilling of pocket-money. I spend many hours in the quiet little South Norwood public library and reading room; one may now visit the shelves and dip into the books at will. To my delight I find a new book by Olive Schreiner, *Trooper Peter Halkett*, which I take into the reading room and devour at one sitting, walking home afterwards mechanically, scarcely conscious of place. With less emotional furore, but an imagination so stimulated that each volume is an extension of personal experience I read everything the library can give me of George Macdonald, Scott, Fenimore Cooper, Dickens and Lew Wallace. Some of the reviews to be seen in the reading room attract me – the *Bookman*, the *Athenaeum*, the *Studio*. And at every visit I con the advertisement columns headed Educational and Personal – hoping for I know not what vague opportunity.

Oliver Twist comes to me as a Christmas present; at the same time Arthur gets *The Last of the Mohicans*. I read and re-read these books. The scenes between Sikes and Nancy, Fagin's trial, and the chapter headed 'Fagin's Last Night Alive' are too vivid and mean sleepless night hours, but Dickens' milder characters make little impression...The America of Fenimore Cooper becomes, for the time, land of heart's desire – the wild life of the forest and the way of the Indian are the ideal. I follow the trail with Uncas and Chingachgook and Hawkeye; the young English officer and the English girls he is conducting through the forest are without interest...The slaughter of the colt, as a safety precaution, makes me wince, makes me resentful. Why should man regard his own life as of so much more value than that of the horse? Man kills deliberately, the horse harms none. This, it seems to me, indicates superiority.

Free scholarships to secondary and high schools are instituted in Croydon this year. Arthur is eligible for the competitive examination. I want him to take it, and urge the matter till he is induced to join a preparatory class held after school hours by one of the class-masters – a charge of sixpence being made for each hour's tuition. Arthur's drawing seems to me very good; his lines and curves are firm and sure, and one of his sketches has won a prize at a Sunday School exhibition. I have dreams of his becoming an architect (artists in stories are nearly always poor and unsuccessful). But Arthur's general school work shows poor average quality, and he is uninterested in the prospect of High School life. Drawing is not included among the examination subjects, and with no flair for phrase-making and arithmetic puzzles a boy has little chance. My brother fails to convince the examiners that he will 'benefit from further education'.

During my childhood I had many opportunities of poring over a pictorial diagram called 'The Broad and Narrow Ways', which illustrated the thirteenth and fourteenth verses of St Matthew, chapter 7. It featured in religious journals; it appeared, framed, in bedrooms and on staircases. I was early impressed with the perilous position of the building labelled 'Theatre'; this stood on the Broad Way, well advanced towards the fiery pit which was the destination of the traveller by that road. Moreover, by Mamma's reasoning, any building wherein stage plays were performed was undesirable, and to be avoided – therefore it was not without misgiving that I went at the age of twelve to see my first play at the Croydon Public Hall. *The Two Orphans*, George Augustus Sala's sentimental melodrama, introduced me to the attractions of the stage. Papa, guided by the same principle which had induced him to take me to a Roman Catholic church at the age of six, had taken me to see this amateur production – but I think he must have been disconcerted by my altogether uncritical appreciation of second-rate dramatic art. To know these wonderful people of the stage – to be one of them – how marvellous! That was the life to live! For some hectic days my mind followed this will-o'-the-wisp. The attack of stage-fever had perhaps one useful effect – I began to read plays.

Papa's experiment is not repeated until I am fifteen. This year Forbes Robertson and his company bring *Hamlet* to the Croydon Theatre. I have read most of Shakespeare's plays. Privately I incline to the opinion that grown people extol Shakespeare more by habit than by conviction. But *Hamlet* is my favourite, and I rejoice when, in spite of Mamma's disapproval, it is proposed that we shall see it.

If the word 'theatre' still recalls 'The Broad and Narrow Way' I can now smile at the memory. But the place, when we enter it, is rather frightening – windowless, dimly lit, the air foul with dust, stale tobacco smoke and other nameless odours. The galleries are without lights, and seen from the pit, where we sit, the tiers of empty seats ascend in curiously sinister fashion to the upper darkness. The iron curtain, painted grey, shuts off the stage, but over the proscenium arch appear the words: 'We Would Give You Supreme Moments'. What are, I ask myself, 'supreme moments'? – and presently the term attaches itself to rare, very rare experiences which I have never tried to name. Moments of strange, utter happiness partaking both of recollection and of promise, associated sometimes with a sudden realisation of natural beauty, sometimes with a dream forgotten at the point of waking. I anticipate nothing of the kind in this ugly, stuffy theatre.

The play begins; the ghost of Hamlet's father looms out of clouds of smoke, quite terrifying. But Hamlet's courage is impressive, and I soon find myself ignoring much of the action and most of the characters merely to listen to Forbes Robertson's voice. Read in cold print the great speeches had moved me only to question probabilities. (How, for instance, could Hamlet talk of 'the undiscovered country from whose bourn no traveller returns' – when he had just been interviewed by such a traveller?) Yet, spoken by this famous actor, the lines come alive, and Hamlet, though incomprehensible, is indeed a real person. My eyes follow him as if he were alone on the stage. Only after the end of the play scene does the tragedy shape for me as a whole, moving steadily towards its inevitable conclusion. I hang on Forbes Robertson's final words: 'The rest...is silence.'

Papa does not comment upon the performance except to make light of the ghost, and to repeat, 'Forbes Robertson is a very fine actor'.

Certain physical matters belonging to a class of information withheld from children and young persons both at home and at school gain in interest and fascination. They are matters treated with the greatest secrecy and intimacy.

No reference to them is ever made in general conversation. Novels and plays hint at them, but any direct treatment stigmatises a book as being unfit for general readers and particularly so for young people. To Evelyn's explanations as to how babies are born are added my mother's directions about personal hygiene on the arrival of puberty. I hear what she has to tell me with impatience and disgust. What an odious, limiting state of things! Are boys, as well as girls, subjected? No, boys are not. This is, I object, unfair! For the first time I wish, heartily, that I were a boy. My mother ignores this, and proceeds, hastily, to advise me of all the precautions and prohibitions relative to the monthly period that she had herself received at my age.

I ask few questions, and remain ignorant of the sexual act until enlightened by my own sensations on seeing the mating of neighbours' cats. My knowledge becomes more accurate when, sent to fetch something from my mother's chest of drawers, I see a book in a bright green cover, with the title *Esoteric Anthropology*. It is odd to find a book among underlinen, and surprising that my mother should possess one with such a learned title. Its illustrative diagrams awaken interest. I cannot bring myself to ask if I may borrow it, but read it in secret, when opportunity offers. It explains, in simple terms, the whole sequence of coition, conception, generation and birth. Wonderfully fascinating – at the same time alluring and repellent. I pore over the diagrams of the queer little frog-like foetus in the womb – but thrust the book back into its place instantly at the sound of a foot on the stair. I could not let anyone find me reading it – unless it were Evelyn, whom I meet at most once a year. It is the revelation of a whole category of experience which seems to belong to a voiceless, sunless world of inexpressible sensation. Sometimes I feel as though I were standing on that world's edge, pricked forward by desire, and I will peer in, or rush away, according to the moment's mood.

In the June of this year my grandparents invite me to visit them at Sevenoaks. The old country town, centre of park and hop land, focus of several aristocratic seats, has a homely but gracious presence. Alpha Cottage, on its outskirts, is square, double-fronted, roomy, with roses in its front garden and a rose-twined porch. Roses! the roses of romance! seen previously only in florists' shops or in distant gardens. In the cottage live Grandma, Grandpa, and the uncles, my father's unmarried brothers. Edwin, the eldest uncle, is an invalid, an epileptic since childhood – his patchy red-and-white face, thin beard and vacant expression awakens a pitying horror. James, the next, is jovial, and keeps a fruit shop in the town. Gambier is the ne'er-do-well, of whom I have heard much from my mother. He will not work. Neither the sustained disapproval of his family nor a penniless condition have persuaded him to a routine, money-earning post. He is well-read, gentlemanly, observant, a good walker and cricketer, no mean naturalist, a gay and intelligent companion. His point of view is that, since he was brought into this world without consultation, and is in no way responsible for his creation, he is entitled to the means of subsistence, and to freedom of action...My grandparents, who live on a small pension, and the uncles, James and Charles, who both contribute to the household expenses, have little sympathy with this philosophy. I notice that Uncle Gambier's meal-time wit is always snubbed by his brothers, who answer him very shortly, and read their newspapers with exaggerated attention. Grandma is a mother-hen to all her sons, without distinction. At meal-times Grandpa is a little absent, a little deaf; he reads Grandma extracts from his paper to which she obviously does not listen...Uncle Gambier addresses himself to me, asking portentous or provoking questions – 'Now, consider carefully! Was Hamlet mad, or not?', or he wanders from one topic of country talk to another – birds, ferns, legends – all interesting. Now and then the brothers are beguiled into listening, but apply themselves to their papers again on realising this.

In the mornings Grandpa will invite me to go for a walk. 'I am not a bad walker for my age', he says – and takes pleasure in the thought of his daily four miles. I do not much want to walk with Grandpa – age seems to me so piteous. He chatters to me, I listen and answer readily – but it is just a chattering in the air, not an exchange of ideas. We cannot really meet – only signal, like ingoing and outgoing ships sighting each other at a distance. After the walk he goes in to rest, and I find coolness in Uncle Charles's office among charts and law-books. Uncle Charles, or his younger partner, Charles Chapman, who is twenty-one, may, if not too busy, invite me to play chess. They are both county club chess men, and I am always beaten in twenty minutes or less. At mid-day dinner Uncle Gambier may say, 'If you will give me the pleasure of your company this afternoon', etc. etc. – and we make a long round in the forest, watching squirrels, following deer, especially a white one who reminds me of the *Ballad of Thomas the Rhymer*. Only when we get home to supper, having missed our tea, do I know how stiff are my legs and how blistered my feet.

While I am at Sevenoaks comes Queen Victoria's Diamond Jubilee. Grandpa is saving himself up for a function later in the day, so after breakfast I wander alone into the great park that forms the town's northern boundary; it is entered by way of a green lane and a small heavy door set in the ancient wall. The morning is quiet, leisurely, like Sunday morning, but quickened by expectancy. The diamond rain-drops of an earlier shower seem to tinkle as they hang from tree leaves. I sit with a squirrel at the foot of a beech tree, hearing distant bugles, feeling as if the ancient wall encloses me within the timeless, the ageless, while the quick noisy life of the day beats a moment out of the present. The bugles will come no nearer, the squirrel will wash its face in the sunshine, the ant at my foot bury its egg, the brake fronds uncurl, day fade to twilight and darkness, night yield to morning, and all the excitement of a Jubilee Day, bands, processions, cheering crowds – up to the last crackle of the festive bonfires – will never enter the consciousness of the creatures of the great Park that dreams through the centuries...Its peace, its remoteness, I leave with reluctance; but I would not miss the programme of the afternoon, a ride to Tonbridge with Charles Chapman and Uncle Charles, to see the county cricket match where Prince Ranjitsinghi plays for Kent. This event fills an excited page in my diary; it is somehow very exciting to be companioned by Charles Chapman whose queer half-broken voice, squeaky or gruff, attracts me.

Home life is by contrast wearyingly dull. I can see no future; have no plans. The chances of adult life rouse nothing of pleasurable anticipation, since my stories fail to win acceptance. A sense of isolation grows. Apparently there is no place for me – I am just to look on at life for a while. Life might be good if we were not poor, but in poverty is no freedom, no choice. I cannot be content, like Uncle Gambier, with a life of dependence upon those who can ill afford to keep me. It seems that poor people are under a blind compulsion to accept any occupation that offers a wage – any monotonous round of drudgery. It is a denial of real living. Girls expect to be married, says my mother. Do they? Who could choose conditions of married life such as hers! I feel that I am not yet as fettered as I may be – my sense of caution increases. Poverty is a prison, but its doors *can* open unless marriage locks them. Then, in marriage, the physical obligation – only to be endured if one wants babies, as Evelyn assures me she does.

What *do* I want? Freedom, opportunity, education, varied experience. These I can only get, it appears, vicariously, through the prompting of books and my own imagination. Do I want friends? Perhaps – of the pattern supplied by Lyndall in *The Story of an African Farm*, by Hawkeye and Uncas in *The Last of the Mohicans*, by other proud and free spirits who look at me from the world of print. Reading is becoming a drug. I touch *life* sightlessly, observation and intelligence turned inward to imaginary scenes and people; pass through the streets in a day-dream; avoid human contact with intention.

What can I do without money to widen real life? There are polytechnic classes teaching languages and crafts, but even their low fees are impossible. It would be foolish to ask my father for an extra penny. He would give me anything in his power, but his insurance commissions bring in scarcely enough to pay for rent and food. My mother's home talk is a daily recital of privation. One day a small black kitten comes in, begging for food. I feed it, but with a burst of anger my mother drives it out – she cannot afford, she says, to feed stray cats. The day following I find the kitten dead in the gutter. I go cold with hate against my mother, as if she were the visible symbol of our poverty.

Papa neither complains nor talks of resignation, but plods on, enduring. He walks daily miles of mean streets, collecting and canvassing; in the evening he sits in his old office writing-chair, reading. His clothes are shabby, but well-brushed, and his hands remain white, the nails well-trimmed. Sometimes, when the day has been luckier than usual, and he is not very tired, he takes out his flute and plays tunes – classical airs, or popular songs that the boys will sing.

The cottage walls are thin, and we must perforce hear much of our neighbours. On one side live a clerk and his wife, with two children, an intelligent boy and a dull girl. The parents are determined that both shall aim at scholarships to the High School, and their evenings are occupied with homework. The boy finds the lessons no trouble, and easily passes the entrance examination; he is the darling of the dark, passionate, heavy-browed mother. The girl is utterly unable to do what is expected of her; the mother insists that sums shall be worked correctly, scolds furiously when words are mis-spelt. Night after night we hear the rising storm of the mother's anger, the girl's protests, entreaties; finally blows and shrieks, and the sobbing of the child ordered to bed in disgrace.

(Twenty years later, visiting the neighbourhood, I make enquiries about these neighbours. The woman is then a widow, supported by the son, a bank clerk. The girl's stupidity has become idiocy. Completely feeble-minded, she has returned to babyhood.)

Kingsley's *The Water Babies* and the tales of George Macdonald still weave for me an acceptable form of mysticism. God the Father, symbol of the urgent unity of creation which I begin emotionally to perceive; God the Son, ideal of humanity; God the Spirit, the fugitive, elusive Power typified by the winds. On the reverse side, the Great Ugliness, Spirit of Evil, represented not now by darkness, but by immobility, obstruction, the power to bind and hold in bondage.

As my sixteenth birthday nears I face the fact that it is essential to search for some occupation which will bring me a wage. It is also clear that the wage earned will be insufficient to support me away from home – my marketable value will not buy me a living in the countryside. A village pupil-teacher post is therefore out of the question, and I have missed the opportunity of the Croydon apprenticeship. If I cannot teach, a junior clerkship or secretarial job seems to offer the only apparent possibility. Dreams of freedom to learn and to write were plainly illusions. Eighteen months of leisure have shown me at least my credulity and ignorance. The only form of writing to which I need apply myself is that of the servile letter offering the sale of my time to business houses.

A large grocery firm gives me a month's trial in its office. There is a slick, smart woman clerk who expects me to run errands for her. I do it stupidly and with a bad grace, hating equally her alternating patronage and neglect: at the end of the month I am discharged, no reason being given. It is another check to my egoism, that sense of personal value which all my little world has fostered from childhood to the end of my school-days. Life may be ugly or grievous, but it is not without compensation as long as one sees one's own reflection comparing favourably with that of surrounding figures. As long as one's *amour propre* can be maintained.

At this point I feel that there is something wrong about the balance of George Macodonald's philosophy, his universe poised so beautifully between good and evil, the scale always tipping slightly to the right side. To all appearances the slant is towards the left. At this point I discover Lewis Morris's philosophic verse in the library; he also is trying to 'justify the ways of God with men'. It is a little difficult:

> If He save from His wolf His lamb, from His tiger His innocent child...
> I think a great cry would go up from an orderless universe,
> And all the fair fabric of things would wither as under a curse.

Difficult, but one degree more convincing. Herein the wolf remains the wolf, the tiger the tiger. Is it like that? Must I surrender as false the satisfying parable of *The Princess and Curdie*?

The actor-manager Wilson Barrett brings his play *The Sign of the Cross* to the Croydon Grand Theatre. Reading in the journals on the public reading-room table I have learned much about this play. Its story fascinates me, partly because my imagination has already found a lurid attraction in Rome of the first century A.D. and the persecution of the early Christians. A magic lantern lecture given at the Horley chapel in my tenth year began it; more recently the final history course in school has stressed the magnificence and cruelty of Rome. I long to see *The Sign of the Cross*, but Papa is discouraging. I can only guess at the reason, but I am intrigued sufficiently to read the columns of letters which appear in the daily papers for and against Wilson

Barrett and his drama. He is accused by many of impiety – of bringing on to the stage matters involving religion, even of daring to suggest a vision of Christ by the use of stage lighting. Papa, so ready to take me to see *Hamlet*, an undoubted classic, prefers to avoid the controversial. I can only stand gazing at the photographs of the noble Marcus and the beautiful Christian girl Marcia shown at the theatre entrance. The caption is thrilling: 'Christus hath triumphed; the light hath come! Come my bride, come to the Light Beyond.' I stand dreaming before the picture, feeling as when I half-believed that the tiny key would open the door to a fairy garden, and with the same suspicion that I may have been tricked. Tricked into accepting a sham for the real, a pretence for truth.

The post-mistress of a little sub-post-office (also news-agent's and stationer's shop) advertises for a junior clerk. I have an interview with her, my mother in attendance. She offers to give me training in post-office work, including telegraphy, in return for general service in the shop. The arrangement is to be an eighteen months' apprenticeship without pay. The need for earning money now oppresses me – it suggests a gain in my diminished self-respect – I am unwilling to close with the offer, but my father advises taking it since it includes a form of training. My hair is rolled up and pinned with many pins; I reluctantly wear a skirt ankle-long. The promised training resolves itself into permission to pick up what knowledge of telegraphy I can in spare time from the acting clerk – my work lies in the shop. The clerk knows, having come here originally on similar terms, that her services will not be required when I am proficient enough to send and receive telegrams; she therefore discourages my efforts to learn, while giving a pretence of instruction.

The shop opens twelve hours a day, except on Wednes-days. An hour is allowed me for dinner, half-an-hour for tea. Few customers enter during the afternoons. The post-mistress retires to sleep in the back-parlour. The telegraphist works crochet, or carries on a conversation in Morse with the man clerk at the Exchange. I stand behind the newspaper counter and scan magazines – such magazines as have never before come my way. One and another catches my aimless glance – I drag them forward and turn their pages furtively, contemptuously. Ignorant as I am, I know this stuff for trash, yet it passes for reading-matter with a multitude of people more illiterate. Something of my school sense of superiority returns as I read, but only momentarily. To appreciate one's level merely in comparison with inferiority is the most utter self-deception.

The telegraphist treats me with a half-indulgent patronage, which I feel is not to be trusted. Nevertheless I cannot help admiring her. She is perhaps twenty years old, with white, fine-textured skin and soft abundance of fine dark hair. Her movements are measured and graceful; she never hurries, even when customers crowd to the counter with parcels just before post-time. She treats the importunate customer with a just perceptible insolence; she is both insolent and ironic with young men who stroll in ostensibly for a paper but really to chat with her. Something about her intrigues me and gives colour to the drab life of the shop.

Among the customers who call for their morning papers is a little, shaky old man. One morning he enters with tears on his cheeks, stretching out a trembling hand for the further news of an event announced to him by the poster outside the shop. 'He's gone, he's *gone*! and we shall never see his like again', quavers he. It is Mr Gladstone who is dead. To me, Mr Gladstone is just a politician of the Liberal Party Papa favours; a past Prime Minister who tried to obtain Home Rule for Ireland. Curious that his death should matter so much to this old man, who perhaps had never seen him.

There is another old man, *very* old, with a hollow like a little cave in the back of his thin neck, and long strands of lank white hair falling over it. He comes for a learned journal – he is the historian Corbett Anderson.

In Dagnall Park, a nearby street, lives the Negro composer Samuel Coleridge-Taylor. He sends telegrams making concert arrangements. Mr Coleridge-Taylor has a soft step, and a soft, husky voice. He is not tall, but has a large head, with a thick black mop of curls. His telegrams are interesting, calling for orchestral instruments with names unknown to me. I sometimes pass in the street his English wife, wheeling the pram of a brown baby son and white baby daughter. I am presently (perhaps a couple of years later) to hear the first performance in London of his *Hiawatha*.

I work eight months at this shop, gradually realising that I am in a blind alley. It is no stepping-stone to any better-paid branch of postal service. I see myself, in prospect, continuing to waste my time, learning nothing of value, enduring a tedious slavery for an eventual few shillings a week. A chance meeting with my former class-mistress pivots me in another direction.

She is married – she invites me to call. I am introduced to her black-haired, black-bearded husband, and also to a large framed portrait of Tolstoy, to whom the pair refer as 'The Master'. They are vegetarians; they do not eat salt. I am a little shy of these peculiarities, and of conversation with a slightly propagandist flavour, but their kindness is great. They discover, by questioning, my position; they assure me that it is not too late for me to take the intending pupil-teachers' examination. Will I send for entrance forms and syllabus, and begin to study?

I turn out of the blind alley and retrace my steps.

Aunt Bec and Evelyn visit us in the autumn of this year. It is two years since I have seen Evelyn, who has recently engaged herself to a man six years her senior. All her talk is of Harry and marriage. Her fresh silk blouses and general neatness reproach my shabby frocks, her clear rose and sun-bronzed complexion accentuates my pallor. She is so delightful – and so different. Looking at her beautiful neck, at the curls coiled high on her small head, I realise that those happy days of childhood at Newhaven were *her* days, and that she was the animating spirit of its world. She, the child Evelyn, not the Evelyn of today. When we go upstairs at night I pull the pins out of her hair and the curls drop below her waist; she laughs, and laughter brings us nearer, but not with the old, easy intimacy that neither asked nor denied. I have lost that Evelyn, and Newhaven will never show me the same aspect again.

I used to envy her. So many opportunities and possessions she had that were out of my reach. But now I do not; that is almost strange. Yet no! not as I understand it. Evelyn is to marry Harry – marriage will define and fix the bounds of her future life within this man's environment. She will accommodate her thoughts and desires to his, live only in his house, spend only his money. She can never be alone again. Perhaps she never has been alone, with the loneliness I knew in those nights of childhood when I lay sleepless beside her, listening to Time and the Sea. For her, marriage will be completion, happiness – she has no doubts. For me there is some other, uncomprehended way.

Days and nights of acute neuralgia, followed by a state of debility and morbid sensation. But except in the case of serious illness, medical advice is an unwarrantable luxury. Meanwhile it is necessary to study.

I pass the intending pupil-teachers' examination, and am appointed as pupil-teacher in the junior department of my old school. The head teacher reminds me of a slender phial filled with ink, white-stoppered. Nothing more human does she suggest. She introduces me to a class of some eighty boys and girls, a mixed company, clean and well-brushed, dirty and ragged, who sit with elbows touching, seven or eight in each long desk, holding slates. One row sits on the floor in front of the desks, their faces scorched by a large open fire in a near grate. The class teacher is chalking a sum on the blackboard – writing down figures to the children's working. Every child is expected to work the sum, hands being raised to indicate a ready answer. The teacher's energy is chiefly employed in urging the slower children to raise their hands; eager pupils who announce an answer figure unasked are snubbed. The head mistress interrupts, orders arms to be folded behind, backs to be straightened; she introduces me by name and commands the class to obey me as it obeys its class teacher. The teacher is advised that I am to give her every possible assistance, to observe her 'object-lessons', and to give a 'criticism lesson' periodically.

On the afternoon of the same day I am admitted to the Pupil-Teachers' Centre, a bare building of red and yellow brick, comprising an assembly hall and classrooms labelled respectively History, Science and Art...The Centre master, Arthur Hillyer, M.A., is small, dark, thin, active, swift in criticism; the Centre mistress dumpy, fair, leisurely, indulgent, with a self-willed mouth and blue-grey eyes that regard the master in manner lazily hostile. There is a young, heavily built, rosy-cheeked assistant mistress whose subject is geography, and who takes a portion of the intensive needlework sylllabus.

The pupil-teachers are of four grades, coresponding to the years of their apprenticeship; all are travelling towards the portentous Queen's Scholarship Examination which should either admit them to a training college, or qualify them to teach as 'uncertificated' teachers on the staff of an elementary school. I am impressed by the dignified name of this examination. Fourth-year students are referred to by the centre staff as Queen's Scholars.

I am so joyful at the escape from my blind alley that nothing troubles me. French verbs and Latin conjugations are more to be desired than novels. The bare walls of the Centre are glorified as the home of knowledge. I shall learn,

I shall acquire. The school-room, dusty and close-smelling, the swarm of dull, fidgety children can be endured with complacence, indeed, with content.

The class teacher, Agnes Mason, attracts me. She has no physical beauty – is indeed extremely plain, and her dress shows little taste for colour or style. Her grey-green eyes protrude slightly, and she walks with a kind of strut. Yet, of the school staff, she alone is a woman I want as friend.

She has a contralto voice, vibrant, which she uses with effect upon her huge class; its variation of tone seems to be her means of control. Neither the sum of her apparent characteristics, nor any single one of them is accountable for her charm. It can only be explained by a kind of vitality which distinguishes her from all the other people of my world. Our way home from school lies in the same direction, and the walk is always too short. Something in that vitality of hers helps me to bring into our talk thoughts previously too vague for words, thoughts belonging to emotions instinctively, or by habitual inhibition, concealed. With Evelyn I could talk of sex, but never of religion; and latterly, in our most intimate conversations there has arrived a point when Evelyn's eyes have become blank, almost as if she had released invisible shutters.

Agnes Mason is the eldest of a family of eight, and her salary is its mainstay. The father and mother are semi-invalid, partially dependent both for income and personal attention. One brother is married, one a school-boy. The other brothers and sisters are adolescents with small jobs, living at home. Their home is a modern suburban house of the eight- or nine-room type, and more than half of Agnes's salary goes to pay its rent and rates. These details I learn by stages as our friendship advances.

Agnes served her four years apprenticeship, passed the Queen's Scholarship Examination, and after two years of teaching and private study sat for the Acting Teachers' Certificate. That was six years ago. She is now earning seventy-five pounds a year at school, and the pianoforte lessons she gives every evening at home bring her a little pocket-money. To my grateful surprise she seems to like my company, and invites me to come for walks twice a week after the lessons are given. Those walks become for me the finest hours of the week. This woman, ten years older than myself, appreciates where I stand, and calls me on. She places at my disposal all her experience and superior knowledge. It is a wonder, a complete amazement of generosity. After inhibition and isolation, I am now to enjoy the lure and promise of companionship, provocation, response. I accept with proud humility, most content to adopt her routine of out-of-school life – the church choir and choral society, the Saturday afternoon concerts of classic music at the Crystal Palace. Out of my year's fifteen pounds allowance from the education authority for 'maintenance' and books, ten shillings is spared for a Crystal Palace season ticket: the crowded, foetid school-room and dingy cottage open on Saturday afternoons to the infinities of great music.

Agnes Mason invites me to join the choir of the Clive Road Congregational church, Addiscombe, where she leads the contraltos. The pastor of this church is the Reverend Benson Evans; its organist, Francis Sisley. I agree, gladly; the quality of my voice and ear prove acceptable, and during the next four years I get useful practice in reading musical scores. Normal Sunday services are fully choral; this church, being associated with the Countess of Huntingdon's Connexion, follows the rubric of the Church of England, but omits Creeds and Psalms. Festivals are celebrated with the performance of special music from the oratorios – *Messiah*, *Elijah*, *The Creation*, Mendelssohn's *Hymn of Praise*; and on Palm Sunday, inevitably, Stainer's *Crucifixion*. There are regular weekly choir practices. From my eighteenth to my twenty-second year this choir dictates my Sunday routine and that of Tuesday evening.

The church is nearly two miles distant from home; Agnes and I walk there in all weathers.

The choir has no point of contact with the congregation, and a rare one with the pastor. The Reverend Benson Evans, walking black-gowned from reading desk to pulpit, reminds me of an Old Testament prophet, but the massive head with rippled grey hair which rises above the pulpit suggests rather Christ as He might have appeared in middle age. In all four years my only contact with the pastor was on those occasions when, after one of the special performances, he acknowledged the service of the choir members with individual handshake. Nor, after the choristers' door had closed behind us on Sunday evenings, would Agnes and I have any further social contact with choir members.

Agnes's passion for music draws me also into the West Croydon Choral Society. It, too, is chiefly devoted to oratorio, though such lighter works as Sterndale Bennett's *May Queen* and Sullivan's *Golden Legend* find place. For a whole winter of weekly practices we labour at Spohr's *Last Judgment*.

I got much pleasure and emotional satisfaction from these musical activities, less from the daily practice of violin technique. But, added to the strain of the school day and the evening hours of study they ran me up an overdraft on my bank of energy that I was only later to realise. I had no one to blame but myself; no pressure was put upon me by family or authority. But youth seldom refers to the state of its banking account, and assumes inexhaustible dividends. The immediate result of this musical self-indulgence was to put creative writing into the background: apart from entries into my diary and an occasional essay dictated by one of the tutors, I wrote nothing during the period of my teacher training. To *begin* the study of the violin at the age of seventeen is absurd; but at that age my self-will and self-confidence were such as to rule out advice against it, even had it been offered by an expert.

My father meticulously kept a diary in shorthand, always making the daily entry before retiring. Mine was irregular, with gaps of months, even of years. The record of 1900 is fairly continuous. There is much about church choral music and Crystal Palace orchestral concerts. On 4 February there is a reference to the South African war...I am trying to feel interest in a remote matter.

The Boers have the best of it, apparently, up to the present, in spite of the 180,000 men we have sent out. We hardly realise the war, here at home, where everything goes on as usual. On Friday there was a rumour that all young men between 18 and 30 would be required for home duty. Our casualties now total about 8,000. We don't comprehend it – how can we? We read in the morning paper *British Reverses; Terrible Losses* etc. – feel shocked for a moment – then go to school and in ten minutes have forgotten all about it. Miss Corney's whims, and the idleness of boys Bone and West trouble us far more than the death of all those soldiers. It doesn't come home to our narrow range of vision.

On 4 March, after a detailed and enthusiastic account of an early performance of Coleridge-Taylor's *Hiawatha's Wedding Feast*, I note the relief of Ladysmith.

Last Wednesday, Ladysmith, which has been besieged by the Boers since November, was relieved. Universal rejoicing – and patriotic brag. The town decorated? with flags. I am glad those poor fellows have been got out of the hole they were in, but I can't call up much enthusiasm. I am a frigid sort of creature.

Then and thereafter I shy like an unbroken colt at any demonstration of mass feeling, especially if it is of the patriotic variety. How *could* Edward Elgar compose *Land of Hope and Glory* or Rudyard Kipling write *The Absent-Minded Beggar*?

The acquisition of a season ticket for the Crystal Palace is undreamed-of good fortune, and a seat in its concert hall, for the Saturday afternoon concert costs only a shilling. I hear a first-class orchestra play superb music – what greater happiness! Haydn, Bach, Beethoven, Handel, Mendelssohn, Raff, Max Bruch, Tschaikowsky illumine and transform my world. Mozart makes less impression –

he is too gay, and I am in no humour for gaiety, be it ever so charming. It is not before the age of twenty, says Olive Schreiner, that we learn to be in deadly earnest and to laugh...The concerto or the symphony is never too long – in the concert hall I am unconscious of time. But my records of this experience are written in the dullest schoolgirl reporting style.

29 April 1900

Yesterday we went to August Manns's Benefit concert. The programme consisted of Schubert's *Unfinished Symphony*; the 2nd movement from Bell's *Walt Whitman*; two songs sung by Andrew Black and the 'Jewel Song' from *Faust* by Lilian Blauvelt; Tschaikowsky's *Suite de Ballet*; *Lord Ullin's Daughter*, ballad for choir and orchestra; Mendelssohn's Violin Concerto played by Maud MacCarthy; and the overture to *Tannhäuser*. I liked Lilian Blauvelt's voice better than when I heard it before. Maud MacCarthy, who is about fifteen, played splendidly. The only fault was to be found with the choir, which was much too weak for the augmented orchestra. The floral tributes to August Manns were numerous, and he was greeted with a storm of applause.

A boy of my own age named Clarence comes into the first half of this year. He wanders with nonchalant air into the Masons' drawing-room during the early spring, sits down at the piano, and improvises. He cannot read music, but has a flair for harmonising a suggested theme, and an audacity that delights in combining incongruous themes into a fantastic medley. Clarence has a round, pallid face, pale blue eyes, lank, fairish hair. His hands are long, thin, damp to the touch. He is unattractive, but has a poise, an individuality, which intrigues. Agnes tells me that he is the spoiled pet of a foolish widowed mother, whom he despises; that he frequents 'bad company' and openly boasts to her of vicious practices. She suggests that as he likes to confide in her we should let him join our walks sometimes, and might encourage him to attend good concerts. I think Agnes's benevolent attitude commendable, and for some months Clarence makes a disturbing third in our intercourse. Disturbing, because as a trio we are stimulated to a pitch of excitement which heightens my perceptions and gives colour to the dullest day, but throws a different light upon my conception of Agnes. She presently allows Clarence to treat her in a way which seems to me insufferably familiar. She indulges him, laughs when she should be angry. It is humiliating to see this quiet, ironic, insolent boy look at her with a kind of contempt. Towards me his manner is courteous, even apparently humble when he sees my irritation.

Mingled with these feelings is a perverse streak of satisfaction when I realise that Clarence is trying to isolate me from Agnes. No one in the past has shown an initial desire for my company. I have turned towards some who have attracted me without intention, but until now no one has singled me out and beckoned. The knowledge that I am found desirable adds warmth to these weeks of spring.

On Saturday 5 May Agnes goes to the Palace afternoon concert, but a near examination obliges me to study at home. At tea-time Clarence calls, and we presently ride up to the Penge gate of the Palace by tram, passing through, South Norwood High Street, where, unknown to me, my little brother Frank is helping a friend who works in a chemist's shop. (A fire breaks out in this shop just after we pass it.) I am in a peculiarly 'exalted' mood all the evening, and Clarence talks with a freakish brilliance very fascinating; we drift in a current of music among the fairy lights of the terraces and North Tower Gardens, where we eventually meet Agnes and agree to stay and watch the firework display. At ten o'clock a tram swings us down Anerley Hill, and I do not notice, as it clatters through Norwood High Street, that the chemist's shop is a blackened gutted shell. The radiance of the evening is still glowing along the horizon when I see the dark figure of my mother standing at the home gate. Have I heard? She and Papa are just going back to the hospital. There has been an accident, and Frank is badly burned...

Arthur tells me how it happened, as we sit awaiting their

return. The errand boy, Frank's friend, was sent to the cellar to draw from an open barrel of methylated spirit. The cellar was dark, and the boys lit a bit of candle, which Frank held. There was a sudden sheet of flame, and Frank rushed upstairs, his clothes on fire. The other boy escaped, but ran down the street, panic-stricken; when able to think he went to a nearby cabinet-maker's yard where he knew Arthur was working. Frank was on a stretcher when Arthur arrived at the burning shop, and an ambulance took them both to the hospital, Frank's face swathed in bandages – his message, 'Tell Mum I'm not so bad!'...and there Arthur lays his face on the table, sobbing, but apologetic – 'You see, he doesn't mean as much to you.' The hours pass; at length Arthur sleeps, his head on his folded arms, not rousing when I push a cushion under them. When it is almost three o'clock the key rattles in the lock of the front door.

A polished elmwood box, smelling strongly of varnish, stands on trestles in the small front room now called my study. I try not to think of what it contains. Boys of Frank's school, with a master, come and stand round, their caps in their hands, silently reading the inscription on the brass plate.

'I done my duty!' Frank's last words. Quaint little boy, echoing Nelson. It was not duty, only the wish to earn a promised sixpence, that brought him to death at twelve years. But there was his consolation, in the thought of a duty done. I, with this new ferment within me, a suddenly-arisen spring of urgent life, turn away, terrified. Nothing could console me, at this point, for early death. It is a horror of disintegration – the dissolution of the self formed by such slow, painful degrees from the flux of the unconscious – this is my *feeling*, for which, at the time, I have no words.

I am offered a week's absence from school, but will not take it, seeking in the restlessness of the children forgetfulness of that dreadful immobility under the lid of the coffin. At night there is no escape from the scent of the new, varnished elmwood, nor from the repetition of the tragic story. Neighbours call, and people from Mamma's chapel and mission hall, curious people, pretending emotions they think they ought to feel. But Agnes does not pretend; she is her quiet, sensible self again. Clarence makes no sign.

From my diary, 11 May 1900

Nine feet deep they have put him. 'Earth to earth, ashes to ashes, dust to dust, in sure and certain hope of resurrection to eternal life.' The Christian theory is beautiful, though I cannot take it in the accepted sense.

Spring has come. Life, and the promise of life everywhere, but Frank dead. Frank's blue eyes and restless little form nine feet deep in that grave. Olive Schreiner's words recur – 'The soul's fierce cry for immortality is only this: "Leave me in the hereafter the thing as it was before. Give me back what I have lost, or give me nothing!"'

(Half my life-time was to pass before I learned enough of the creative processes to realise the childishness and stupidity of that demand. In May 1900 I felt pity, resentment, horror, but little sense of personal loss. My young brother and I had never really met. His nature was simple, responsive, uncritical, happy; he enjoyed his part in the multiple small undertakings of home and school, accepting what came with a natural gaiety. What, I wonder, might life have done to change Frank, had he reached manhood! A futile conjecture – seventy years and two world wars left him in the nineteenth century. He lives only in my memory – little brother Frank.)

I exchange the sadness of home for the magic of great music and the illusions prepared by the sexual instinct for eighteen-year-olds. Clarence remains in the background for three weeks. Then there are other walks and concerts not lacking their thrill, but it presently becomes clear that he and I shall not reach any greater degree of intimacy. His audacity attracts, but his nature repels; he is selfish and vain, and I resent the pose of cynicism he affects, and dislike the touch of his always clammy hands. Yet, when in

July he leaves the neighbourhood, it is as though a spring
inside me had run down.

This June there is a Handel Festival at the Crystal Palace.
Men in black and women in white, the massed choirs pack
the galleries ascending to the great organ in the Centre
Transept. At mid-day, the air quivering in hot sunshine, I
walk up through the grounds from the Penge entrance as
the Hallelujah chorus is being sung – a paean beating down
like the fierce sunlight. Arriving on the top terrace I pause
for breath and then pass into the North Tower garden.
There is no crossing of the Centre Transept today; it has
become a vast concert hall, thronged by devotees of Handel
who have come from all parts of the country, but especially
from the northern counties; somewhere among them are
Aunt Bec and Evelyn, come for the day to hear *Messiah*. As
soon as the last *fortissimo* Amen has died away Agnes and
I go to meet them at the pre-arranged spot, under the great
clock at the end of the South Transept. The crowds are
dispersing: I have no difficulty in finding Evelyn, now taller
than her mother, and wearing her curls piled high on her
head, crowned by a small floral toque. I admire, silently, her
blouse of pale rose silk, and the poplin skirt of deeper tone.
Aunt Bec, as always, is in black. They kiss me conven-
tionally, and I introduce them to Agnes, who presently
forges ahead, the pink roses in her picture hat nodding, to
find a side booth which will offer tea and seats until time for
the Newhaven train.

Nearly two years have passed since Evelyn and I last met.
She is now like a rose almost full-blown, and she has
nothing more to say to me than the rose. She makes me feel
old – so long ago seem the days when, with laughing face
and flying curls, she raced me along the Piddinghoe road,
and always won. She shows me her engagement ring – says
she is marrying Harry next year and that I must be her
bridesmaid...I look from Evelyn to Agnes, the latter older
by nine years, see sharp features, peaked nose and angular

frame, ill-suited by the flower-besprinkled delaine dress and lace fichu – and know that the active, enquiring mind lighting the grey-green eyes brings to me more of beauty than the physical perfection of my cousin. With the departure of the Newhaven train I wave goodbye to the one intimate friendship of childhood.

From my diary, 16 September 1900

Life is dull and commonplace now. The days go by, full of monotonous work. In the present calm even flow of existence, I look back and wonder at the excitement of the first half of the year. Stormy sunsets and summer lightning have been succeeded by grey, quiet autumn days. The glow and sparkle of living have died out. 'To every action an equal and opposite re-action!' Perhaps the third law of motion is one of the first laws governing the intricate machinery we call life.

In January 1901 there is a note on the death of Queen Victoria.

27 January 1901

It was reported on Tuesday morning that the Queen was dead, and Miss Corney publicly announced this to the school. At mid-day we found the report to be wrong – but she died at about six in the evening.

The affairs of royalty usually concern us very little; but now we are thinking more about the Queen than we have done in all our lives. She who was old before we were born seemed part of the natural order of things. It is strange to hear prayers for the *King* and to read of *His* Majesty. The King was proclaimed in Croydon yesterday. Silver the Vigilant put in an untimely protest and was mobbed by the crowd...Everyone is wearing black. There is a feeling of novelty in the air; change is the order of the day.

Nothing of homage or of personal loss enters into my feeling for the Queen. She means little more to me than her picture in a history book. The concentration of my school history and geography courses upon the British Empire has failed to awaken in me any active sentiment for that institution. The big WE and OUR applied to it seems a sham. I do not own, and am never likely to own, a single Indian palm-tree or Australian gold nugget. Nor do I wish to rule or dominate other nations. *Kim* and the *Jungle Books* I love, but am bored by Empire Day celebrations. Yet sun and moon are scarcely more constant and regular than the rhythms˄of British national life at the period, and youth moves to them, unconsciously.

The potency of books read in one's nineteenth year is determined less by their literary quality than by their emotional appeal and the answer they make to the mind's questioning. My list includes Drummond's *Ascent of Humanity*, Grant Allen's *Evolutionist at Large*, Carlyle's *Essays*, a *Life of Tolstoy* and Oliver Wendell Holmes's *Breakfast Table* series. Novels include those of Hall Caine, Wilkie Collins, Conan Doyle, Harold Frederick, Sarah Grand, Maxwell Grey and Mrs Humphry Ward. The Centre literature list only mildly interests me. I am not ready for Thackeray's realism, and am irritated by Kingsley's Protestant partisanship in *Westward Ho!* I like Goldsmith, especially in *Citizen of the World*. Nothing late-Victorian, nothing controversial enters into this syllabus. As a prize-winner twice running in the annual Biblical examination I am invited to choose my prize books – but Authority demurs when I ask for the musical score of Gounod's *Faust*, and presents instead a fine edition of Tennyson. (In later life I approve Authority's judgment.)

There is no reference library at the Centre, but research is not required of us. We are wedded to text-books, Latin and French, work innumerable exercises in grammar and paraphrasing, and read those languages with individual and unconvincing accent. I gain a general idea of world geography and a more detailed picture of English history; I share in class reading of Shakespeare and memorise some lyric verse of Tudor period. English literature is otherwise tabulated in a text-book of some three hundred pages.

Any glamour which may have invested the teaching profession is dispelled by the end of my second year of apprenticeship. I feel that I am a cog in an instruction machine framed to manipulate masses of human material. The head mistress puts this fact into a sentence: 'Remember! *You* are the mind – the children are the matter you work upon.' I am to mould the human material of Whitehorse Road Junior School into the shape for which it is required by the social and economic pattern of the period. A vague realisation, not to be expressed in talk or writing at present.

Our department receives annually from the infant school two classes of sixty children in their eighth year, and will admit a possible twenty or thirty more of the floating population. The children normally remain two years; on leaving for the senior school they are expected to have acquired a vocabulary of words in common use, to read, spell and write these correctly in composition or dictation; they shall add, subtract, multiply and divide numbers up to 10,000, and show logical power enough to solve 'problems' combining the four rules. They must write in a clear, uniform, sloping hand.

The teachers concentrate, without consideration of the pupils' health or their own, on getting the results expected of them by authority. They are kindly persons, ready enough to bandage a bruised knee, to deal with any small, patent, immediate form of suffering; they grumble in private over their packed classrooms, bad ventilation, draughts; they accept with almost unquestioning acquiescence the standards imposed upon them by the approved syllabus. Their compulsion is that of pleasing the visiting inspectors, their fear that of presenting for examination, at the end of the school year, children incapable of gaining the average mark. The spiritless, docile child of average ability and regular attendance is the *good* child who passes easily through the school. Obedience, receptiveness – these are the qualities most valued.

My work as pupil-teacher lies chiefly with the children designated 'duffers'. They are nearly all badly nourished and worse clad products of an extremely poor quarter; a few are better off children who attend irregularly (these are objects of extreme dislike); the rest are recently admitted pupils below the school standard for their age. I am required to teach the 'duffers' reading, writing and arithmetic, without reference to the official time-table which dictates periods for object lessons, history and geography lessons and singing. Except on bitterly cold days we stand on the stone floor of the lobby outside the classroom – six or eight at a time – to be specially instructed; the head teacher closing her eyes to an illegal practice unless inspectors are reported in the neighbourhood. I have also to tack seams for little girls to sew; this occupation sometimes gives me the chance of listening to Agnes Mason's 'scripture lessons'. Agnes has grasped the idea of presenting Bible history in every-day setting, and amuses herself and any casual listener by stressing details to the point of incongruity. My occasional 'object lesson' interests me; it is even enjoyable to feel eighty pairs of eyes turned to gaze on my specimens, and to see the delight of the child called from the press in the desks to demonstrate by action 'things that burn' and 'things that won't burn'. But I know I am not 'keeping order' on these occasions – the class teacher sits near, usually marking a pile of exercise books. The controlling power may depart, at a tap of the head teacher's knuckles on the door. When this happens my nerves tighten – can what I am teaching sustain the interest of the class? Eyes must *not* wander, feet must *not* fidget. What will happen if the teacher is away more than a few minutes? Why should these children obey *me*? They don't want to obey – they want to run out of those desks, to shout and dance round. They *must* not – *I* should be shamed, discredited, if they did! With difficulty I drag my mind from the hideous suggestion back to the matter of the object lesson; the wandering interest of the class returns in its train...

Once each month a cab draws up outside the school gate

117

and from it emerges, with some difficulty, the Clerk to the Education Committee, Barrow Rule and an assistant. The Clerk is very lame, and hobbles awkwardly along the floor of the main room to the head teacher's desk, but supports his disability as cheerfully as does a lame blackbird, and faces the interested class with a quick grin followed by a quick scowl. On the desk his assistant places two bags of money, and a child messenger is sent round the school to summon each teacher in turn; it is pay-day. The pay-sheet lies upon the desk; under the eye of the Clerk and Miss Corney each teacher signs and is paid her salary for the preceding month. I receive my allowance, one pound five shillings per month during the second year of my apprenticeship, one pound thirteen shillings and sixpence during its final year. The fine golden coin puts sunlight into the gloomiest day. The young college-trained teachers in their first year of full-time service receive five sovereigns each per month. This, to me, represents riches.

These rates of salary were not actually as absurd as they may seem to teachers in the present year. The catastrophic fall in the value of the pound since 1914 is not always appreciated.

There are divisions among the school staff. Set hard against the head teacher is the senior assistant, a big-framed, bony woman in her fifties. She will brook no comment or criticism from the Head, to whom she is senior in service. They mutually detest one another – the school quivers with their animosity. During the second year of my apprenticeship I am sent to help with the senior assistant's class. Except when angered, a good-humoured bluster marks her manner with the children. Miss G.'s reading-lesson method is characteristic of her teaching attitude. The sixty pupils stand, each child holding its open primer on an extended left hand, upon the forms of the desks – this gives Miss G., who is tall, the opportunity of watching fore-fingers move along lines at a convenient height. The reading is done in chorus with a pause between words; Miss G. walking the while along the rows, to tap lightly with a short cane the fingers of any pupil who has 'lost the place'.

This woman is very kind to the child who is ill, or hurt, or neglected at home, but can be brutal to any who fail to appeal to her sympathy. There is a particularly pretty, dainty, eight-year-old girl in her class – a mother's darling, with long lashes and ringlets, wearing fine embroidered pinafores over fresh, frilled frocks. Lily shrinks from the more unclean children, and wrinkles her nose with disgust at the scent of a boy in dirty corduroys, edges away from the person of a desk companion, and cries frequently. These things infuriate Miss G. 'Lily 'Awkins, move *up*! None o' that, you little snob. Don't you give yourself airs here my lady! I won't have it!'And when the child is in tears – 'Joe Bailey, y'd better fetch my umbrella – it's in the corner. Lily 'Awkins is raining again! We'll want it.' A joke appreciated by the corduroyed lad.

There are three young teachers, recently from college, upon the staff. One of these finds favour with the Head. The best classroom, the most intelligent class are allotted her; the Head is known to converse at length with her, privately, in the lunch hour. This is Miss G.'s great grievance; she does not recognise the existence of the 'favourite', except to stare scornfully after her when she passes.

The school would be intolerable but for Agnes. I endure for two years; in the meanwhile my old senior department takes, in retrospect, an increasingly desirable aspect. Eventually I ask Authority to transfer me there, and the request is granted.

Four years have elapsed since I left this department, and one of my former class-mates is serving the last year of her apprenticeship. I remember how Phyllis cried when, in the week of her probation, she had to face our giggling class. She is now teaching with grave assurance and the

5-2

confirmed approval of Miss Smythe. Beside her I feel a raw junior. I am conscious of a complete change in the Head's attitude towards me – a puzzling and perplexing change. Presently I realise that I am no longer the superior pupil, the prize-winner, the good child. I am a member of the staff upon whose efficiency the school grant depends – a staff completely subordinated to the purpose and direction of the Head. It is a very different position.

There is no coaching of dullards in the senior school. I am required to relieve the class teachers in turn for set periods, and to give prepared lessons from the approved syllabus. The Head tells me that the secret of good discipline is *tact*. This, I am sure, is indisputable, but acceptance does not help dispel the terrible nervousness that grips me when I stand before the big groups of girls, so quick to perceive and take advantage of weakness. Out of sheer envy I begin to hate the solid personality of Miss Smythe, which shames my instability. In her presence I feel as if I had bitten the wrong side of Alice in Wonderland's mushroom, and am shrinking small and smaller. Her calm, level voice stills with a sentence the stormiest class, and from her centre of assurance she looks at me with faint, unspoken reproach. The eyes of all the girls turn with hers to me, complacent, hiding an amused smile. She calls me to her desk later, and as I stand before her she leans back in her chair, chin supported on hand, clear brown eyes searching my face. She tells me that I am disappointing her, bids me imitate Phyllis's manner with the girls. I dread school, as the possible grave both of my self-respect and hopes.

In desperation I go to the Education Office and ask again for a transfer; my Centre reports being fortunately satisfactory, Authority complies...An old, very shabby school of the two-storey type; my work lies in the junior department, on the upper floor. Three hundred boys and girls massed in a main room and two classrooms opening from it, with stair exits out of main room only. I teach a class of forty, under the kindly eye of the Head, Miss T., whose official desk is close by. Miss T. is gaunt, hollow-cheeked; the afternoon sees her face always painfully flushed with the pink of fatigue and impure air; but she is as strong-willed as sympathetic, and comes to the aid of any over-wrought younger teacher without reluctance or patronage. She has not forgotten the difficulties of the road to her well-deserved headship; she knows well the absurdities of the system she serves, and will earn no advantage for herself at the expense of her staff. Possessed with a sense of proportion that will permit no drive for showy results, she manages to endow even the instructional machine with a human aspect. There is continuous hard work, but no over-strain in Sydenham Road school; its atmosphere is one of cheerful compliance. Gradually my self-confidence returns.

During the latter years of my apprenticeship I attend the Pupil-Teachers' Centre on three afternoons per week and on Saturday mornings. It is still run by the Centre master Arthur Hillyer, M.A., and the Centre mistress Ellen Holden, between whom there is a quiet but obvious antagonism. Mr Hillyer is thin, dark, tireless – of a super-activity necessary to the task of steering some two hundred students at four different stages through courses in mathematics, elementary physics and chemistry, Latin and music – the last-named involving the Saturday morning choral practice. His home-work includes all accountancy connected with the running of the Centre. I never talk with Mr Hillyer; I listen to his incisive, ironic voice from the lecture platform, and in study-time he will slip behind my desk and drop a corrected exercise book over my shoulder. The exercises are always usefully corrected – with diagrams if necessary – in red ink. Miss Holden is a pussy-cat, comfortable and leisurely, claws always well hidden, a quiet purr if stroked the right way. The form of her history lessons is unvarying; first a reference to the chapter in the text-book previously set for home-work – have we any questions to ask relating to its content? We always have many, for the longer we can prolong this stage, the shorter will be the strip memory test which follows, and we sit in repose while the purring voice recapitulates well-known data. The lesson ends with an indication of the next home-work quota. French grammar and exercises are also 'home-work' – but Miss Holden hears us read from a book called Charlin's French Course, in which preposterous and unrelated sentences are rendered respectively in English and French on pages facing one another. Miss Holden would seem to ignore the existence of Mr Hillyer as far as this may be possible. The Centre entrance for girls and boys is placed at either end of the building; Mr Hillyer, shabby old gown flying, enters from the boys' end; Miss Holden, smiling gently, moves in among the late-comer girls. All classes include both sexes, separated by an aisle; girls on the right, boys on the left.

Beyond the Centre walls I have no association with my class-mates; it is without social activities of any kind. There are no facilities for sport or recreation, and only in my final year a physical training mistress, clad in a short green tunic, and obviously without corset, appears, to demonstrate on the lecture platform exercises recommended for children.

Of my class-mates, one only has some contact with me in later life. He is a thin, angular Scot, Arthur McLeod, a true student, with literary tastes. I enjoy hearing him read from a Shakespeare play, and am happy when Miss Holden chooses me to read with him the scenes between Coriolanus and his mother. For the most part, these boys and girls, in training to become teachers, are not interested in study. It is, for them, a 'must' – the boring road to a paying job. Sometimes I think their indifference may be merely a pose. What other way than knowledge gained through books can enlarge the narrow circle of daily experience? To me, at this stage, it scarcely matters what one learns, since one's ignorance is abysmal and the field of knowledge infinite. Having trailed, through childhood, not clouds of glory, but the fog of a disintegrating theology, having emerged into adolescence conscious of widening horizons, how can one *not* wish to explore? The strange sounds and syntax of foreign languages, the hypotheses and ordered terminology of physical science would seem to coincide with certain laws of my inner life, learned by observation and experience. Common rhythms, swinging through the several planes of nature and mankind – high tide, low tide, attraction, repulsion – 'to every action an equal and opposite reaction.'

Agnes Mason describes herself as a Deist. She rejects the Christian doctrine and says that in attending church she has a duty only to the choir. Her attitude seems to be shared by other members. The organist and chief soprano draw salaries, and treat their church-going as a commercial proposition. The leading bass regards church music as a hobby. This flavour of insincerity is unpleasant, but the lure of the music helps me to compromise. The act of worship may be feigned, but the rendering of a Beethoven Mass or a Mendelssohn *Lobgesang* must justify itself, both for performers and listeners. I love the quiet of the church, my seat in the choir stall, the absorption of choir and congregation in the harmonies of a classic score, and the feeling of peace and detachment from personal and petty things.

Since childhood I have longed to play a musical instrument – latterly the violin. Now, in my nineteenth year, I buy a small, cheap fiddle and resolve to take lessons. It is an utterly foolish resolve. (Had I then been able to afford the advice of a first-class teacher, he would certainly have pointed out that my wrists and fingers lacked the strength necessary for good tone, and that the fingers, small and thin, would slip between the strings when double-stopping. Moreover, at nineteen it is far too late to begin the study.

Should I have taken such advice, had it been offered? Doubtful, since I was accustomed to easy success in what I undertook personally, and my real capacity had scarcely been challenged. A young, inexperienced violinist undertook to give me cheap lessons; as a teacher he was without qualifications, and for more than a year my practice hours were a complete waste of time.)

In the summer of 1902 Agnes Mason and I are invited to join a holiday arranged by the organist, Francis Sisley, and one of the sopranos, to whom he is engaged. The propriety of Edith's mother demands that Edith shall have a female companion on this holiday, and Agnes is approved; the invitation is extended to include me. Details are all arranged by Francis Sisley. We travel by train to Rye, and occupy for a fortnight a cottage on the Winchelsea road. The cottage is long and low; it faces the river Rother which has yet two miles to flow before it reaches the sea. Down at Camber, on the empty miles of sandy shore, we have a solitary tent, so lonely, so far removed from the cramped life of home, open to sun and wind and the voice of seagulls. A toy train takes us from Rye to Camber, and we are more than content to spend the first days of the holiday on the warm sand, and in and out of shallow, curling waves tipped with dazzling foam. Later we explore the ruins of Camber Castle and visit Winchelsea, always walking, meeting few other visitors. During the second week we are joined by one of the choir tenors; there is then a brilliant moon at night; we drift along the river, singing the hymns, the bits of oratorio we love best. The long cry of owls punctuates our pauses. The gently moving oars only disturb the glowing surface of the river to fling phosphorescent jewels into the night. At midnight we return to the cottage, elated. Agnes, Edith and I share one bedroom, the two men the other; we talk long before going to sleep. We have made a small breakaway from Victorian holiday tradition, and it excites us.

My cousin Evelyn's wedding day is fixed. Authority, in the person of Barrow Rule, the kind old Clerk to the Education Committee, writes granting me 'leave of absence to act the bridesmaid'. I take an early train to Newhaven and arrive in time to help Evelyn put on her ivory silk wedding gown. She looks charming, is in the gayest of humours, and pins at my throat a brooch shaped like a golden bird with seed-pearls in its wings, the gift of the bridegroom. I receive it in silence, but Evelyn does not notice, and bids me go downstairs and thank Harry, who has just arrived. I leave her in Gran'ma's big front bedroom (where we used to play with our dolls and laugh at the telegraph poles that seemed to be marching over the downs to the sea), and descend to meet her future husband. He stands, a strong, stocky figure in wedding garb complete with buttonhole, on the hearth-rug in Aunt Bec's parlour. His feet are planted a little apart, his hands behind his back, and he is talking to Gran'ma with an air of well-controlled impatience. He turns quickly to me when the introduction is made, and immediately claims me as cousin, smiling assurance. I am polite and distant, and at my obviously forced thanks his smile becomes ironic; the entry of the second bridesmaid, laughing and fingering his gift with evident delight, is a welcome diversion.

The marriage ceremony takes place, not in the chapel where the bride's family worships, but in the parish church, 'because it is Harry's wish', Evelyn has explained. I stand resentfully behind her in the aisle, holding her bouquet of pink carnations. If only she were plighting her troth to a bright-haired, handsome boy, her complement and comrade, I should not feel so depressed. I resent and reject the mature, heavily-built figure by her side, who takes her 'to wife' with his air of quiet authority. I am glad when the formal wedding-breakfast is over and they are gone.

There is still an hour before my return train is due. The house is silent. Gran, Gran'ma and Aunt Bec are at home, but it is so lonely that I want to be away. Gran'ma is lying down, resting, Gran sits in his armchair stolidly smoking his long churchwarden, smoking-cap over his brow. Aunt Bec, from the window-seat in her parlour gazes out at passers-by; sometimes she looks back at the confetti-strewn carpet. Except for the confetti everything in the parlour is as I have known it always – Uncle Will's painted ships sail over their blue seas, the Chinese helmsman steers his junk, the bright foreign birds perch in their glass case, and the portrait of Uncle Will smiles eternally. But the key-board of the piano is closed and Evelyn's music put away. I see my first ghosts – two children at the piano, singing the old sea songs.

August Manns is dead – last of the great orchestral conductors of the Victorian age. The stocky figure, the long white locks falling over the black velvet jacket, the assurance of beat – these will be remembered and missed as long as the Crystal Palace remains a home of music. Nor is it many months before his orchestra is disbanded, as a measure of economy. The concert hall remains empty except when a London symphony orchestra pays a rare Saturday afternoon visit, or the Dulwich Choral Society gives one of its winter evening performances – Sullivan's *Golden Legend*, German's *Merrie England* or Coleridge-Taylor's *Hiawatha*. Coleridge-Taylor is now conducting the Croydon String Players' Club – which plays to full audiences in the draughty old Public Hall where long ago I went to receive my useless and unnecessary school certificates. I wonder whether I shall ever qualify for admission to the String Players' Club. I greatly admire the beautiful bowing arm of the first violin, Christine Chabot, and enjoy, this spring, the fine pianoforte playing of a young, emaciated composer and pianist, William Hurlstone.

The Crystal Palace Company, in debt, appeals to more popular taste. Stunt shows appear on the terraces and invade the gardens. An object like a giant roundabout is erected; instead of the horses of the circus roundabout it dangles cone-shaped boxes with propellors, which are revolved fast enough to give the sensation of flight. It is advertised as Hiram Maxim's Flying Machine.

Agnes and I look further afield for Saturday recreation. We have discovered Richard Jefferies' Open Air philosophy and read his books. There is now a series of small hand-books indicating the possibilities of woodland paths and downland tracks, with avoidance of road-walking. We seize these and begin happily to explore the countryside. As soon as I am free of the Centre on Saturday mornings we board the Purley tram (now electric) and start over Riddlesdown; the length of the walk is determined merely by the time of sunset.

My brother Arthur is now nearly eighteen, and his future has become a family problem. Since leaving school he has drifted in and out of unskilled and temporary jobs, finding neither personal interest nor training. He lacks initiative, and tends to adopt my Uncle Gambier's attitude of irresponsibility. Uncle Charles and his partner Charles Chapman decide to take Arthur in hand. A post is found for him in Sevenoaks.

Charles Chapman's vision of the British Empire is of a world-wide dominion wherein men of all colours and races will peacefully unite to play chess and cricket. Kipling is his prophet and Kipling's *Stalky and Co.* his manual of conduct. He proceeds with Arthur's education along the lines indicated, using as primers the *Barrack-room Ballads* and *Soldiers Three.* Half a year later my mother receives a letter from Arthur, posted in Dover; he has joined the Regular Army as a gunner and is leaving on foreign service. This information is a blow to her self-respect. The redcoats of the fort at Newhaven did not stand high in the estimation of the townspeople; she saw them as lazy, swaggering youths, good for nothing but to chase girls and lounge at street corners! My father looks troubled, but bides his time; not entertaining for a moment her suggestion that we should buy Arthur out.

In the ranks of the Army one is relieved of decisions – one has only to obey orders and to look smart. These obligations are new to Arthur, and the novelty pleases him. One is quit of the boring business of earning a living by some mechanical or tedious work lasting the whole day. In the Army there are spells of real hard work, but there is also much leisure – time to lounge and chat with other men, time to write racy letters and to *draw*. Materials found if an officer can be interested. Among the other chaps there are small distinctions to be won. And there are the *guns* – creatures of fine line and immense power, to be served and controlled.

A troopship takes my brother to China. During the next five years he writes me an occasional letter which reflects the eastern setting of the ordered, leisured, subordinate life that contents him.

At intervals of perhaps three months comes a morning when the school-room door is suddenly opened and a loud voice gives a good-morning to Miss Towell. Rising from her desk, the Head shakes hands with the largest woman I have ever seen. This is Miss Morland, sister of the Mayor of Croydon, and herself a formidable member of the Education Committee. Her family, formerly considerable landowners, are of Quaker tradition, and take most seriously their civic responsibilities. Miss Morland, I am told, is a 'blue-stocking' – which means, in this instance, one of the few women of Miss Morland's generation with a college education. She has a real desire to improve our school and teaching conditions on broad lines, but since public funds are not available, resorts to investigating cases of especial need among the children. Her great voice booms from class to class. She is so tall that I, being of middle height, can only look at her face if I raise my head, and this it seems rude to do. She wears a tweed jacket and skirt, long, but shorter than that of an ordinary woman, with thick stockings and heavy shoes. The school-room is smaller for her presence in it.

Years later, I sit in the public gallery of Croydon Town Hall; the Borough Council is in meeting on the floor below. Alderman Harold Morland, its chairman, sits in the high seat of the Mayor, beyond the table end. He is then an old man, in the final year of his office. There is a great deal of noisy argument among the Councillors. The Mayor may not be listening – or he may – but he does not interrupt. Then out of a silence which suggests the exhaustion of the Councillors the Mayor speaks two sentences, in the tones, not of a Mayor, but of an old king. There is a sigh of relief from the floor and a rattling of papers; that matter is done with; the agenda can proceed.

Twice, before my twenty-first year, I see the acting of Henry Irving, both times in company with Agnes, and at the Lyceum Theatre. He plays Mephistopheles in *Faust*. I am sure that he is a most convincing devil – but what *is* the devil? and who or what originated 'the moral law'? I am back with old problems of my sixteenth year. Our second visit is to a performance of Tennyson's poetic drama *Becket*. In this there is much to enjoy, and I can forget everything subsidiary in the action of the drama. I have a first sense of the *inevitability* of tragedy, given the existence of opposing forces. There is the rainbow, but though it is born of Rosamund's harp-chords, it will not stay for Rosamund. Gleam upon gloom becomes gloom upon gleam. But who wills the tragedy? Is it the king, impelled by the queen, or is it the magnificent Becket himself – more magnificent in death than in life? I carry away an abiding mental picture of Henry Irving in his final scene.

> Not twenty steps, but one,
> And fear not I shall stumble in the darkness.

At Whitsuntide of this year, 1903, Agnes and I walk by the woodland paths of Farley and West Wickham from Croydon to Sevenoaks. But the tracks end on Westerham Hill, by an inn called The Saltbox, and we must follow seven miles of high road, dusty and tiring. We finish the twenty-two miles walk empty of energy, and the effects of over-strain show themselves a month later, when I am due to sit for the King's Scholarship exam.

Grandma is dead, and the invalid Uncle Edwin, but Grandpa and Uncles James, Gambier and Charles still live in Alpha Cottage, employing a house-keeper. Grandpa's walks are now limited to the ten-minute daily stroll and the seat by the Vine cricket ground from which he can watch sun and shadow on Polhill. The old town is little altered, but a short street of small new villas ends blindly on a bluff rising on the adjacent edge of Knole Park. The tops of tall trees rooted in the valley below are level with the end house, in which Agnes and I lodge for our week's holiday. For the first time I hear the full chorus of English wild birds in a spring dawn. It begins, well before sunrise, with a solo call from a blackbird and its answer from his rival; is taken up by thrush, robin, warblers, tits and cuckoo. It would seem, indeed, to be a Hymn to Joy, an acknowledgment of the God of creation. It delighted St Francis in his day, it delights me now for a full half-hour, then ceases suddenly, unexpectedly, as it began. 'The name of the chamber was Peace.' I sleep for three hours before time to dress and breakfast in May sunshine.

I overtax my strength during the year preceding the K.S. examination. Teaching, with full responsibility for the class, on eight half-days of the normal week, evenings given closely to study and violin practice, the Saturday country walks, averaging fourteen miles; two church services on Sunday. My diet at this time is vegetarian, discouraged by my mother, and unsupplemented by additional proteins. I have new and unpleasant sensations – breathlessness on a hill slope, the fear of falling, a tendency to clutch at fence or railing and to hesitate before crossing a road. The hard beating of my heart will wake me at night, terrified, wondering whether I am going to die.

Such symptoms intensify as the week of the examination nears.

Past exams have found me pleasantly excited and free from apprehension; now I sink with shame at my feebleness. On the opening morning I am nearing collapse, but my mother urges me to try and reach the examination centre; she will come with me and interview the supervisor. He is kind, shows me to my seat, bids me do what I can; my mother amazingly thrusts a small bottle of brandy into my hand, the mist clears, and my mind, though not my hand, steadies. The ordeal begins with a hand-writing test – my large-hand effort resembles that of a fly escaping from the ink-pot and painfully freeing his legs between the guide lines on the paper...The light dims nearly to darkness, and I am only aware of a hammering machine, my heart, and a roaring in my ears which is not really sound. A gulp at the brandy bottle warms and steadies me – the nervous fit passes and presently I can concentrate, fairly, upon the arithmetic paper. At the end of the session my mother's anxious, sharpened face appears, and I am able to smile at her – the first morning is over. Each successive session begins with a similar battle. The papers are all attempted, but in the end I am sure that I have failed.

...Days and months of weakness follow – of being nothing more than a detestable body full of wretchedness and distressing sensations – a body to which all mental and emotional power is subordinated. Sight of print, even of book-titles upon a shelf, is physically nauseating. A vague, frustrated desire to escape from home, to get away from the people who look at me with such concern – who offer contradictory advice. The dragging misery of the school hours! Three months – then comes a long envelope bearing the Board of Education stamp. I have passed the King's Scholarship examination, but in the second class!

The chagrin of a second-class pass! But my mother is more than content with the answer to her prayers. A post and a salary are assured me.

POSTSCRIPT TO
ADOLESCENCE

There are yet two years of study before me in preparation for the Acting Teachers' Certificate. About half my Centre class-mates will spend that time in a training college. Not in a university, with the opportunity of making social contacts which should widen their experience of life, but in a government-subsidised boarding establishment where they will meet only the trainees of their own profession, and where the lectures given will relate to their work as elementary school teachers. The fees of such colleges are small in comparison with those of university, but in my case the payment of any fee is out of the question. Nor have I the least wish to enter a training college. The tales told during school lunch-hour by recently returned teachers have not tended to lighten the impression made upon my mind by a reading of Hardy's *Jude the Obscure.* The alternative is study at polytechnic evening classes after the day's teaching.

I am appointed to the Dering Place Mixed School, South Croydon, at a salary of fifty pounds per annum. This school is new, and in a quiet situation. It stands on a slope, its building and play-grounds stretching the length of a short, blind street terminated by the garden walls of some large houses on the top of the rise. Its plan is the same as that of Whitehorse Road, with the addition, at either end, of small rooms respectively for head teacher and staff. The head teacher's room is furnished with official desk and arm-chair; the staff-room contains a pitch pine table as sole furniture. This superior accommodation distinguishes the new school from the earlier ones. But Dering Place has also advantages of position; it is on the southern edge of the town, adjacent to the open green space of Russell Hill, and but ten minutes walk from the wooded mound of Croham Hurst.

The school's head master, Philip Smith, is a wiry, impetuous man of middle age but youthful enthusiasms. Impulsive, inconsequent, he is liked by the staff as much for weaknesses as for abilities. School-days amble along easily under loose rein except when inspectors are reported in the neighbourhood. There is now no formal inspection upon set dates, no testing of individual pupils as during my Horley school-days. Instead, the visitation is without previous notice, and report is made upon the general discipline of the classes and the standard of such teaching and children's work as may be conveniently made manifest to the inspectors. If these appear in one school of a given area it is probable that other schools will shortly be visited, and warning goes round – it is a matter of *esprit de corps*. Given such warning P.S. begins to frown and bristle, becomes preternaturally aware of shortcomings otherwise ignored; his rein tightens, the staff responds, and there is a spate of manifest activity lasting until the visitation is over. P.S. alternates spasms of lassitude and energy; seized by the latter he will dash into a classroom, release or expel the teacher, galvanise the class with an experimental lesson just conceived. No German is taught in the school, but P.S. has placed on the wall before the desks of his senior class the legend, in German capitals, WENN ICH RUHE ICH ROSTE (when I rest I rust).

On my first morning at Dering Place I face a class of fifty-six boys and girls of seven or eight years old. I attempt to teach what the class syllabus dictates, and use all the tricks learned from observation of teachers' method – tricks to engage the attention and impress the memories of the children crowded together in the desks. During the school-day, every volt of my energy is expended on the disciplinary and mechanical. The aim is the class average of attainment. The individual child means to me little more than a name on the register, an average of sums right or wrong, of spelling mistakes in dictation.

My fifty pounds salary has meant a move from the slum-side box in which we have lived for eight years to a small house in The Crescent, Selhurst. I walk to school and back, four miles, on the five week-days, attend polytechnic classes in South Norwood on three evenings each week and on Saturday mornings. The tutors require much homework, and an hour a day is too little for the practice of violin studies. But the nervous symptoms of the previous year disappear, and this, I think, is due to the regular exercise of my daily walk.

Francis Sisley, being well satisfied with our Rye holiday, plans another on similar lines. We shall stay at Shoreham, Sussex. But this holiday is a miserable failure. The summer is wet and chilly; our rooms in the boarding house are unwarmed; Edith has a raging toothache. I sit in a corner of the dreary parlour and read *Adam Bede*. George Eliot is enthralling enough to draw my mind from present conditions, and I love her pictures of farm and village life, but the story is infuriating. I loathe the Methodism of the saintly Dinah, and long to forbid the banns of her marriage to Adam Bede – whom I should have respected more thoroughly had he remained faithful to the twice-betrayed Hetty. For Arthur Dimsdale I have nothing but contempt, and scourge the author for false sentiment in making him the means of Hetty's reprieve from the death penalty. Reprieve, indeed! rather condemnation to a worse fate – a living death. This is the mercy of a community calling itself Christian, of a nation priding itself on its sense of justice. For the hour, for the days following, against the grey cloud and almost incessant rain, I see Hetty Sorrel, alone, always alone with her great fear, and I realise the isolation of one rejected by family, damned by its moral law.

The *Faust* legend haunts art. Goethe's drama is followed by

Gounod's sentimental adaptation of the story in operatic form, and by Berlioz's terrible *Damnation de Faust*. Under the spell of the music I never question the right of the theme to its prominence, but in dispassionate silence feel that the medieval spirit exaggerated beyond measure the significance of the sexual act in its human manifestation. Why should Mephistopheles be assumed to set such store by this 'sin'? Obviously the sexual instinct is that which ensures the continuity of the human race, but, like the other instincts, it is subject – or should be – to the control of reason. Only when it is not, as in the case of Arthur Dimsdale, is there a selfishness that can be called sin. So, in my twenty-third year, I see this matter.

I am now twenty-two. The fears of childhood and the emotional flurries of adolescence are behind me. The basis of objective living is routine. It is so with all my world. One week is like another – a time-table existence. As a teacher I escape from school routine for two months of each year, and during one fortnight of this time I can leave the suburb and stay by the sea. I know that the possession of wealth ensures a wider orbit, but the world of wealth is remote, completely removed from mine. Much nearer is the world of extreme poverty. It is rather as if I am walking firmly along a low dyke which crosses a morass. If I pass the impending examination my salary will increase automatically by a few pounds per year for some ten years, as long as I serve the suburban education authority; but a post in the country or by the sea would mean reduction. I am apparently without ambition; my childish dreams of authorship, of recognition in a literary world, were unrealistic; I have no desire for the headship of a school.

What is my life on the other plane – that of the spirit and the imagination? I decide that only therein is the way of escape from one's objective limitations. One builds one's palace of art, one gazes into the magic mirror. Reality and romance are separate, two distinct, if parallel, phases of existence.

But presently I am to see a figure who would appear to identify the two planes.

INITIATION

In the beginning was the word – the printed word. When I think back into childhood and infancy to trace the influences which contributed to the make-up of the amorphous creature of my twenty-second year, this seems obvious. Lying in my cot, I must have gazed, day after day, at the bright colouring of the framed illuminated Biblical texts with which our bedroom walls were hung. These texts, and the rhymes in nursery books, were memorised very early. Veneration for the printed page was inherited from my father and grandfather.

The Bible was God's book, peculiarly sacred; but a measure of authority invested everything in print. Until, at five years, I could read for myself, both parents habitually read to me – Mamma from *The Peep of Day* and *Line Upon Line*, Papa from Longfellow and other poets. These attentions ceased later, and Mamma, but never Papa, objected to my absorption in 'book-reading'. (I still keep the old, clear-print copy of the New Testament which was my prize from Papa for reading, without mistake, the tenth chapter of St John's gospel, a favourite chapter, being all about sheep. My name, with the date 13 April 1887 is written in my father's fine, firm hand-writing on the title-page.) Thereafter the fascination of the printed word increased – I read, or dismissed as uninteresting, all books upon Papa's shelves – preference being given to poetry and history. Only Eugène Sue and Harrison Ainsworth were forbidden as being too exciting for a child who slept badly. The daily paper was taboo, but not the weeklies *Christian Commonwealth* and *British Weekly* – the latter posted regularly to Papa by my grandfather after reading. Also available to my eighth and ninth years were huge bound volumes of the *Illustrated London News* and *Sunday At Home*, dating from the sixties. During my tenth year appeared the first issues of the *Strand Magazine*, *Titbits*, *Answers* and *Pearson's Weekly*, in blue, green, yellow and pink covers respectively. Papa brought these in irregularly and incidentally. I was particularly attracted to the *Strand*, in which the Sherlock Holmes tales were serialised, and I looked long at the sequence of photographs depicting well-known personalities from childhood to middle-age. How queer the transformation! The only library available in Horley was that of the Sunday School, which lent out to children a nauseous collection of goody-goody books, which I read, but detested.

To assess the influence upon one's mind of particular books is not easy. But there is no doubt that in my experience the Bible came first. It was there all the time. On Sundays it was read aloud in chapel and Sunday School; on week-days a Bible lesson began morning school; passages had to be memorised. During my last three years at school, and again at the Pupil-Teachers' Centre we were coached for an annual examination in Biblical texts, history and geography. The Ten Commandments, basis of our moral training, hung on the school wall before the assembled school. The Holy Land seemed more real to my imagination than Europe. The diction of the Authorised Version of the Bible became as familiar as that of common talk, and Biblical characters as real as those of my family. Next in point of influence (up to my ninth year) was Bunyan's *Pilgrim's Progress*. Although the appeal of the story came first, I could not entirely ignore Bunyan's theology, and without any imposition of creed I learned very early to believe that 'the things which are seen are temporal, but the things which are unseen are eternal'. The abstract was no less valid than the concrete. No confusion there – the confusion from which my childish mind suffered came from the paradox presented by religious teaching – I was under penalty to love an unlovable God, and to believe what my reason rejected. Much of the influence exercised by Olive Schreiner's *The Story of an African Farm* is accounted for by the fact that the book presents two characters also in revolt against the tenets of contemporary religion. I felt no longer alone. The other book impressed upon my tenth year, Lew Wallace's *Ben Hur*, somehow delivered the personality of Christ from association with unacceptable dogmas formerly, in my mind, woven about it. But at ten, one *feels* rather than *thinks* in relation to such abstractions.

George Macdonald's fairy tales built me a bridge from orthodox Christianity to Buddhism as presented by Sir Edwin Arnold in his *The Light of Asia*; over this bridge I passed from religion to the poetry and art which illumined adolescence. The light was fitful, directed backward into history, tending to ignore the present.

Turning to the influence of contemporaries, that of my father – least self-assertive of men – was paramount. From the beginning I had from him a sense of security, of rightness and justice, conveyed merely by his presence. A quiet word from Papa was more effective than a long scolding from Mamma. My mother's qualities were not so evident to me in childhood as in later years. Apart from her Bible, *Enquire Within Upon Everything* and a *Home Medical Dictionary* she had little use for books, and during my school-days believed that I should sleep better if I read less – which was probably true. I never wished to be like Mamma, or to live her kind of life.

After his trading failure a small feeling of pity crept into my regard for Papa, but without lessening my fundamental faith in him. From the beginning of school-days my brothers and I shared in common little more than our meal-times; the boys made friendships with which I had no concern. Two of my teachers definitely influenced me – Miss Mary Ann Smythe, head mistress of Whitehorse Road School, Croydon, and its senior assistant mistress, Miss Nellie Peck. From Miss Smythe I gained experience of a real personality, and a sense of the sublimity of epic poetry, also a conception of the Bible as literature. Nellie Peck, the lively, attractive daughter of a borough councillor, always beloved of her school class, was a Tolstoyan and an advocate of good causes, especially that of the R.S.P.C.A., whose pamphlets she introduced into the classroom. The grime of Whitehorse Road was forgotten in her presence. The accidental meeting with Miss Peck during my six-teenth year was a deciding factor in my career. She was then married to a schoolmaster, Jack Hooker, and a tea-time at their house introduced me to Tolstoyan Socialism. A large portrait of 'the Master' hung on the wall. We did not meet again until 1934, when at another tea-time we revived memories of Nellie Peck's 1893 school class. At that point she and her husband were preparing a transfer to South Africa.

Into this category of personal influences come two more emotional ones, those of my cousin Evelyn Lydia Robinson and my staff colleague Agnes Mason. The first was dominant for seven years: although Evelyn and I met only during summer holidays, we wrote frequently, and when at the beginning of a holiday we met at Newhaven railway station, it was as though we had only just parted. My love of Evelyn was based on admiration mixed with envy. What I represented to her I never learned, but for me she focused all the magic of the South Downs, the sweep of warm wind over their ripening corn, the forest of sailing ships in the harbour and the mystery of the sea beyond the bar, a heaven of translucent blue and dazzling cloudlets, and the peace and friendliness of Orwell House. Standing beside Evelyn at the piano, near enough to catch the scent of curls that danced to her tune, singing a sea shanty that called up Uncle Will's lost ship, I knew a content and happiness rarely repeated in later life. Nothing of a sexual nature entered into our personal association, but I was intrigued by her endless interest in babies and pregnant mothers – an interest I did not share, but which contributed much to my knowledge of obstetrics. My reaction, at fourteen, was summarised in a contribution to Evelyn's 'Confession Book', 'Love is the only *excuse* for marriage.'

The influence of Agnes Mason was that of the experienced upon the inexperienced. I found that with her I could confidently discuss matters relating both to life and religion. Her training as a teacher had been on the same lines as mine, but in an older and more primitive school building, and she had seen her transfer to Whitehorse Road as a rise in the world. She had enough personality and independence of spirit to hold her own against Miss Corney without antagonising the head mistress, and a vitality and forthrightness which inspired confidence in children, and pupil-teachers. I shared her love of music, admired her freedom of mind, and as our friendship developed, enjoyed, for the first time, a sense of comradeship. In the early days it was strange and wonderful to me that she should enjoy my company, callow as I was at eighteen; and it was flattering that she should be interested in my thought. Later I realised how, with ten years of school drudgery behind her, and bound by a sense of duty to support her family, she needed the touch of youth to stimulate diminishing vitality. An enquiring mind and a love of nature and art had saved her from being drawn into the vortex of the petty; she had resisted the demands of school and family upon her time, to the extent of reserving week-end leisure, and filling this with whatever intellectual activities came her way. Her interest in philosophy was genuine but superficial; her love of music emotional rather than interpretive, and her pianoforte-playing was without nuance. But none of these shortcomings were evident to me in the beginning of our friendship and its measure of companionship contented me until my twenty-second year.

Ambition, for the assistant mistress, could take only one form – the desire for a headship. I had no such desire, though I sometimes played with the fancy of a little school and school-house of my own, between the Downs and the sea. But until fully qualified I must stay in Croydon, and my final was nearly two years distant. I had pulled out of the depression surrounding the King's Scholarship period with just enough energy to carry me through the day's work without worry or resistance. Omar Khayyam, read first at this period, expressed the mood:

> Unborn tomorrow and dead yesterday,
> Why fret about them if today be sweet.

Today may not be sweet, but it is no longer intolerable. There are compensations, both spiritual and material. I know companionship, and a fine sense of freedom comes with the Saturday exploration on foot of the still remote Downs and Weald. At home there is a relaxed and contented atmosphere, and new amenities – even a bathroom. My parents' anxiety for their children's future is lessened; I am on a straight path to economic independence, Arthur's letters tend to show that he is qualifying for advancement in the Army, and is fascinated by life in Pekin.

I get no satisfaction from the practice of the violin. My bowing remains inept and my playing utterly toneless. I have little confidence in the young violinist who has undertaken, for pocket money, to teach me, and under whom I have studied for eighteen months. Now he leaves the district. A member of the church choir suggests that I try to get lessons from H.B.M., a violinist of local repute. I seek an interview. H.B.M. is not encouraging, and my audition does not last for five minutes. He tells me that I know nothing of violin technique, and cannot even hold the bow correctly. If he is to teach me I must start from the beginning, and forget everything previously taught me. I have the impression that he would prefer to refuse me, and yet his manner somehow supports my intention to insist on learning to play. We agree on terms, and he rushes away to catch a theatre train.

Apparently there has been a re-discovery of Edward Fitzgerald's presentation of the *Rubaiyat*; it figures in review columns, and copies appear in every bookseller's shop window. Its rhythm, colour and imagery haunt me, and the audacity of the philosophy appeals, but not the philosophy itself. Even for me Khayyam's moment is too brief a point of time – I cannot be so trivial a thing. Against Khayyam I set Gautama Buddha of *The Light of Asia*; and yet Gautama's conception of Nirvana is too remote from activity to be acceptable.

At the Dering Place School my class numbers a total of fifty boys and girls of seven and eight years. The individual child may mean to me little more than a name on the register, an average of sums right or wrong, of spelling mistakes in the dictation exercise. I neither accept nor reject the class approved syllabus as a whole. It seems to me that children should be taught to read, write and speak clearly – these are the means of self-expression. They may not *want* to acquire these means, since they are too young to value them – hence some measure of compulsion is permissible. There is nothing in the syllabus that comes into the category of art; at best the children make pencil drawings in outline of an object set up before them. If colour is introduced at all, it is limited to the use of hard, greasy crayons. My chief criticism of the syllabus is levelled against its arithmetic impositions. I see no reason at all why children of seven and eight should be compelled to manipulate numbers far beyond their comprehension. Do the adults who frame the syllabus know *anything* of the working of children's minds? My training course for the current years includes the educational theories of Froebel and Pestalozzi, but there is little evidence that their ideas have reached the staff of Dering Place School.

Rising in the chalk of the North Downs there is an intermittent stream to which the country folk give the name

Woe Water. Traditionally it appears once in seven years, but actually the frequency of its rise varies with the seasonal rainfall. Its course is casual, variable; it makes its way across meadow and pasture, through gardens, through the basement of houses recently built for people without knowledge of its vagaries or by speculative builders indifferent to them. It crosses main roads, turns lanes into water-courses, and so comes down to Purley, where, after flooding the school play-ground and isolating the schoolmaster's house, it subsides into a prepared channel.

When, during March, we hear that Woe Water is rising, Agnes and I plan our next Saturday walk to start from Purley, and to follow its course upstream, as nearly to its source as the hours and miles allow. The day is one of intermittent bright sunshine, with horizons of azure blue and silver beyond bare, windswept downs and plumed fir-groves on hill crests. It is fascinating to trace the streak of gurgling water – now lost to view, now emerging from a bank, running alongside, disappearing into a copse, re-discovered flowing from a disused gravel pit, coming briskly down a sandy lane, trespassing in the gardens of a great house. My Saturday is one of detached content. I feel free of all bondage, all obligations – happy to be like Woe Water, without known source, without set channel, inconsequent, indifferent to anything human.

I have now much more satisfaction in the practice of the violin. A very few lessons have convinced me that my new tutor, H.B.M., is both an expert violinist and a good teacher. I no longer scrape through dreary pages of technical studies, but must concentrate upon small, essential points of technique. The short lesson over, my master rises, swings his instrument into position, and I learn what the Bach 'Air on the G string' , or some other immortal melody, sounds like played on his Carcassi by strong, efficient hands. I begin to think of H.B.M. as *Dominus*. I look at him less casually, and see the finely balanced proportions of body, limbs and head. He is tall, but not too tall, his thick, dark hair is shapely, and brushed back from a high forehead; his eyes are dark blue and long-lashed, reminding me oddly of an eight-year-old boy in my school class. His age is, perhaps, thirty-four.

During succeeding months I learn something of his family, meeting its members incidentally. Living in the house with H.B.M., his wife and four children, are his father and sister. The father, a retired City merchant, a Scot, will greet me with old-world courtesy. The sister, Laura, brings me a cup of tea, with apologies, sometimes, for H.B.M.'s late return from an afternoon rehearsal; Laura has the heavy black hair and high colour of a colleen. The wife may be of Spanish descent; the children, aged from thirteen to five years, are fine youngsters, but noisy and quarrelsome.

The routine features of the week tend to arrange themselves at relative distance from the forty minutes of my violin lesson. I rush away from the bleak school-room as if I shall never enter it again. Tired, I play badly, with unsteady bowing-arm and stumbling fingers. H.B.M. becomes indulgent, gently humorous. His self-assurance annihilates mine through much of the lesson; only towards its end is the balance adjusted, but as we close the instruments in their cases and talk of general matters I recover, and lack neither grip nor elasticity of mind. I can, and do, interest H.B.M. – the fact restores my self-respect.

I see him as soloist on the concert platform, as leader of the orchestra in local opera. Increasingly I admire his power and poise. His evening route to the railway station crosses mine on the way to Polytechnic classes; occasionally we meet and exchange a greeting, but what can one say in a moment become suddenly so unaccountably significant! On such an evening the lecturer's voice fails to hold my attention. Mr Carrick is a heavily conscientious teacher, who gives instruction at high pressure; head of a large boys' school, he has little energy left for evening teaching; I feel that he is whipping himself to the task...When the literature professor lounges in to take his place, the class relaxes. The young Cambridge graduate is indifferent, pleasantly cynical. We are glad that he does not care whether or not we get honours in English. He lectures lolling in his chair, sometimes balancing it perilously on one leg, and does not rise to write an illustration on the wall-blackboard behind him, but turns and scribbles over his left shoulder. Yet there is something provocative, stimulating, about him, which affects the composition of the essays he suggests that we might, at our leisure, attempt to write. I am even pleased when he is lazily complimentary.

When a new, strong influence enters one's life, its pattern changes. There is a re-orientation of its lines: as when, among the iron filings of a magnetised field, a fresh magnetic force comes into play, and all the filings re-arrange themselves in relation to the modified stresses of earlier compulsion. Whether this general movement is sudden and chaotic, or gradual and in orderly progression, change is inevitable.

I never questioned the right of H.B.M. to effect this change. The Wise Men did not stop on their way to Bethlehem and argue the Star's right to rise. Nothing in my previous experience had brought with it so definite a sanction. Suddenly an inert and aimless present was vitalised; I sensed a living organism in place of a mechanism. My life was to be illumined by the sun of its own time as well as by the reflections of past glories.

Because of its ambiguity I have always avoided the use of the word *love*. There are, said Olive Schreiner, as many kinds of love as of flowers. But I begin to think that the feeling I have for H.B.M. may be one variety. And when I realise that I am stepping into his world as he into mine, I am very glad. In a way it is the fulfilment of a promise. His strength calls forth a strength latent in me; his mind stimulates and complements my own. Through the lens of H.B.M.'s personality I see life during the succeeding five years.

Four winters of Crystal Palace concerts have introduced me to a range of classical music. My listening is all sensuous – a symphony is a magnificent dream of rhythm, tone and colour. H.B.M. objects that I ought to study the form of the works I hear; he will give me lessons in harmony and counterpoint. I work the exercises diligently, but they are no more than note-puzzles to me – tedious note-calculations that add nothing to my appreciation of music. Music is a magic, an illumination. I want to hear the symphony, the sonata, the tone-poem as a *whole* – each is something transcending its representation on the score, or the sum of its themes and their development. I ought, when writing down the notation of chords, to hear them in my mind, but I cannot even pretend to myself that I do.

Presently H.B.M. is writing me brief letters – letters that are simple postscripts to our too short talks after my lessons. They arouse unjustifiable suspicion in my mother's mind. Fearfully, reproachfully, she challenges me, hinting at dishonour. It is as though she had thrown dirty water over a delicate flower or a fair page. In reaction I am coldly, contemptuously angry, and bid her never again mention H.B.M. She has superimposed her own mistaken image of him upon mine, and faint though the impression is, I cannot completely erase it.

Dishonour! What is dishonour? It is a lowering of standards. This intimacy of ours lifts – it does not degrade. It brings to us both an enhanced quality of life. To end our friendship would be a senseless waste. It *ought* to be ended, says my mother – H.B.M. is a married man. What is that to me! I do not want to marry him. Indeed, I am glad that the bounds of our association are defined by the fact of his marriage.

I have no urge to produce children. I should never find satisfaction and fulfilment in family life. Of this I am sure, but it is not the whole reason for my rejection of the married state. There is a more deeply seated denial. Perhaps I claim a single-mindedness that marriage would preclude. I have glimpsed the possibility of spiritual adventure – there is a fugitive radiance that must be followed; there are thoughts to capture. Thoughts which should be exchanged with those of H.B.M.

His art and thought, I soon discover, are both subordinate to the business of earning a living. When we meet first, he is playing nightly in the orchestra of the London Gaiety Theatre, much bored by the banalities and interminable repetition of its musical comedies. From his talkative sister, Laura, I learn presently of his marriage at seventeen – a romantic, runaway marriage, from which the romantic flavour has long evaporated. The wife, says Laura, is slovenly, an inept housekeeper, and the children are undisciplined. (Laura, though Irish in appearance, has a typically Scottish dislike of poor housekeeping.) Rehearsals and teaching fill H.B.M.'s days. Before marriage his education was specialised – the academic training of a professional violinist; and it seems strange that the ideas of poets and philosophers, familiar to me, are new to him. I am humbly proud of the deference he pays to my limited literary research. We exchange books, and I am introduced to Emerson and Thoreau. The latter's forest hermitage delights me – evidence that it *is* possible to escape from wage-earning and the city. Emerson's individualism attracts, but there is much in his philosophy too profound for the experience of my twenty-two years.

The next year, 1905, passes for me like a quiet radiant summer day. H.B.M. and his influence are fitted into the pattern of my life and I am content. I have again the illusion of stability.

At twenty-three I am still virtually blind to all that

happens in the world of public affairs. My community sense
is dormant; in theory I acknowledge a duty to the community – mine is discharged in the school. Any kind of
social and political movement advanced by mass demonstration I avoid sedulously, fearing and hating the emotional pressure of the mass mind. I am indifferent to
politics, and unaware of the international scene, except
as the eastern aspect of the latter may be incidentally
reflected in my brother's letters from China. My father
awakens, rather surprisingly, to the possibilities of the 1905
General Election.

His satisfaction and hope in the spectacular Liberal
return induce me to take a fleeting interest in Parliament as
an institution ...but I see it rather as a venerable debating
chamber devoted to the culture of the fine phrase than as a
power house of national progress. I know, of course, that
there is a framework of Acts of Parliament within which
individual action is limited, and that Conservative and
Liberal Parties compete for the right to alter the shape of
this framework; there are also Socialists who aim at working-
class representation. But nobody of my world, my father
possibly excepted, imagines that an election, or anything
said or done in Parliament, will alter the pattern of our daily
existence, or add to its scope any perceptible measure of
good or ill. Cowper, it seems to me, was probably right:

> How small
> of all that human hearts endure
> that part which laws or kings can cause or cure.

But before this year is over H.B.M.'s feeling for me
begins to move urgently to the physical plane. The
kaleidoscope of my values is shaken, as much by the
realisation that this was not unexpected, as by its fact. We
are entering another phase of intimacy, which may prove
untenable and will certainly be difficult. The old, I protest,
was better. I plead with H.B.M. for a controlled friendship
which we can defend against all challenge, because it harms

no one – discounts no earlier ties. To myself I re-state my own conclusions – mind must control bodily instincts, or human beings sink to animal level. The key word is *sublimation*. In our case its use as a rule of conduct is essential. It is not for me to be either wife or mistress – and for H.B.M. to become my lover would be a denial and repudiation of H.B.M. as I have imaged him.

Writing in 1970, a decade after the general recognition of the period then dubbed 'the permissive age', I try to imagine the reaction of twenty-two-year-olds to the preceding paragraphs. Born at a time in history when the Christian morality is discounted equally with that of the older Jewish tradition – at a time when contraceptives are available to all and the sexual act has become almost as incidental as a cup of tea, I can only assume that reaction to be 'much ado about nothing'. I cannot hope to convey to them the depth and power of emotional states contingent upon community and individual inborn loyalty to traditional moral standards of sixty years ago.

The press reports a nine-days' wonder from the United States. Two brothers named Wright have invented a flying machine capable of lifting itself from the ground and carrying pilot and passenger a short distance in the air. It has no gas-bag, like a balloon, but is driven by a petrol engine; it can be steered in any direction. My father reads this report aloud with unusual excitement, declaring that the problem of human flight is at last solved. My mother regards the invention as an impious encroachment upon the province of the Almighty (unaware that in less than five years' time she will watch with amusement little dragon-faced planes purring over an improvised aerodrome at the foot of Croydon's Duppas Hill).

Between H.B.M. and myself there are more months of stress, of strenuous attempt to establish our intimacy upon a basis acceptable to us both. It fails. But this summer the joint house-keeping in the South Norwood house is given up. H.B.M.'s father needs a more peaceful life, and this is impossible in the proximity of riotous children; Laura wants an orderly routine and an end to kitchen-sharing. They move to Purley; H.B.M. and his family to Wimbledon. Temporarily my lessons are discontinued.

I am baffled, depressed and angry. Baffled by the apparent impossibility of maintaining our friendship on my own terms, depressed to misery at the prospect of life without him, angry that he refuses to struggle any longer against the demands of a passionate nature. In this mood I pass the two months previous to my final examination. Stone-walled against the emotional problem, my energy rebounds into the field of impersonal study. The exam, taken in the operating theatre of the London Medical Institute, lasts a week; my concentration on the papers is good enough to surprise me, and the required essay gives plenty of scope for my imagination. Between papers I walk the Embankment, pleasant in June, and stray into the Savoy Chapel. August holidays follow the exam, with a fortnight in Jersey. But unchained, my mind reverts to H.B.M., and fancy stages future possibility of renewing violin lessons. Wilfully I choose to visit Jersey this summer because he knows the island well, and I feel that he has part in the giant cliffs of red granite that wall the deep blue sea on the south-west – that he is at home in the narrow flower-bordered lanes. In Jersey H.B.M. seems only just out of sight.

In September the examination results appear. I am now fully qualified to teach in any elementary school in the country, either as assistant or (if opportunity occurs) as head mistress. So much freedom is achieved. But at this point I make no move to leave the suburb.

There are changes at Dering Place School. Philip Smith, its Head, marries a member of staff, Alice Cox, and shortly afterwards receives an appointment to the borough's new school, in Davidson Road. Agnes Mason gets a transfer from Whitehorse Road to Davidson, as does Arthur McLeod.

In Philip Smith's place comes James Morrison, son of the manager of a Cumbrian coal mine. He is a quiet, thorough organiser of methodical mind. His relations with staff and pupils are characterised by intuition, consistency, sympathy. Henceforth the working of the school will be that of a well-oiled machine. James Morrison's ideal is harmony in efficiency, his aim to get the best results that can be obtained from the educational system as it is. He is little interested in theories that will not bear, here and now, immediate testing.

The last week of Philip Smith's jurisdiction is one of discipline relaxed. A staff meeting called at play-time by J.M. on his first morning is rendered almost impossible by explosions in the play-ground. Dozens of boys are firing 'caps', having discovered that a leather sucker attached to a door-key will serve in lieu of a toy pistol. J.M. coolly ignores the nuisance, then and for the week following, without protest, and makes friends with his boys. After that there is a science lesson with a social moral, and finally prohibition, upheld with absolute consistency.

Corporal punishment is the ultimate form of correction. P.S. would, according to his mood, cane or refuse to cane either boy or girl sent to him by a class teacher. J.M., upon the request of a woman teacher, will punish a boy, and such punishment is no pretence. He will not cane a girl, but will delegate authority to a woman assistant if desired; it is rarely asked.

My class now numbers fifty; it cannot be said that I see it as fifty individuals. Here and there a small individual sticks out of the mass, more or less persistently. There is eight-year-old Ernest, a serious midget, always on the doorstep when the charge-teacher arrives in the morning, always the last to leave. Ernest, more methodical than I, is naturally the class librarian. The book-cupboard is in his charge, and there is never a book out of place; he keeps a record of the number in each set, he distributes and collects them as required. Play-time never sees Ernest in the play-ground; his little pale face flushes with resentment should a teacher send him out to play; he can always find a job, real or imagined, at the book-cupboard. Ernest is also my school memory; he lets me forget no detail of the daily routine. There is Maud, blue-eyed, golden-haired, vivacious, a joyous tom-boy, probably not yet aware of her illegitimate birth, though it is mentioned in whispers by members of the staff. I make the experiment of taking Maud, with Kathleen, a sober little maid recently orphaned, for an Easter week of country holiday. It is not an easy week, and I discover how superficial are school-time habits and manners.

There are the 'home' boys – always referred to as such. Swarthy, passionate Rowland, whose speech is perfect; and Sidney, fat, flabby and Cockney, with an amazing memory for Bible data. They represent a group of some forty pupils from a nearby institution for illegitimate and unwanted children. The 'home' is run on humane lines and some measure of freedom and choice of occupation are allowed. But the house in which they live is too small to provide scope for the activities of forty healthy children, all kept on a full, stodgy diet, and the restless 'home' boys are not welcomed in any class, nor by other children less well-nourished. These latter, often thin and threadbare, nevertheless maintain a caste superiority which isolates the unfortunates. Every summer a contingent of the older boys leaves the home for Canada – this Canadian exodus is the great event of the year. With a new suit of clothes and a copy of the Bible they are dumped upon a Western farm to labour, at thirteen years of age.

My imaginative perception of H.B.M.'s nearness passes; as the autumn term drags on I know only the emptiness of his place in my life. Then bills upon a hoarding advertise local performances of an opera – he is leading the orchestra. I cannot deny myself the sight of him – Agnes and I take tickets. He does not know that I am present, but his wife, also in the audience, sees us and invites us to tea in her new home. Provisionally I accept. There is a fire-lit tea-time, *en famille*, on a raw Saturday afternoon in November. H.B.M. and I say little to each other directly, but there is a mutual radiance between us which pervades the party. I am happy in the hope that the situation may be saved. He enquires of my violin study – I say it is blundering on without direction.

Eventually the lessons are resumed. I turn with joy to Kreutzer technicalities, and practise the Bach double concerto with determination. It is presently possible to buy a better violin – an old, composite fiddle which H.B.M. finds for me.

This year my cousin Evelyn invites me to spend some days of the Whitsuntide holiday with her. We have not met since her wedding day, six years ago. She has two children and hints at the probability of a third.

A square-built, roomy country house, with a large garden which occupies most of her husband's time when at home. The 'living-room' a place for meals, needlework and children's play. In the parlour an unused, untuned piano – Evelyn says that she never plays now – has no time, and Harry is not interested in music. The two little boys are exacting, but Evelyn is serenely patient, completely absorbed in her motherhood and apparently unaware of any world beyond her home. I marvel at the difference between us, pity the ungainliness of her heavy body, feel anger when Harry calls her, peremptorily, to attend to some duty. But Aunt Bec, also on a visit, is obviously satisfied with Evelyn's choice of life, and is very sure of Evelyn's happiness – there, on the spot, is her husband.

Evelyn will never wait, together with the birth of a child, the return of a ship that is sunk in the China Sea.

We sit, after supper, in the living-room, Evelyn at her needlework, Aunt Bec knitting, Harry hidden behind his newspaper, but throwing some enquiry or suggestion relative to family concerns every now and then at his wife, or commenting with condescending pleasantry upon a remark of mine. I feel remote. My thoughts revert to H.B.M. – to my joy in his sensitivity, in the mastery of his music, the vitality of his personality and its response to mine. Silent, I turn to his image – a guest of whom these three know nothing.

But how completely the child-world in which Evelyn and I played has disintegrated – this thought gives me a chilly feeling of unsubstantiality. At the end of my visit I get into the return train with relief – I am going from a dead to a living world.

The year is 1907 and I am twenty-five. Time seems to stand still. The routine of home life is as regular as that of the school under the control of J.M. My mother's house-keeping and little social round of chapel and Sunday School, my father's going forth and coming in, his evening reading and the gentle, superficial chat which always conceals his thoughts – all are unvarying. At the beginning of the school year each member of the school staff turns to the first page of the class syllabus, and enters fifty or more new names upon a new register – the names presently become familiar, the children bearing them can be distinguished; as the months pass a more or less individual outline of each child is imaged in the teacher's mind. Twelve months – the syllabus is covered, the children 'pass up'. Their outlines fade, fifty more are in their desks; the wheel has turned full circle.

My friendship with Agnes is now also one of routine. I know so well her reactions to my moods, her poses and prejudices, her generosities and jealousies. Our com-

panionship has become rather habit than choice, yet
neither she nor I seek other friends. We share our books,
concerts, holidays, and there is seldom a third person in our
company. This summer the holiday is spent at Sidmouth in
Devon – I retain an impression of pine-trees clutching
crumbling cliffs, a deep blue sea glimpsed through their
branches. Perhaps a clearer impression is of the book read
during this holiday. Agnes has borrowed from Arthur
McLeod a copy of Lord Dunsany's just published fantasy
The Gods of Pegana, illustrated by H. Sime. Text and
illustrations strike a new chord and suggest a new dimen-
sion, of which I am a little afraid. But the book accords well
with my overall mood of this summer. The escape from
reality is through the romantic to the fantastic; and
Dunsany's fantasy, which dwarfs the human scene, is the
expression of a fatalism, on the edge of which, since I am
young, it pleases me to play.

The study of the violin may continue for ever! On each
Saturday morning I go by train and electric tram to the
small modern house in New Malden. Under H.B.M.'s
tuition, more formal than in earlier days, I acquire a pretty
average technical skill, closing my mind to the fact that my
fingers lack the power necessary for sustained tone. The
written exercises in harmony and counterpoint fill several
books, but I cannot relate the notation of a chord to its
musical sound. Sometimes, when a point of theory will bear
an interpretation in terms of general philosophy it becomes interesting – as, for instance, that a musical phrase
tends to move from concord to discord, and thence
through a more or less complicated series of resolutions
to concord again. This, I half dare to hope, may be true
of life.

When one tends to entertain an assurance of the per-
manence of conditions or institutions, they are on the point
of change or departure. The Sabbath, rest-time of the
Creator, occurs as a principle in nature and human

experience, to be followed, inevitably, by unforeseen development.

At the beginning of 1908 two fresh influences enter H.B.M.'s life and mine – Wagner and Nietzsche. In February the *Ring* is produced at Covent Garden Opera House. H.B.M., to his satisfaction and joy, obtains a seat among the first violins, near the leader, and devotes himself to an intensive study of the *Ring* scores. His enthusiasm for Wagner, and desire that I should share it, reduces the formality with which he has latterly hedged my lesson hour. I am more than willing to study the *Ring*, haunt the Wagner section of the public library, and read E. F. Benson's rendering of *Walküre*. Further, I discover George Bernard Shaw's commentary on the *Ring*. Agnes and I secure seats in the gallery slips for *Valkyrie* – for the first time the cycle is to be sung in English. All unaware of the power of Wagnerian magic, my imagination enters the plane of supermen, gods and heroes. The vast conception sweeps my mind – a hurricane of music and emotional colour, testing its roots as they have never been tested before. The high noontide of common day is a pallid gleam beside this glory. What a miserable travesty of life is that of humanity! 'Ye shall be as gods!' *or* Ye shall be as dwarfs, driven by the economic whip to labour, dwarfed mentally, emotionally, conditioned to the mediocrity of suburban life, to the petty routine of factory, office, schoolroom! 'Lord,' say I to Wagner, 'it is good for us to be here.' And how good it is to be saluted, from the orchestra, by the violin bow of H.B.M.!

But there is no abiding place among gods, heroes and *Walküren*.

In April and May the *Ring* is sung in German, and Richter himself conducts *Rheingold*. I have a cycle ticket. Looking down from gallery slips into darkened theatre I see Richter as the magician bending over the faintly illumined, magic score. With the lowering of the lights all noise from the auditorium has ceased; the initial chord of the opera rises out of profound silence. The stage performance does little to deepen the spell; but if the Rhine maidens too obviously swim behind screens of green gauze, I close my eyes until the music has effaced that impression. On the second evening after *Rheingold* I hear *Walküre* again, this time anticipating the musical interweaving of the leitmotivs, and such is the power of the spell, fantastically identifying H.B.M. with Siegmund...Unreal school-days divide the stages of the music-drama. When the curtain has fallen upon *Götterdämmerung* I am exhausted, sleep in the train, and stagger home from the railway station.

In the company of Wagner's admirers and critics I meet Nietzsche. He is too drastic an iconoclast to be a welcome companion while one holds on to any cherished legacy of Christian philosophy. He dwells, or seems to dwell, at high Stoic altitudes, in a region of winds too bitter for those accustomed to a lower plane. Yet I greet his revolutionary spirit with great respect. Only when he attacks women do I see him as a giant in bonds. 'When thou goest to a woman, take a whip!' It was his own total dependence upon the care of women that he wanted to scourge, unhappy Nietzsche!

With the end of June the opera season closes: H.B.M. returns to his desk at the Gaiety. He seems tired and dispirited – in a mood of reaction from the stress and excitement of the spring. This weariness of his calls up in me a protective instinct which tends to lessen again the formality of our association as master and pupil. I beg him to take a holiday, but he says he cannot afford one. And the father in him is concerned about the future of his eldest daughter, now sixteen. I have seen her in the past as a charming, wilful, lovable child. At sixteen she is untaught, undisciplined, with a flair for the musical comedy stage. Her mother dreams that she may make it her profession and become 'a leading lady', but her father has no such illusion, knowing that while she is a fair dancer, her voice lacks power and quality. She can only remain in the chorus. Perhaps it is the Scot in him that loathes the prospect of this life for his daughter; but it is too late for him to assert any parental authority in the matter. I learn this on a Sunday afternoon which we spend together upon Hayes Common.

I see no reason, when H.B.M. tentatively proposes that we may at least share an afternoon walk, to refuse. It is understood that we walk as friends, not as lovers. He has so little chance of enjoying sunshine and 'the wind on the heath'. So we go to Hayes, and I am shown the big old house by the Common in which he and Laura spent their childhood; and we visit his mother's grave in Hayes churchyard. It is a happy afternoon, into which no discord enters. Later in the season, when the oat-fields beyond Riddlesdown are whitening, I propose another walk – one which begins at Purley, ascends Riddlesdown, and turns north to the village of Sanderstead, dropping into a narrow valley through a small, dense grove of larches. In the larch wood the light is very dim, and there is no sound but the murmur of gently swaying boughs. We pause a moment, listening to the music of the trees, then descend the steep path, cross the valley, and climb the rise to the village. Beyond Sanderstead church the long downhill road brings us to the Swan Inn at South Croydon, and the electric tram which will take me home.

For this year's summer holiday Agnes and I have chosen Pagham Harbour and the hamlet beside it. The map of Sussex shows Pagham to be an inlet, half a dozen old cottages and a small inn. We book accommodation at the inn. On impulse, I suggest to Agnes that we offer to take the two little girls of H.B.M.'s family, aged eleven and seven, with us to Pagham…there is no prospect of a holiday for them otherwise. Agnes agrees, dubiously, to the proposal. The offer is accepted; the children are willing to come, anticipating a different kind of seaside holiday from the one we are preparing for them; but their disappointed reaction

to Pagham is immediate. No pier, no Punch and Judy, no
sweet stalls, no donkey rides, no other children to play
with! The elder girl feels that she has been cheated, is bored
and sullen, the younger puzzled and unhappy. After the
first day on the sea-shore they have no further interest
in anything it offers, nor in the picnics and games we
improvise for them. Accustomed to a modern house, they
see the inn as an ugly old building. Why have we brought
them here! They are only appeased when, at the end of
a week, we curtail the holiday and take them home. I
am ashamed of my own stupidity in the matter; how little
have my years of teaching taught me of a normal child's
mind!

In the late autumn of this year, 1908, Agnes tells me of a new
assistant master recently appointed to the Davidson Road
school. His name is David Lawrence – a young Midlander
of college training but small practical experience. She says
he avoids, or is avoided by, the other men on the staff
(Arthur McLeod excepted) and looks lonely and unhappy.
She talks to him in play-time, and reports that he has
'original ideas'. (Agnes, in her flair for the novel, is a
veritable Athenian.)

Agnes invites David Lawrence to her home for a social
evening with the family, and asks me to come and be
introduced to him. A memory of Clarence and my
nineteenth year inclines me to refuse, but Agnes is insistent. I call, and am shown into the drawing-room; the
new-comer is discovered in the centre of a family group,
father, mother, two sons and three daughters. David
Lawrence, seated on the floor, is telling fortunes with cards,
chattering clever nonsense in three languages. When I am
introduced he rises, and for a moment his interest is
focused upon me with a peculiar awareness: it is as though
he were isolating me from all present; then he returns to his
fortune-telling patter...My call is short, but I carry away the
impression of a tall, slim, lank figure, of thick, straight,

ruffled hair, of keen, deep-set blue-grey eyes under a high forehead and heavy brows.

Our week-end excursion range now extends to the North Downs, the Weald, to Putney Heath and Wimbledon Common, to Thames side and Hampton Court. Electric trams will carry us to Purley or to Wimbledon; Purley is the jumping-off spot for a day on the Downs. One turns up a lane on to the short grass that grows over the chalk, leans one's arms on a meadow gate and looks back at mist and smoke hanging over the town, and further north, the Crystal Palace towers glinting through the mist. We shake the dust of the city from our feet, and turn southward to walk miles of turf and track, to laze in a hay-meadow, to eat sandwiches sitting on the low, rounded wall of an old churchyard, to climb a steep, grassy hill and rest on its summit, feeling like God surveying all that He has made, and finding it good. The country roads, which we avoid, are white with fine grit, which covers the hedgerows when disturbed by a farm-cart, a heavy wagon, or the infrequent motor car. Less often I choose the more sophisticated west and north-west routes, but they are easily accessible after my Saturday morning violin lesson at Malden – and indeed the birches of Putney Heath owe little to human inter-ference, other than that of migrant gipsies.

H.B.M., whose state of depression has not passed with the summer, goes down with influenza during the autumn. For some weeks he does no teaching, and I see him only when Agnes and I pay a social visit. But with the coming of winter his energy returns and the lessons are resumed. I am distressed to see that the hair has turned white over his temples.

The schools are closed for the Christmas holidays. Two days before Christmas, in a twilight that is heavy with yellow fog, I call at the Malden house for an afternoon lesson. H.B.M. himself admits me and ushers me into the small drawing-room, where tea is laid by a comforting, rosy fire. He takes my coat, and I open my violin case, but he demurs. No – we are going to have tea together. I enquire about the family – it has gone, one and all, to a party. He is gay with an irresponsible gaiety that he has never shown me before. Yes, he was invited to the party, but there is a theatre performance tonight and he has only an hour and a half before train-time. He piles my plate with Christmas fare, and insists on pouring me three cups of tea. When we can eat and drink no more I object that I came for a lesson – may I have it. Without answering, he takes me in his arms and pulls me to the settee...I know that the sex impulse – which I think of as 'the beast' in him – has broken loose. Against it I pit every volt of my energy, which is reinforced by anger. There is a physical struggle lasting two or three minutes, then he lets me go, staggers across the room, picks up a cigarette. I am breathing hard, and silent. It seems as if there is silence everywhere. When he speaks it is to say: 'That is the end. You think I am a beast! So I am and I can't help it!'

The tension is broken. We face the position. *What* asks he, are we going to do?

Physical passion, as the impersonal, creative force necessary to ensure the continuance of the race, had never been starkly presented to me. Like the majority of my generation, I had received no comprehensive biological teaching. I was equally unaware that the Creator's command, 'Increase and multiply, and replenish the earth', is primarily imperative upon the man – who is less able than the woman to opt out of this obligation. My early religious training had divided soul and body, and presented the body as the inferior, rightly subordinate to the soul. The literary patterns of the period mostly enhanced this teaching. They tended to exhibit physical passion as a gross manifestation, linking man with the animal, but, in the case of man, properly controlled by reason and the will. Love was either divine or human. Religion imposed no prohibition against *spiritual* intimacy, for which it claimed complete essential detachment from bodily functions.

I cannot see the matter as H.B.M. sees it, nor understand the urgency of his nature. Whatever exchange is between us is, and must be, of the spirit. His personality is the lens through which I perceive beauty. If Keats be right, and no one seems to challenge him, denial of the means to the perception of beauty is also a denial of truth. This cuts out the issue of our complete separation. As far as I can apprehend our future, it will be one of increasing struggle.

Early in 1909 I pass my twenty-seventh birthday. I am still scarcely aware of the world beyond my personal experience, totally unaware that the rhythm of the outer world affects mine. I have built my palace of art – a very small one – but even such building is limited by one's income. Poetry, history and fiction are the means of escape from a drab present to a colourful past – a past divided from the mundane concerns of today by the No Man's Land of the later Victorians. *Their* period, my studies have led me to believe, cannot yet be recognised as History, since people and happenings are too recent to be seen in perspective. My day-to-day life is an individual fragment of the present – a present which interests me so little beyond the personal radius that current events pass unheeded. My reading of journals is limited to the bookish and music sections of reviews found on the tables of the Braithwaite Hall (central Croydon's reading room) and I rarely listen to my father's after-tea summary of the day's news.

The actions of the Suffragettes are shouted from the house-tops, but I am not moved by the gospel according to Mrs Pankhurst and her daughters. It is an injustice that women may not vote, but I cannot feel that the vote is worth the price paid for it by these women. Into the flame of their enthusiasm for 'the cause' the Suffragettes fling individual dignity, beauty, reserve and poise – attributes that no woman should sacrifice.

With the school staff I am on friendly terms, but this means nothing more than chance association in school hours. The school provides no social life, either for pupils or teachers. It lacks a playing field; hence there is neither cricket nor football, and at 5 p.m. each school-day the play-ground gates are locked.

There are teachers whose lives are devoted to a heroic wrestling-match with the conditions of their service; who pour their whole energy into the task of humanising and modifying the curriculum and supplementing the inadequate supply of books and material provided by the capitation grant. They are highly esteemed by a management desirous of justifying by pleasing examination results the system of child-herding and cheap education – a system as short-sighted and wasteful as it is humanly deplorable. These teachers become so narrowly specialised that their minds are bounded by the classroom and they regard the system they serve as having the fixity of natural law. They groan and grumble under it, but honour it by an acceptance that avoids challenge...They are martyrs without vision.

About this time I notice some signs of a progressive spirit in the educational world, the beginning of a desire to adapt the system, as far as that may be possible, short of revolutionary change, to children's capabilities, to teach them on the lines of child interest. I attend a conference arranged by a teachers' association in which idealism is rampant. The enthusiasm of planners for new schemes inclines one to forget for the moment the limitations imposed by crowded classrooms and the paucity of apparatus and materials. No general improvement takes place, but teachers and children fortunate enough to be located in a new building are better provided. The new school is the new toy of the local authority – its pride, its shop window. My school, Dering Place Mixed, is the last to be built in Croydon on the old, two-class main-room plan. Henceforth each new school is provided with a central hall for assembly, physical training and organised play, and in the classrooms dual desks with back supports replace the long ones with forms. It would seem that the old schools are pinched to pay for the new glories.

During my childhood at Horley there came one autumn a fair to the village, and camped in a meadow, thrusting flames of naphtha into the evening dusk and rending its silence with bray of roundabout organ and shouts of showmen. Leaning behind the counter in the deserted shop I listened to the noises of the fair blended by distance, and enjoyed a sense of remoteness from the hurly-burly of the fair-ground. The best of the evening was mine. Swings, roundabouts, stalls, strange gipsy faces – it seemed I could sense them better than if I had gone with the crowd. On the fair-ground I should have been submerged in a raucous mass of perspiring people, and dazed by the flares and the din. I still feel this satisfaction in staying apart from crowd activity, in playing the remote observer. Yet, this spring I have a sense of being drawn, by some external volition, into the momentum of a force I do not comprehend, impelled along a path which is not my own.

There is no opera season at Covent Garden in February this year. The grey weeks of late winter creep by un-recorded...I teach, read, practise the violin, play sonatas with Agnes. On Saturday mornings I go to New Malden for the usual violin lesson.

H.B.M. and I have patched up a semi-formal kind of association. I put out of mind, as far as possible, the memory of that shattering December evening. But I cannot uproot a small but growing fear of some inevitable change in our relationship. The present condition is a kind of truce, and the balance between us is shifting, due partly to my conviction that worry, overwork and his feeling for me are reducing H.B.M.'s vitality and grip. I cannot deny that what is for me the supreme joy of friendship in association imposes on H.B.M. an exhausting degree of physical control.

Agnes's interest in the young Midlander, David Lawrence, continues, and he spends more social evenings at her home. She tells me that he lodges in Colworth Road, Addiscombe, with an attendance officer and his wife, and that she thinks he is writing a book in his spare time. At weekends he takes long walks. On a fine Saturday in April she arranges that we shall meet after my lesson and introduce David Lawrence to Wimbledon Common and Putney Heath. He is polite and gay; he offers to carry my violin, but this is not permitted. When we reach the Common our talk turns upon Algernon Charles Swinburne, the poet, who died recently. The house he shared with Theodore Watts-Dunton stands on the edge of the Common...I have read Watts-Dunton's *Aylwin*, but scarcely anything of Swinburne's, with whom young Lawrence seems very familiar. While we sit under a clump of silver birches, on Putney Heath, he takes a small book from his pocket, and I hear, read with a restraint that intensifies its exultation, the Chorus from Atalanta. Within me there is an echoing exultance, an excitement that I hold tightly in check. This morning H.B.M. told me that he has secured a contract to play in the Covent Garden orchestra during its long season – April to the end of July – and that he may be able to afford a few days' holiday in August. Will I spend it with him, by the sea? He asks with a kind of desperation which makes me afraid for him – I feel that I cannot, and dare not at the moment, refuse. When I assent he tells me that he has not seen the sea since the days of his boyhood, when the whole family used to migrate each summer to Freshwater, in the Isle of Wight. He would like to visit the old place again. H.B.M., and an island – what a vision to warm the sunlight of a spring day! My horizon expands; the deeps of the blue sky become illimitable.

So Swinburne's poem is curiously apt. The spring

sunshine glints on the bark of the silver birches as David Lawrence reads it.

> For winter's rains and ruins are over,
> And all the season of snows and sins,
> The days dividing lover and lover,
> The light that loses, the night that wins.

The talk following is gaily ironic, but Lawrence seems to sense the undertones in my mood, and meets it with a peculiar and penetrating sympathy. Something of wonder stirs in my perception of this young Midlander, whose intuition is so strangely acute.

When the opera season begins, Agnes and I wait for hours on the stone staircase to secure seats in the gallery slips for *Tristan und Isolde*.

Each succeeding generation seems to suffer a more or less violent revulsion against the poets and prophets of the period immediately preceding its own. The reaction against Tennyson was particularly marked, but has sufficiently abated now, sixty years after the poet's death, for one to confess to an appreciation of his Idylls of the King *without evoking pity.*

I knew the Tristram of *The Last Tournament* and he of Matthew Arnold's *Tristram and Iseult* long before I came, this May of 1909, to Wagner's presentation of the story. The music of the opera, with its lure of love and death, enchanted me less than that of the *Ring*. The magic of the overture was dispelled by the stridency of the second act. The opera expressed an idealisation of death which I was not prepared to admit. The third act brought no conviction.

Later in the season we see D'Erlanger's *Tess*, featuring death in an aspect equally unacceptable. I recall Hardy's conclusion as it appears on the final page of his novel – 'the President of the Immortals had finished his sport with Tess' – and instinctively reject it. I choose life, convinced for the moment that life *can* be very good.

Returning from the opera on a June evening, I find my mother waiting up for me. Weeping, she reads a letter from Aunt Bec – my cousin Evelyn has died in child-birth. Again, as in the case of my little brother's death, my feeling is scarcely sorrow – rather, one of intense resentment against the frustration and futility of this early end. The companion of my childhood vanished in adolescence, but why should the woman who succeeded her die – as I see it – unnecessarily? Evelyn had been in poor health since her last pregnancy – she should not have borne a fourth child. Her husband's lust has cut short the life she entrusted to him. It is all *wrong!* I refuse to join in my mother's expression of sympathy with the widower. He is guilty of a kind of manslaughter more detestable than that of the jailed criminal who has killed in a moment of desperation.

The monoplane flight of M. Blériot across the English Channel, in July of this year, stimulates my father to unusual conversation. His tired eyes become quite animated as he talks of this event and its portents. History is being made, and because he is aware of this, he is participating. I have to live through another five years before I can appreciate his point of view.

Four weeks of summer holiday begin on 30 July. For the elementary school staff these weeks are the climax towards which each school year turns. The freedom, leisure and opportunity they afford is the unique advantage of the teaching profession; they help to raise it, in the common scale of values, above occupations allowing at most an annual week off, with pay. The married teacher, with family, can seldom take more than a week of sea and country air; the teacher with lighter responsibilities may manage a fortnight; but the annual saving on a maximum salary of £120 per annum will hardly finance a month's travel. School holidays out of England are still the exception.

Agnes and I plan well in advance. This year our choice is Cornwall. We engage rooms in a cottage at Treknow, near Trebarwith Strand, arranging to take them from 6 August. A week before, on 31 July, I travel alone to Freshwater, in the Isle of Wight.

I have never before concealed my movements from my parents, but now it is necessary to tell them some half-truths. Do they believe that the grilling school-days of July have left me so tired that I want a few days alone, before the longer holiday with Agnes, who is bringing a lively, volatile chatterbox – a girl from her school staff? I never know, but my mother's expression is unhappy...It happens, oddly, that David Lawrence is taking his mother and sister to Shanklin on this Saturday – at a chance meeting with him some days earlier he has mentioned his holiday plans, and even made the suggestion that I might travel with his party. But I am in no mood to meet strangers, and rush off before breakfast to catch the first train of Saturday 31 July to Portsmouth.

H.B.M. plays that night at the closing performance of the opera season, and reaches the Island on Sunday at noon.

Of our five days' experience in the Island enough has been written. Perhaps it was not unique – perhaps it only anticipated that of many lovers who, during the World War that was coming, were fated to compress the happiness of a life-time into a few glowing days, and to part under the shadow of death. But something of its intensity and detachment, together with the memory of his own actual proximity to the scene, fired the imagination of D. H. Lawrence; his subsequent attempt to realise it is embodied in the manuscript originally entitled The Saga of Sieg-mund, *later published (1912) as* The Trespasser.[1]

[1] See Appendix (p. 222) for my Freshwater Diary, which Lawrence read and used in the novel; this material was also interpolated in my own *Neutral Ground*, which I finished writing in 1918, and which was first published in 1933.

I see H.B.M. for the last time on the station platform at Wimbledon, the night of 7 August. Agnes and I, on our way to Cornwall, change at that junction; he comes there to meet me. I am shocked at his appearance. The sunlight of the previous days has badly blistered his forehead, unprotected by a hat, and his expression of misery alarms me. We walk to the end of the platform in disjointed talk which seems meaningless, but ends with words I never forget – *'Dear, whatever happens to me, remember, you must go on!'* I beg him to write to Cornwall – he nods, and turns away.

That night H.B.M. dies, by his own hand.

In Cornwall I wait four days – no letter comes; then I return, going to New Malden with a premonition of tragedy. The headlines of a local paper seen at a newsagent's shop confirm this. There is then only the question as to how to dispose of myself – to forget and be forgotten...The tide-rush in Trebarwith Strand...? At Waterloo I ask for a ticket to Camelford, the nearest station, and am told that there is no night train...I am very tired and dizzy – the crowds around are like swarms of wasps, with curious bright eyes. I must get away from them, find my bedroom and go to sleep. *'There is no god found greater than death, and death is a sleep.'* Automatically I make my way home.

But sleep is not death, nor any way to death – it leads to renewed activity of mind and body. Exhaustion passes, and I return to full consciousness and the torture of thought. Death, my reason insists, is the surrender to destruction and disintegration. Suicide is a violent denial of life – a deliberately destructive act. H.B.M., in an extremity of mental torture, willed and carried out the destruction of his body. It, with its ungovernable passions, had become hateful to him. Judged by the tenets of *my* ethical code, it had been found guilty and condemned...When I come to see, in order, the steps leading to his act, and to enter into his state of mind, I realise that he had no hope of any mystic life beyond. To make a complete end, to cease to exist, was the best that might be desired – for him. But he wanted me to go on living, and assumed that I should do so. One of his last acts was to write a couple of lines leaving to me his Carcassi violin.

My parents haunt me, lest I shall kill myself if left alone, and when they know all the facts, beg me not to blame myself. My father seems to imagine that I am suffering from a sense of guilt. No explanation is possible. I cannot see myself acting, under the same circumstances, and with the knowledge I possessed at the time, in any other way. They need not fear for my life. Although its prospect gives me nothing to desire, I shall continue to live, because this was the wish of H.B.M., and because death offers no whit more than life.

I draw memories about me like a thick veil. All my power of imagination is concentrated upon fixing within my memory, to the last detail, our days in the Island, and their physical and emotional content. The present is blurred, as one might walk in a cold fog, half-seeing human shapes pass. When my visions of the past fail, and sense of loss becomes anguish, I will sometimes taste the anodynes of mysticism. The appearance, at such moment, of W. B. Yeats's book *The Secret Rose* may become a portent.

I turn with hate upon Agnes when, during the last days of the August holiday, she begins to try drawing my mind towards the thought of work at school. Yet on the opening morning of the autumn term it is easier to return mechanically than to face new conditions absence would entail. Let the machine run! There is no point of contact between home and school life. The staff has no knowledge of the tragedy, and half-curious enquiries as to my health are soon forgotten when the press of routine work begins, dispersing the sociable atmosphere of the first morning. And I, stepping again on to the old levels of daily existence, feel as if I am moving backward in time. This is a former phase, its content unchanged. The maps on the walls, the exercise books on the desks, the cypresses of the deserted garden seen through the higher window-panes – here they remained, unconsciously awaiting my return, all through the days and nights of that eternity – the first week of August. Here are the children, equally unconscious – to them I am the same grown-up, immutable being who directed their work and play before the holidays. The Little Things – with their clamorous demands on my attention, with their day-long demands on my energy – they drag me away from that island of memory where I would abide for ever. The children become the synonym for all that belongs to the present and temporal.

I spend the autumn evenings at home in my fire-lit room. My only activity during September is the writing of a digest of introspective musings which takes the form of a serial letter to H.B.M.

12 September

Strength to embrace the commonplace – to feel it moulding my mind and body to its own image...strength to see your likeness, and the vision of life and love fade...strength to live and die hoping nothing, fearing nothing, expecting nothing. Praying one prayer, that never may any delusive promise of happiness make me forget my destiny.

Words, words, words!

A letter comes from H.B.M.'s sister Laura. She asks whether I, pupil and friend of her brother, can throw any light on his sudden, shocking death. Her father, she writes, is terribly distressed, being unable to account for his son's act. 'We knew he had debts, but we were always ready to help him.' And Laura suggests, 'If my father could attribute H.'s action to a brain seizure, to a natural cause of any sort, he would be easier in mind.'

Four years before I had met them both, several times, when the family was living in the South Norwood house. Laura is of a simple, frank, practical turn of mind, loving equally a tasty dinner and a tasty scandal. The father is a kindly, sensitive old man, with what is called an old-world courtesy. I cannot refuse Laura's invitation to visit them – it seems another opportunity of keeping in touch with H.B.M.

They both want to clear the memory of the dead from what they see as the sin and disgrace of suicide. I feel that H.B.M., so much more mature than they, would wish me to give them what comfort I can. I tell Laura, briefly, of the four burning days in the Island, stress the fact of H.'s blistered forehead, and show my still scarred wrists. She is grateful, and seizes immediately upon the possibility that her brother's state of mind on the night of his death was due to sunstroke. Father and daughter develop the theory to their great relief. And I am told of the pencilled note expressing my lover's wish that I should have his violin. (The instrument has been left with an agent for sale; with the connivance and help of the father I am ultimately able to buy it.)

Opening the case for the first time I can scarcely believe that H.B.M. is not present, so closely is the violin linked with his personality, so much it retains his natural scent. Yet, I reflect, he was but the latest of the old Carcassi's sequence of masters. What of the others, now forgotten! My unskilled hands can merely take care of the fiddle for a season.

Agnes tries to turn the current of my life back into its old channels. Her task is a thankless one. I want only to be left alone. I could better tolerate the presence of a stranger. She extends to my memories something of the jealousy that she did not always disguise earlier. She fails to see that my adolescent feeling for her could not continue indefinitely. Our intercourse was originally vital, a genuine exchange of the essential gifts of friendship. She influenced and taught me out of the experience and fuller knowledge of her ten years' seniority, and my gratitude and admiration provided a return which bridged the difference in our ages. But now it seems that she has nothing more to give me, or I her. That which was vital is dead. It is another tragedy which at this point I accept without trying to understand.

Presently Agnes brings David Lawrence with her when she makes her evening call. He will sit down in a fireside chair, head thrown back, arms hanging over those of the chair, legs stretched across the hearth-rug, while Agnes and I play Mozart sonatas. The playing is very unsatisfying – Agnes's hard *fortes* and meaningless phrasing, my tonelessness. When the sonatas end we talk, desultorily, or Agnes and David talk, and I am silent. It is Agnes who will go to the kitchen to fetch coffee, or who makes it if my mother is out...and then the young man will suddenly bring a book from his pocket, with 'Listen! will you hear this?' Half a dozen lines from a poem...'What do you think of it? Shall we go on?' Or he will hand me, without speaking, a small thick note-book and point to a poem on the open page. There is always something arresting about these manuscript poems, something which lifts for a moment the weight of my inertia, jerks the sullen set of my brooding mind from its concentration upon memories. I am aroused to discussion – even, after the two have gone, to some reflection on what has been said.

David Lawrence is not without place in those absorbing memories. He had entered during the anticipatory springtime, that April day on the Heath, and I had spoken of him later to H.B.M., calling him *Wunderkind*. Now, in the autumn, he returns, with no less delicate a perception of the autumn in my heart. At first I am only aware of his unobtrusive sympathy, then of a tentative endeavour to re-awaken my interest in literature and art, as related to personal experience. He will lure me from the isle of memory with the quiet voice of the sea itself.

> In Salamis, filled with the foaming of billows,
>   and murmur of bees,
> Old Telamon stayed from his roaming, long ago,
>   on a throne of the seas,
> Looking out on the hills, olive-laden, enchanted,
>   where first from the earth
> The grey-gleaming fruit of the maiden Athena
>   had birth.

Voice and rhythm enter into the pattern of my dream – that memory of an island where I saw romance and reality not as two eternals but as one eternal. On the mist-curtain enclosing that island I see the forms of the Greeks, and hear, mingled with the pulsing of waves on its beaches, the tragic chorus of Euripides. Through Gilbert Murray, through Lawrence, the spirit of irony and pity inspiring Euripides brings the classic tragedy of the Troädes into touch with an individual tragedy, and they are woven together into the fabric of my life. Lawrence begins with the Chorus – then he ventures 'Will you hear the whole?' – and I lie hour-long in my chair on the opposite side of the hearth, conscious of the flicker and glow of the fire, which ever and again reddens David Lawrence's high forehead, the thick, straight, goldenish hair above, the bushy eyebrows over deep-set eyes, the high cheek-bones and slightly sunken cheeks.

One winter evening David is left alone in my room for a few minutes; he seizes the nearest writing-pad and is writing in it when I return. The pad is replaced and our talk goes on. When he leaves he asks if he may take the pad with him – he has begun a new poem and wants to copy the lines written into his own college note-book. I consent – then he suddenly passes me the pad, and watches me closely as I read:

> All the long school hours, round the irregular hum of
>   the class
> Have crowded the immeasurable, ensanguined spaces
> That roar unborn, that hold the unborn me

Travelling, resolving in immensity. All the faces
Of the boys have troubled me, have lit a white spark of
    disquiet...
Snow stands on the window sill like tufted grass
And soiled snow muffles and hushes the streets.

Only a fragment, a promise of new thought, but something like a surge of gratitude arises in me – a rare enthusiasm, which David senses with pleasure. I beg him to finish the poem. A few days later he brings me completed 'A Snowy Day in School'. (To how many weary, disillusioned teachers may it since have brought a renewal of faith and vision! Reference to its final form as published in the 1913 edition of *Love Poems and Others* shows how the original, subjective idea was given objectivity by concentration upon the relationship between master and boys.)

But David rarely mentions school, and I never have occasion to enter his classroom.

My mother encourages Lawrence's visits. For her he has always a gay raillery, with a sympathetic undertone. I fancy she sees in him the suggestion of a grown son – her lost Frank. His age is that of my brother Arthur, twenty-four. But my father shows a nervous avoidance of him, and puts up a defence of light sarcasm if the young man attempts to engage him in discussion.

I close my writing-pad when D.H.L. comes in. He asks, tentatively, what I have been writing. It is only the long 'letter' to H.B.M. But during the autumn I have finished a brief, retrospective diary of the first week of August. The writing of this has been self-indulgence – an opportunity to live again those precious hours; to enshrine them in words. I have chosen the words, balanced the phrases, very carefully. When David Lawrence asks if he may see a bit of my work I tell him there is no *work*. But the claim his intuitive sympathy has established is strengthened by the coincidence of his presence in the Isle of Wight during those five days. I give him the diary. There is a new urgency in his voice when he returns it. 'What are you going to *do* with these prose poems?' he asks. I reply – nothing. They are written, it is enough. He declares, and insists, that the act of expression in writing pre-supposes a reader, and that human experience is the property of humanity. I only know that my impulse was to use the medium of rhythmic prose to enshrine what I had found beautiful.

David has a cough which he disregards, but which gives my mother concern when he appears on cold, wet nights. In February I hear from Agnes that influenza is keeping him from school. On a Saturday afternoon I call at his lodging in the Colworth Road, Addiscombe. His landlady says he is better, but still in bed, and shows me to his room,. He is hoarse, but obviously glad to see me, and declares that he shall be out in a few days. There is a thick brown-paper parcel standing on the floor by the wall; he asks me to lift it on to the bed. Unpacked, it is the manuscript of a longish novel, with the title *Nethermere*. He says it is his first novel, which has been accepted by the firm of Heinemann, but is returned to him for a final revision. Will I read the manuscript and give him my impressions? Especially marking passages that show prolixity.

Gaunt and pallid, but full of energy, he delivers the MS. to me three days later. As I read the close, cursive, always legible script, my mind is lifted again from the personal, and sent on an excursion into a new country, the English Midlands, to see Lawrence as Cyril, the impersonal, almost bodiless intelligence, the observant wanderer, moving among a little community of Midland folk.

The raw February days mark a fresh stage in our relationship. Hitherto David Lawrence has been content to minister to the needs of my sick mind, and I to accept his ministrations. Now he makes his first demand on my activity. We enter a phase of co-operation which brings us together more frequently. I have a copy of the pianoforte score of *Walküre*, with its libretto printed in German; he suggests that we might improve our German by reading simple lyric verse, and he brings along a small collection bought for twopence on a second-hand bookstall. The German verse, long discussions relative to the revision of the novel, and other books he brings for my reading, may occupy three evenings a week. From *Nethermere* I get incidental impressions of his home life, but make no effort to co-ordinate them.

The earlier poems in my collection *Songs of Autumn* were written during the autumn and winter of 1909–10 – but these were not shown to David.

He returns to the subject of my Freshwater Diary later – comes with the request that he may take it and expand its theme – use the poems as basis for a more comprehensive rendering of the story. He will bring me the work as it grows; nothing shall stand with which I am not in agreement. It shall be a finished study in full accordance with my suggestions. He is very eager. I think of the music H.B.M. should have lived to write. Indubitably David Lawrence is a poet. The power of grasping subtle analogies, of apprehending new rhythms, of capturing truth in symbols, is his in very great measure. There is an element of wonder in my contemplation of him, and in the coincidence of his appearance at just this juncture of my life. I consent.

One evening during this spring of 1910, D.H.L. brings me the first chapters of a manuscript he has called *The Saga of Siegmund*, saying that here is the beginning of a composition which must be a saga since it cannot be a symphony. He asks me to scrutinise it in detail, as I have done the manuscript of *Nethermere*. I cannot do this; my part in his work is that of guide: David must see and feel very clearly the personality of his subject. He must know Siegmund as I know him. It is the one thing I would do – realise for D.H.L. the living image of H.B.M.

Life finds a purpose. The closing words of the Chorus in the *Alcestis* become charged with a personal significance:

> There be many shapes of mystery,
> And many things God brings to be,
>   past hope or fear,
> And the end man looked for cometh not,
>   but a path is there where no man thought,
> So hath it fallen here.

At the spring week-ends of 1910 David Lawrence and I ramble over the Surrey hills, pondering and probing the three major mysteries – life, love and death. The presence of H.B.M. seems never very far away. Each Saturday morning we meet – at Purley, or Addiscombe, or Penge – all jumping-off points into open country. David knows the flora of the lanes better than I, and our talk is often mixed with incidental study of botany. I have a sense of peace, a detached kind of happiness; he is serious and whimsical by turns. One day we pass in a lane a fallen elm-tree, blown down by a gale but not utterly uprooted – a small thicket of bright green shoots is rising from its horizontal trunk. Perhaps my life is to be like that of the elm.

Sometimes, on our downland walks, David's mind reverts to his earlier experience, and I hear, casually, something of his Nottinghamshire home and its people. His talk is like an appendix to *The White Peacock*, but concerns chiefly the girl Emily, with whom Cyril, the narrator, has a detached kind of friendship. The original of Emily, I gather, is a farmer's daughter, Jessie Chambers, with whom David has shared his reading and study since their joint period at the Ilkeston Pupil-Teachers' Centre. She is now teaching in a Nottingham school, and keeping in close touch with David by correspondence. My very partial interest in her story is quickened when I hear that this friendship is being challenged by David's family, who voice local public opinion. 'They' declare that the time for a boy and girl friendship is over, and that David ought either to become engaged to Jessie, or put an end to the connection. It seems that he is miserably uncertain which course to follow. He seems to forget the personal problem only by absorbing his mind in the *Saga of Siegmund* tragedy.

One evening he brings me a recently written short story; its opening sentence runs: 'Muriel has sent me mauve primroses.' The 'Muriel' of the story is evidently Jessie Chambers. Thereafter J.C. is known to me as 'Muriel'; the change is the first instance of D.H.L.'s flair for relating name and personality. Between our three selves she is exclusively 'Muriel'; all her letters to me during the period are so signed.

David does most of his writing late at night. Self-absorbed, I scarcely notice how the *Saga* is taxing his nerves – imposing highly imaginative night work upon the strain of a wearing, noisy school-day. He tells me once that he writes half-drunk, but this I discount as a touch of the pose, which, evident a year ago, has almost disappeared. He brings the manuscript to me, chapter by chapter, as written. The intuition it shows, the rare symbolism, fill me with wonder. My regard for David Lawrence begins to be mingled with awe. Again romance and reality join hands.

He reads aloud to me the 'Ave Atque Vale' of Swinburne – reads it as if it were a ritual elegy for H.B.M.

> Shall I strew on thee rose, or rue, or laurel,
> Brother, on this that was the veil of thee?
> Or quiet sea-flower, moulded by the sea...?
>
> Not thee – O never thee, in all Time's changes,
> Not thee, but this, the sound of thy sad soul,
> The shadow of thy swift spirit – this shut scroll
> I lay my hand on, and not death estranges
> My spirit from communion of thy song...
> Is it well now, where love can do no wrong...

O sleepless heart and sombre soul unsleeping
That were athirst for sleep, and no more life
And no more love – for peace and no more strife!

It is to me an opiate, this verse. I wake suddenly on a day
when David and I are wandering in Kentish hill country. At
the top of a green hill which falls away to meadow, David
challenges me to race down the slope, passes me and turns
in my path, catching me as I try to check. Recovering
balance, I laugh, but David clasps me longer than is
necessary, and when we move, holds my hand fast, pro-
tectively and possessively...We are silent. That evening
I write in the letter to H.B.M. an entry with a new note.

8 May 1910

In spite of everything, life and spring claim me. O Destiny! put no
more dreams into my sleep, for even in my sleep I shall laugh at the
dreams.

I try to face our position objectively. Into what kind of a
relationship are we drifting? What are our feelings towards each other? Mine for David – affection and admiration sometimes touched with awe when I realise the
subtlety of his mind and the scope of his imaginative power.
His for me – I argue that his present reaction is induced by
the writing of the *Saga*. He is putting himself, imaginatively, into H.B.M.'s place; the conditions are both abnormal and temporary. I must not confuse the man with
the artist. When this work is finished he will see me from
another angle and in other light.

I determine that I will spend the first week of August in
Freshwater, occupying the rooms H.B.M. shared with me
last year. It is a kind of affirmation of his right in me; it is
also a final test of his spirit's persistence. Years ago I had
asked him whether, if I were ill and sent for him, he would
come; his reply had been, 'I would come to you from hell!'
During the months since his death I have half-hoped for
some intimate sign from him; it has not come. Nothing I
read about the cult of the spiritualists inclines me to try their

181

methods of 'communication'. Eleven months of separation have virtually convinced me that the dissolution of what I have known as the personality of H.B.M. is complete, yet the idea, born of the *revenant* tales and ballads, that our island may retain some emanation of his being discernible by my consciousness persists; it recurs in spite of my conviction of the greater wisdom of Euripides, and of an inner voice which warns me of a mystery not shown to babes, nor to be revealed in these terms.

Two days before the schools close for the Whitsuntide holidays, David, from his classroom, sends me a painful letter, scribbled on school drawing paper. It has neither address nor date. Its content makes the relationship between David and Muriel seem very clear to me, and it indicates the intensity of the strain imposed upon David by the writing of the *Saga*.

I had a letter from Muriel yesterday morning. She knew she had won. She wrote very lovingly, and full of triumphant faith. Since when, I have just lain inert. It is extraordinary, how I seem to have lost all my volition. She will take me as she would pick up an apple that had fallen from the tree when a bird alighted on it. I seem to have no will; it is a peculiar dull, lethargic state I have never known before. And now Muriel writes and says she will come on Saturday, and bring me an excursion ticket, & go home with me by the 6.25. And, I say 'Bien – venez,' – No more. And she will come. But the time might be next year, or in the after-death, or never, so it seems to me unreal. I cannot feel it beforehand. Till Saturday I shall merely wait in lethargy; I can do no other. Yet I have a second consciousness somewhere actively alive. I write 'Siegmund' – I keep on writing, almost mechanically: very slowly, and mechanically. Yet I don't think I do Siegmund injustice. Somewhere I have got the ballad of 'Sister Helen' – Rossetti's – beating time. I couldn't repeat it, but yet I beat & beat through the whole poem, with now and again a refrain cropping up:

> 'Nay of the dead what can you say
> Little Brother?'

or again

> 'O Mary, Mother Mary
> Three days today between Hell and Heaven'

and again

> 'What of the Dead between Hell & Heaven
> Little Brother.'

You are part of his immortality. That is what would make me go wild, if I woke up. You see, I know Siegmund is there all the time. I know you would go back to him, after me, and disclaim me. I know it very deeply. I know I could not bear it. I feel often inclined, when I think of you, to put my thumbs on your throat.

Muriel will take me. She will do me great, infinite good – for a time. But what is awake in me shivers with terror at the issue. Whatever happens, in the near present, I can't help it – I cannot.

You will sleep with Siegmund on the holiday. A revulsion from me, and put out your arms with passion into the dark, to him. And he will come – more or less – as sleep and inactivity.

When I finished the Bacchae, on Tuesday night, the last words:

> 'And the way shall be pointed out, strangely
> It shall not go either this way, as ye expected,
>   nor that way, as ye thought:
> But elsewhere, unthought, unknown.'

Bien – I leave it. I must rise up and teach. I cannot see you before the holiday. Yet Agnes wants me to go to tea tomorrow. I may not.

Vale

D. H. Lawrence[1]

Returning after the May holiday week David is his normal self again. He writes to me on the second day of term:

Davidson Rd Boys School
South Norwood s.e.
1st. June 1910

I am wearing a pink carnation. Poor Agnes, she looks woe-begone. So far, I admire her. Now, I am urging her to begin to work – paint, write letters, play. I think she will regain her independent individuality. If not – well. But don't be too kind to her: it will weaken her.

Heinemann was very nice: doesn't want me to alter anything: will publish in Sept or October, the best season: we have signed agreements concerning royalties, and I have agreed to give him the next novel. Will he want it? This transacting of literary business makes me sick. I have no faith in myself at the end, and I simply loathe writing. You do not know how repugnant to me was the sight of that 'Nethermere' MSS. By the way, I have got to find a new title. I wish, from the bottom of my heart, the fates had not stigmatised me 'writer'. It is a sickening business. Will you tell me whether the Saga is good? I am rapidly losing faith in it. – Oh, I am rather disappointed that Austin Harrison has again omitted to put my story in the Review: I expect he's forgotten – mislaid it.

I assure you, I am not weeping into my register. It is only that the literary world seems a particularly hateful yet powerful one. The

---

[1] Holograph in possession of Humanities Research Center, Texas University.

literary element, like a disagreeable substratum under a fair country, spreads under every inch of life, sticking to the roots of the growing things. Ugh, that is hateful. I wish I might be delivered.

I shall not see you till Saturday. Then, unless you deny, we will go into the downs. I will look for you at the Grey Hound at 10.0 oclock. If it should be wet, I will come round later in the morning – unless you deny – & we'll go somewhere.

You don't know how inimical I feel against you. C'est moi qui perdrai le jeu.

Vale

D. H. Lawrence

What we cannot bear, is deliberately to allow those we care for to think ill of us. It is a high test of courage.[1]

The postscript puzzles me, but I do not ask for an explanation. David's relations with his family and Midland friends are not my concern. But the tone of the letter's final sentence rankles. I am playing no 'game' with David.

Early in July the writing of the *Saga* is finished. The MS. has been shown, during the holiday week, to Muriel; her reaction to it seems to have disappointed David. He tells me now that he is sending it to Ford Madox Hueffer. I hear nothing more of it for many weeks. Our evenings of reading, English and German, continue; the good local library supplies us with current publications – poetry, philosophy and fiction; and David haunts Glaisure's bookshop in George Street, Croydon where pocket editions of the classics, well-bound, can be bought for a shilling. We exchange admired works – I lend David Olive Schreiner's *The Story of an African Farm*, he brings me H. G. Wells's *Tono-Bungay*, Arnold Bennett's *Old Wives' Tale*, E. M. Forster's *Howards End*, Walter de la Mare's *Henry Brocken*. Each, in its own way, is an illumination.

The long, June Saturday walks may begin at Purley, then a village; taking the track to the left of its tram terminus we climb Riddlesdown. Behind us, to the north, the Crystal Palace glitters in sunshine through a shawl of silver mist, ahead lies an illimitable prospect of sunshine and shadow – the uplands of Surrey flowing down to the Weald. David is

[1] Holograph with Texas University.

a good walker, and swings along, developing an idea or following a line of thought as we go, but his thought never blinds him to the nature of the path or the variety of the plant life at our feet. Once, to his delight, he finds a wild orchid. Riddlesdown is left behind; we are on the downs above Warlingham, where the tracks are merely those made by the few wandering sheep and goats. We plunge north into a valley of tangled copses and rank under-growth, to climb tediously again up into the sunshine warming gratefully the short turf of a hill summit. It is noon, and time to eat. David's landlady has given him sandwiches, I have biscuits and apples, and we share the food, sitting by the edge of a field of marguerite daisies, which, by our very feet begins its descent to the Weald – the sun-lit Weald of scattered red farmhouses linked by dusty white roads. Seen from our height it vanishes in a blue distance to the south. But we do not go down, we take a western track which slants, presently, into the Kenley valley, and so back to Purley…Or, if the day be wet, we may take a tram-ride to the Thames Embankment and visit the Tate Gallery. I have loved the Tate since childhood, when my father would take us there – my brothers and I – on a Bank Holiday, leading us first through the slum of Nine Elms, perhaps to quicken our sense of contrast.

David regards dubiously my preference for Luke Fildes, Landseer, Holman Hunt, and in general for pictures which tell their own simple story. He leads me to the Botticelli Madonna, whose beauty enchants him. But my mind cannot yet bridge the centuries to meet with that of Botticelli. David loves the immortal trees of Corot – and so do I. A day or two later he hands me his pocket-book open at pages carrying two new poems – 'Corot' and 'Michael-Angelo'.

We propose to see an opera at Covent Garden Opera House, but the gallery slips are all sold and we cannot afford more expensive seats. How shall we spend the evening? (Six years later, when writing the novel *Neutral Ground*, my memory recalls in detail the pattern of that dismal night, and it is woven into the story.)

David is in an oddly irresponsible mood, and suggests that we go to a 'jolly old music-hall'. I refuse; the Puritan side of my unconscious strongly objects to music-halls. I release David to go if he wishes. He will not leave me, and we board a bus going to Hyde Park. A band is playing; we join the crowd of people strolling up and down the Broad Walk. David is fascinated; he stares, smiling, into the faces of the passers-by; his face has an expression I have never seen on it before. I hate my whole surroundings – the alien crowd, the painted faces of women, the stridency of the band, the hot glare of the coloured lights. I stop, release my arm from David's, and tell him I am going home. 'You don't like it?' he queries, still with that strange smile. We take a crowded bus to Victoria, and a train to Selhurst without having spoken again, and I wish him good-night at the garden gate without offering my hand. We have come, I feel, to a point where our paths divide, and on the day following write, telling him so. He replies (21 June):

Once again, Helene, I must answer your word: you had better not see me again. Once again I say 'Bien' and proceed to disobey.

You see, you are very hard. But if our alliance breaks down often in the beginning, like a new machine, it will be the stronger in the end, for we repair and strengthen the weaknesses when they are discovered to us. I will be patienter and 'plus sage'. In the evening we are very wise concerning the past day, but we're never wise enough for the coming morrow. Eh bien![1]

In mid-July David announces that Muriel is coming to spend a week-end with him. Do I want to see her? Should I like to meet her?

I am not incurious. We arrange that he shall bring Muriel to meet me on Hayes Common, for an afternoon walk, but I set out with misgiving, even prepared to dislike one whose

[1] See p. 236 for the rest of this letter. Thinking it destroyed, I had quoted briefly from memory here, but the full text has just been rediscovered and brought to my notice.

claim on David is evidently so strong and subtle. She may resent my presence – and how detestable if I seem to intrude upon their older connection. Yet each of us has David's portrait of the other – I know her as 'Emily' of *Nethermere* – she has just read the manuscript of the *Saga*.

The afternoon marks a stage in my education. Indubitably, Muriel belongs to my world – she may enter it in her own right. I sense that she brings to it a new element. Light and colour, movement, joy and anguish that world knows; her presence will ensure it *warmth*. Not sun-heat, nor the unreliable blaze of a fire that scorches or sinks to ash, but a glow that relaxes, comforts, sustains…(In retrospect I always see her in a claret-red dress – perhaps it was the colour she wore on the afternoon of our introduction.) She is taller than I, but her shoulders are a little bent. Dark, silky hair waves over her tanned forehead and rests in little curls on neck and temples. She has a slight, gipsy tan, under which emotion may bring up a sudden flush. Her brown eyes, even when she smiles, are sorrowful – they have a grieved expression, as if, impersonally, she were always conscious of the pain of the world, This David Lawrence has recorded:

Some people, instead of bringing with them clouds of glory, trail clouds of sorrow. They are born with 'the gift of sorrow,' – sorrows, they claim, alone are real. You read it in their eyes and in the tone of their voices. Emily had the gift of sorrow.

'It fascinated me, but it drove me to rebellion', comments the 'Cyril' of *The White Peacock*.

My reaction is not that of rebellion. Muriel, ready to transmute my sorrow into beauty – even to see me as beautiful on its account – draws me at once within the orbit of her own life; induces her vision to be, for a while, my own.

We return to David's lodging for tea. He, in cynical mood, lies on the hearth-rug and rends with slashing criticism a book of modern verse. It would seem that he is not pleased with the afternoon's development. I leave them immediately after tea. David sees Muriel to the railway station, and calls at my home later. He asks questions – what do I think of Muriel, what is he to do in relation to her – and what of ourselves?

I tell him that I think he will ultimately go back to her – how, I wonder, being conscious of her *quality* of life, can he do otherwise? He is cynical and impatient. It is almost as if he had hoped I would declare myself *against* his marriage to Muriel. As if he had expected me to produce evidence against her.

I feel that at the moment his desire is towards me – in such measure as I still represent the 'Helena' of his *Saga*. But there is no rest, no assurance in this love of David's, which will ultimately make an impossible demand upon me. A demand not only for passion given and reciprocated, but for the absorption of my being in his. 'He for God only, she for God in him'; I think he knows that he is asking the impossible, and refuses to admit it.

We are indebted to Arthur McLeod for the loan of new books. He is the only male member of the school staff sharing a common interest with David – love of literature. I recall, from my student days, a memory of Arthur McLeod – thin, lanky youth – whose obvious love of Shakespeare and fine intonation secure him the chief male parts when the plays are read in Miss Holden's English class. We read *Coriolanus*, and I am proud when the part of the hero's mother is allotted to me. Arthur McLeod is now senior master at Davidson Road; his imperturbable manner and tone of quiet authority make him a power in the school. Outside the classroom he would seem to have two interests only – his mother, with whom he lives, and his growing library. His fancy is for the latest and best in poetry, philosophy and fiction; and he will loan generously to those few friends who appreciate his taste and can be depended upon to return borrowed books in good condition: among whom he counts David Lawrence and Agnes Mason. I never seek a direct loan from 'Mac' but many of his books come into my hands before being returned by Agnes or David.

When the schools close for the four weeks of summer holiday I go down to Freshwater, alone. I have been able to secure, for the first week of August, the rooms H.B.M. and I occupied last year – our sitting-room and the little room over the rose-covered porch where he slept. The landlady knows nothing of the tragedy, which was reported only in the local press, and she is discreet enough to ask no questions.

On each of the five days I follow the course of our wandering a year ago – time might be repeating itself. I deaden my sense of desolation by working at a rhythmic translation of the *Walküre* libretto, and again by the futile gesture of the letter-diary.

August 1910

It is a year by the reckoning of days. By your wish I have lived, yet your last words do but echo the demand of the Life Spirit that moulds and modifies me, finding through me some painful manner of expression. My former vivid sense of you is blurred, and clear impression of your voice, tone and touch is fading – yet still I close my ears against the inexorable command – follow Me, and let the dead bury their dead!

another entry:

On the other side of the marsh stands the church behind its elms. I take the road crossing the marsh, and little bright fish swimming near the surface of the water, and long-horned shrimps below, dart from my moving shadow. Standing by the church-yard wall I look at the gravestones. One is a double stone, recording the names of Jane and Robert Allen, 'drowned after 20 days of marriage'. An echo of last summer comes to me in the tone of my own voice: *It is good when life holds no anti-climax...*I know better now. While life endures, light and darkness will alternate – and ebb and flow, and birth and death...*The graph of existence is not to be expressed by any finite straight line.*

On the third day at Freshwater I am called back suddenly into the present by a letter from David Lawrence. He writes from his home, Eastwood, Notts. The letter is a scrawl of thick characters, in marked contrast to his usual even, slanting hand-writing.

Lynn Croft,
Eastwood
Notts
Sunday 31 July

Liebe Helene,

How are you?

I began to write to you at sunset. Now it is starlight, big, scintillating stars; it is nearly midnight. I am as miserable as the devil.

But how have you found the Island? How often have I thought of you. I wish with all my soul I were with you in Freshwater – but the incongruity! How sick it makes one feel!

Muriel met me. She is very pretty and very wistful. She came to see me yesterday. She kisses me. It makes my heart feel like ashes. But then she kisses me more and moves my sex fire. Mein Gott, it is hideous. I have promised to go there tomorrow, to stay till Thursday. If I have courage I shall not stay. It is my present intention not to stay. I must tell her. I must tell her that we ought finally and definitely to part; if I have the heart to tell her...

Then, when she looks at me so forlorn, I feel I must kiss her even to gladden her a bit. But I do not want to go tomorrow.

I am a rather despicable object. But can I hurt her so much. I wish I had not come home. I wish fate would not torture me with these conjunctions – and you in Freshwater.

Never mind – we shall pull through everything all right. Do not forget me, and do not smile too wearily as you read.

Auf wiedersehen

D. H. Lawrence

The writing is so bad because Mater is waiting for me to go to bed – won't leave me up.

This letter presents an aspect of David which seems almost to reverse our former relationships. Since last October I have been dependent upon him for force and direction; he has recharged my depleted energy. This exhibition of weakness, of indecision and self-distrust, are contradictory. Passively I have accepted the fact of his presence at my side all these months, assuming no concern or responsibility on his account. He has lured me back among the living; now it seems I have to begin again to use my own volition, to make decisions, perhaps for him as well as for myself.

Our minds are extraordinarily intimate and their perceptions reciprocal. In the beginning he fantastically associated his idea of me with Rossetti's *Sister Helen*, and our physical relationship has been, all along, that of brother and sister: but since the early summer of this year I have been increasingly aware of the demand that he, instinctive man, makes upon me as woman. I cannot definitely ignore it, but there is no physical response from my own body. My desire is not towards him. I do not want either to marry him and bear him children, or to be his mistress.

I am now twenty-eight, and in no other sense than this immature. I think I cannot be 'woman' in the ordinary meaning of the term. Apparently I represent a variation in human type. The old, childish feeling of 'aloneness' remains. Whence came the folk-conception of the changeling, the half-human?

On impulse I write to Muriel, inviting her to spend some days at my home before her holiday ends. She has never seen the sea from the south coast. I want to show her the places where the happiest part of my childhood was passed.

We make a day's excursion to Newhaven.

Muriel's presence fills me with peace. It is induced by the low, musical tones of her voice, her reflective manner, and her dark, innate warmth. Sometimes she slips into an absent mood, and moves almost like the blind; again, she will seem suddenly happy in being with me, and I hear her laugh, low and full as her voice. Our talk today is all of personal relations, of David, of her old home, the Haggs farm, centre of her association with him; and of my childhood with Evelyn by the sea. She draws me, very gently, to talk of H.B.M., and of how the *Saga* came to be written. Presently she asks me to tell her, if I can, what David *is* to me. I try to explain, perhaps as much to myself as to Muriel...

How can *he* be other than infinitely content to be with her?

The August day is sunny and breezy. We sit in a little hollow of the cliffside, sheltered from the wind, and as we talk, watch the sea foaming in Seaford Bay like the petals of a giant marguerite daisy... And at night I bring Muriel home, and see with secret satisfaction that my mother and father are both responding to her like pimpernel to the sun – their faces relaxed, their voices full of pleasure.

Some change in my relationship with David is inevitable, I know, when we meet again after the August separation. September makes this obvious. The grace and tenderness of his bearing towards me now show rarely; he is sullen, or irritation flares suddenly into pitiless criticism or fierce irony. An undiagnosed illness of his mother fills him with foreboding, adding to the depression caused by indecision over future relations with Muriel and myself.

I lie awake at night thinking miserably of the situation. My sense of responsibility is stirring. It was so easy to admit David into the zone of intimacy between my lover and myself – David the sensitive, impersonal artist. I should have foreseen that he might endanger his impersonality, but grief is stupid, and his understanding, his comprehending sympathy, were healing. The onus of the position is with me – I am three years David's senior.

If it were *merely* a sexual debt I have incurred it might be paid. Then, eventually, David and Muriel could marry. Would they complement one another – would they be happy? I feel that Muriel believes so; but David, sometimes uncertainly and sometimes emphatically, denies. And at this stage I am unaware of what later is seen to be the deciding factor – the hostile attitude of Mrs Lawrence towards a marriage between her son and Jessie Chambers.

The gloom of the early autumn is relieved for me by Muriel's letters. She continues to write both to David and to me.

In my memoir of Jessie Chambers I comment:

Her letters confirmed my original impression of her rare quality and intuitional power. They also reflected the suffering inflicted upon her by the long conflict with Lawrence. Their conflict was inevitable: social principle and the inheritance of a sternly Puritan code obliged her to dismiss as intolerable the suggestion of a physical intimacy less binding than that of marriage; nor did she lack the desire of the normal woman for a unique personal right in the man to whom she would devote her life.[1]

Muriel writes to me, early in October:

I have just read David's poems in the *Review*.[2] That first one is the very accent of the David I knew until a few months ago. Times and times without number he has left me to walk over a wet meadow with water on one hand and black woods on the other, and all heaven and earth shaken in my soul...

He talks to me so distinctly from that printed page that it is only with difficulty I can restrain myself from answering him; the effort to restrain gives me a rending sensation. But we have talked like that long enough – let it go! Nevertheless it seems strange. I find myself wondering stupidly what has happened. I look at his portrait – I seek in his features for a clue to the puzzle, but shake my head – the portrait lacks the swift changes of expression.

David is my Sodom and Gomorrah. Like Abram, I seek in vain for the five just men. Nay, I am reduced to looking for *one* just man. I do find *one* just man, of noble stature; he is essential truth, like the truth in the poems. But the loveable men of everyday common human truth and honour, they are not to be found, and that one great noble man is not able to save the cities; rather, he is likely to be lost in their ruin.

You will forgive me that I am so troublesome. You are another star in my bowl, one that neither David nor I saw when he wrote that poem.

Muriel invites me to spend the mid-term break at her home, Arno Vale Farm, Mapperley, Nottingham. (The family had left the Haggs farm three years earlier.) Arno Vale, originally Swinehouse Farm, lies in a green hollow approached from Mapperley Plains by a steep and irregular pathway winding through hilly pasture. The path ends by the gate of an orchard fronting the house. Stack-yard, cow-sheds, stable and barns lie behind.

The farmhouse is not large, and there is no guest-room. But I see nothing unusual about being invited to share

---

[1] Published as *D. H. Lawrence's 'Princess': A Memoir of Jessie Chambers*, in 1951 by The Merle Press, Thames Ditton, Surrey.

[2] The *English Review*, edited by Ford Madox Hueffer. The letters of Jessie Chambers to Helen Corke (holograph) are in the Reference Library of the University of Nottingham.

Muriel's room and bed. (Most middle-class bedrooms of the period were furnished with a large double bed, intended to accommodate two persons. Preference for the single bed – for two single beds per room in the case of schools or families, scarcely became general before the end of the First World War.) So I sleep with Muriel at night. During the days we take long walks, and Muriel will show me all the scenes of her childhood and student life with David. *The White Peacock* – the proofs of which David and I have recently corrected – becomes life rather than literature.

Muriel's mother is small, pale, with soft brown eyes and compressed lips. She welcomes me very kindly, as does the farmer, but I am, and remain, a southern stranger. These people merge into their environment – it is all one to me. I still tend to sense human beings through the medium of art and seek direct contact only with the artist. But there is a vitality about this Midland farm life which it is good to share.

Meals are taken in the big farm kitchen, but the small parlour is now regarded as Muriel's study and sanctum. She draws to the hearth an old settee and low armchair, and here we read and talk through the long evening, enquiring of each other's experience, exploring the maze of personal reactions, particularly in relation to David. Snow is falling, and in intervals of silence I hear the rustle of snowflakes on the window. I sleep in a low-pitched room facing the stack-yard, and wake long before dawn, when lanterns shine up from below, their beams crossing the ceiling. Steps cross the stack-yard to the cow-sheds; then I listen to the contented lowing of the cows, and the sharp buzz of milk against the sides of pails...

The Chambers' family numbers seven – four sons and three daughters. Three grown sons work on the farm; the fourth is a small, delicate-looking boy of twelve years, who is oddly attracted by my violin, and can be discovered listening by the door when I am practising. I hear him beg to be given a violin and lessons; Muriel promises that he shall have them. She is also determined that little David shall be sent to the new high school recently opened in Nottingham. (Both intentions were carried out. Nottingham later knew David Chambers as Professor J. D. Chambers, Ph.D. of Nottingham University.)

Muriel has written short stories; it seems to me that her writing is finely intuitive and her natural style that of the best kind of essay. The stories lack the dramatic touch so evident in those of Lawrence...Beyond showing them to me she makes no effort to publicise them. (Lack of faith in their own ability seems to have characterised both Lawrence and Jessie Chambers. But Jessie's admiration for Lawrence's work led her to take the initiative and submit his poems to Ford Madox Hueffer, then editor of the *English Review*; but, as far as I know, Lawrence never made any attempt to introduce Jessie's writing.)

On an October Saturday whose sun-heat and colour have surely been borrowed from August, David and I take a train to Brighton, walk up over the cliffpath to Rottingdean and scramble down on to the beach by way of a rope ladder left there by coastguards. Along the beach we walk to Newhaven. It is not a pleasant walk; the beach seems to be one on which ebbing tides cast their refuse of rotting seaweed and dead fish. We talk little; I pick my way over slimy stones, David, with a kind of desperation, leaps over large ones. Arriving at Newhaven we cross the harbour by the bridge and make for the Bishopstone and Seaford road. We are tired and hungry; as we reach Seaford the sun is setting behind the old fort over the bay. I walk up to the door of a tall boarding house by the end of the esplanade and knock, hardly expecting a response, since the holiday season is over. But the door is opened by a hungry-looking woman with a thin, flushed face, who doubtfully admits us. Yes, we can have a meal, and beds. We want, I say, two bedrooms. She silently leads the way upstairs and indicates rooms at either end of a long corridor. She places a cold meal on the long table in the dining-room, furnished only with table and chairs, and lighted by a single candle. As she leaves, she points to two candlesticks on the hall table, and then the front door slams behind her.

I look at David; he has slumped in his chair, but responds when I urge him to eat. We have nothing to say to one another. My mind is behaving oddly; this place, it assures me, is the Seaford of my childhood, the Seaford of the great clean beaches washed by foaming tides eternally working to grind and polish beautiful pebbles for children's play; its atmosphere carries the scent of Evelyn and Aunt Bec. But what have they to do with David, who is sitting, his face wan in the candle-light, staring at nothing? I rouse suddenly and say I am going to bed. David fetches and lights the candles left on the hall table and follows me upstairs; I say good-night and close my door as his steps recede along the passage.

I sleep at once but wake at dawn, in a cold fright. The uncurtained window is shrouded outside by dense fog. In a half-light the room is deadly still. Shivering, I listen for a sound – any sound; the cry of a sea-gull or the bark of a dog would have reassured me. But there is no sound; I am sealed into a cold cell and the house is a dead womb. Half-consciously I make for the door and glance down the dim passage. At its other end, perhaps, is David. By the time I reach his room door I am awake and conscious of the position. David is asleep; through the closed door I can hear him muttering in his sleep. I must not wake him; I return to my room. There is now a promise of more light in the east. The fog is lifting. I dress, and in an hour's time am on the beach, where David presently joins me, the gloom gone from his mood.

At the end of the half-term break David and I return from Nottingham by the midnight train. Muriel comes with me to the railway station; meeting David she is all too cognisant of the situation and his grief. We have a compartment to ourselves; David flings himself down in a window-seat; I take an opposite one. There is nothing to be said, and I cannot approach him for fear of imposing upon him the exhausting struggle with his sexual desire, so urgently towards me. He understands, and composes himself, as if to sleep. We arrive at King's Cross before dawn, and walk in silence to Victoria.

In 1964, when the *Complete Poems of D. H. Lawrence* were published, I read for the first time the one entitled 'Excursion Train' – David's record of this journey.

One of the first of his poems David had shown to me was 'End of Another Home Holiday'. It is an expression of pity for his mother's limitations and of his sadness in outgrowing his home world.

> Ever at my side,
> Frail and sad, with grey, bowed head,
> The beggar woman, the yearning eyed,
> Inexorable love goes lagging.

Inexorable love! The fiercely possessive little woman feared and hated the artist-soul in Jessie Chambers, and the intuitive power that stimulated and supported the artist-soul of David Lawrence. The self of her son which was remote, incomprehensible to her, she denied and rejected. His spirit must be bound within the circle of *her* world, where she might dominate and control it. Jessie, of her very nature, opposed the maternal tyranny. The Lawrence family, revolving unconsciously round the mother, its power-centre, was inimical to Jessie's de-centralising influence.

David, imaginatively endowing his mother with his own young, acute, abnormal sensibility, saw her pitiful and tragic as Hecuba; her illness, this autumn of 1910, intensified this pity. His utter reaction towards his mother implied revulsion from Jessie Chambers. His mother should remain his eternal love. His wife, since sex must be appeased, should be a girl of simple type, who would never challenge the maternal claim.

'It doesn't matter who one marries', David has insisted to Muriel.

One day during this November he takes out his pocket-book and shows me a new poem. It is entitled 'Snap-dragon'. He stands watching me as I read it.

> She bade me follow her to her garden, where
> The mellow sunlight stood as in a cup
> Between the old grey walls: I did not dare
> To raise my eyes to hers; I did not dare look up
> Lest her bright eyes, like sparrows should fly in
> My windows of discovery, and shrill 'Sin!'

By any standards of mine it is an admirable poem; I see very clearly the old garden, glowing in the sunlight of late autumn; I sense the subtlety of the young man's approach to a woman whose beauty is not that of autumn. Any other, more personal impressions I keep in check, and merely assure the poet that I think the poem one of his best.

Later in the month David tells me that he has betrothed himself to the girl of the garden. On one of the darkest week-ends, his mother drifting to death, he had by chance met Louie in a local train and been for the moment diverted by her charm and vitality. There was a longstanding friendship between them, dating from his and her college days. On impulse he had proposed to her and she had immediately accepted him.

In early December Muriel writes:

Do you remember the hour of your arrival on the Sunday we came down together? It is just about that time now, and the sky is pale gold through the big window and blue-grey through the little one that looks over the crew-yard. The sunshine today has seemed so precious I could almost long to go out and gather an armful of gold before it all sinks behind the high hedge. But I am not so impetuous nowadays; I know that the sun is faithful.

I did hear from David. I saw him also, last Sunday. I suppose you will have seen him by now. I think I must not talk about him at all. At present I am not strong enough. If an artery were cut you would tie up the end of it, wouldn't you! Well, I must not undo the band, lest I could never get it on again.

It is wonderful how old sayings come back with stores of new meaning. The sins of the parents visited upon the children – well, it is so – and who can help it! Because my forebears had a terrible degree of intensity nobody can help that it should be handed on to me. And David is strangled in his mother's tragedy; he has to pay the cost for her. So we *have* to pay our dues and it isn't much use talking. But many things become extraordinarily full of meaning which used to be very dim.

(After Mrs Lawrence's death I do not see David again until the beginning of the spring term. With his sister Ada he spent the latter part of the Christmas holiday in Brighton where, incidentally, they met the head master and his wife. This meeting resulted in better social relations between Lawrence and his chief, and to Lawrence's introduction, through Philip Smith, to a Croydon society with literary pretensions, where he was presently invited to lecture.)

Muriel will have me spend the after-Christmas holiday at Arno Vale. The days are sunny, the nights bitterly cold, with occasional snow-showers. I write, elsewhere:

My most vivid memories are those of the evenings on the farm. There is early supper with the whole family in the big kitchen – spasmodic talk and awkward silences – the young Midlanders shy of the foreign southern guest. Supper over, Muriel takes me across the hall into the parlour, now tacitly recognised as her study. The rich glow of a fire piled high in the old-fashioned grate gleamed on the mossy trunks of fruit trees visible through the square-paned windows. When the table lamp was lit a portrait of David and one of his drawings appeared on the parlour wall. Muriel would wheel forward the red settee, and since I could not be persuaded to lie on it, would bring also to the fireside the Duchess's low chair (which had a romantic story, and discovered to the family, soon after purchase, the Duchess's embroidery scissors at the back of its seat!).

Muriel and I were so much attuned to one another that we could talk frankly of intimate matters, read one another's written work, or just remain silent, listening to the rustle of a light snow on the panes, or the flicker of the fire...Now I am shown the first section of a story called, provisionally, 'The Rathe Primrose' – the moving study of a young soul too early awake to the beauty and terror of existence. And there were other short stories, based upon family history or her own experience, but no poetry and no imaginative work. She wrote with simplicity and a delicate realism, drawing her material chiefly from home life.

Our holiday ends with three days walking in Derbyshire. The first night we spend at the cottage of Muriel's married sister May. The last night of that strange, transitional year 1910 sees us tramping the dark road to Matlock Bank, the Trent tearing alongside over its unseen, rocky bed. Then an unbelievable funicular railway swings us up to the door of a dimly-lighted hydro, and we look down from the high window of a big ice-cold room at starry, clustering lights in a valley as deeply inscrutable as the dark sky.[1]

In January *The White Peacock* is published, but David seems to have lost all interest in it. A pre-publication copy which he had secured for his dying mother had arrived too late, and remained unnoticed on her bed.

David has reverted to his Eastwood self so fully that we meet almost as strangers at the beginning of the spring term 1911. He resumes calling at my home, perhaps from inertia, or because a later identity asserts itself when freed from the suppression of the Eastwood atmosphere. Gradually we build again a bridge of mutual comprehension. He brings me books, and we analyse and discuss them, sometimes crystallising a satisfactory definition or two from the argument. His preference is now for French and Russian authors. I read Maupassant, Baudelaire and Flaubert for the first time. Some of Baudelaire's poems convey a sort of rank beauty. I am too ignorant of the French language to appreciate the perfection of Maupassant. *Madame Bovary* makes no appeal to me – I dislike both subject and treatment. David insists upon the value of its masterly technique. Turgenev's characterisation in *Fathers and Sons* I can readily admire. Of modern English poetry David brings Ernest Dowson, who is lovable; and the Aubrey Beardsley drawings illustrating the volume have a fascination which I admit without understanding.

The essential of great art, David now constantly affirms, is impersonality, objectivity, and an unassailable technique. My early conception of art defined it as the embodiment, in word, sound or material, of beauty. By

[1] *D. H. Lawrence's 'Princess'.*

'beauty' I designate that quality towards which the flower of one's life instinctively turns. I assumed that the artist, with finer perception and greater sensitivity than the ordinary being, selects the more significant experiences of life, and presents them, clean of commonplace, in art-form, for the joy of such as have eyes to see or ears to hear. My own writing, slight as it is, has always been an attempt to sign and seal, in rhythmic form, the beauty I recognise, either in comedy or tragedy. David now challenges this conception. An art-form, he declares, is justified whether it excites loving or loathing. Moreover, the *subject* of a work of art takes a place of secondary importance in relation to its technique. He quotes Flaubert's dictum to the young Maupassant: 'When you can so describe this horse that no one may ever mistake it for another horse, believe that you can write.' He is obviously accepting French models.

Ford Madox Hueffer's criticism of the *Saga* has been taken very much to heart...The work is too molten, says the critic – by which I suppose he means too much the stuff of life itself. David has no defence ready. The arbiter of elegance has spoken, and David feels like one of his own school-boys sent back to his desk with a reprimand for indifferent work.

Early in the year he tells me that he has begun a new novel, with his home life as its background. Its title is *Paul Morel*.

In February Muriel writes:

I have been wishing you were here all today and yesterday. Arno is looking more charming than I think you have ever seen it. A sprinkling of snow lifts the outlines of the hills into prominence, and under the sunshine our valley is brilliant and glittering. The ponds are frozen; I have been sliding upon them; the lower pond with the branches of a willow drooping over the ice brings back to me the far end of the mill-pond at Felley Mill, as David and I found it one winter day.

I dread Spring, yet look forward to it. I am happy in the repose of winter when all is sealed and sleeping, and the wonder of nature is only superficial. Yet I look for snowdrops piercing the soil, and the thought of daffodil bulbs lying buried gives me a sudden breathless feeling, and I watch for Spring with love and dread.

Oh, I wish we could establish some means of communication other than this of sitting down to frame words! Why can't I, watching the log blaze, and having so many things to say to you, just capture your thought? It seems so natural and so simple. I used to think I could really effect it with David; I believe, at times, we did manage it. The snapping of that cord with David was the strangest of all things in the break with him, and has made more difference to me than anything else – it has given me psychic freedom.

How curious these things are!

With spring we resume Saturday rambles in the country. The Addington and Farley woods, the North Downs, Limpsfield Common. They are still remote from traffic and the crowd. We seek by-ways and walk silently, not disturbing the small wild creatures. In April we pick primroses in Farley Woods. I ask David – sitting on his haunches beside a tree-bole, what of *The White Peacock*? He turns up to me a white, expressionless face and shakes his head. 'I did think it would give me a start' is all he says.

The White Peacock has given David at least an entry into London literary circles. He makes the acquaintance of young Ezra Pound, red-headed eccentric, and brings me a corrected proof of Pound's book of verse, *A Lume Spento*. The poems have a quaintly medieval flavour and much self-consciousness. David receives an invitation to call on a woman poet, Rachel Annand Taylor, and lends me a collection of her poems, *Rose and Vine* – subtle and musical compositions. Especially appealing to me is one entitled 'Resurrection', beginning:

> There shall no blare of heavenly trumpets end
> The long, long lapses of oblivion.

David is also invited to hear Florence Farr declaim the poems of W. B. Yeats. Something in the séance irritates him beyond bearing: on the following evening it amuses him to lampoon the company and the recital for my amusement. I resent his treatment of Yeats.

Tolstoy, Turgenev and Conrad come into our reading just now, also E. M. Forster's *Howards End*; and the

American *White Whale* story, the violence of which seems
to attract David. Wells is represented by *The New Machia-
velli*. I find the book a tonic; the freedom and energy of
Wells' mind so charge his writing that realism is real
without being drab, and the presentation of middle-class
life escapes boredom. Wells is dynamic; he generates
activity. But I am not ready for Shaw – *Man and Super-
man* repels me. David brings a public library copy of
Schopenhauer's *The World as Will and Idea*, in which he is
interested, but into this book I can dip casually – no more.

Sometimes the self of me that loves mysticism will ask if
there can be an intention behind the circumstances which
have brought the three of us together at just this point in
our lives. According to the mood of the moment I humour
or flout the supposition, but it persists. I cannot deny the
existence of a Creative Power, quick and active in the
personality of the few, dim in that of the many; this Power
would seem to glow into incandescence on the impact of two
or more sensitive and vital beings. By its light mankind
moves forward; it is what Tennyson called 'the gleam'. The
truth it discovers to the individual he can record; through
him new knowledge is communicated to the race.

While the mystic is dominant in me I write several poems.
And I am impelled to try and express the state of my mind
while in Cornwall during four days of August 1909, when
waiting in vain for a message from H.B.M. It evolves as *The
Cornwall Writing*. But, although David has shown me his
'Mother' poems, I cannot submit anything so intimate to his
irritably critical judgment. At this time he has no will to
approve either Muriel's writing or mine.

At Whitsuntide I go again to Arno Vale – a night journey,
when the Midlands glide under an early summer dawn, and
the still, powerful life of the trees takes on a deeper
significance as it emerges from the darkness. I rest in
the consciousness of this slow, silent power of the trees...

Nottingham railway station is awake in sunshine at five o'clock, but drops asleep again as the north-bound express draws out. Muriel meets me, and an early tram swings us up to Mapperley Plains. Morning is sunny over the meadows set for hay, and the fruiting orchard trees... We wander round hedgerows – and Muriel shows me a throstle's nest, the nestlings lying on their hard clay bed – and a spinkie's, woven of moss, fine grass and downy feathers...At the farm I am shown how to milk. This is not the farm of *Nethermere*, but I look at it through the medium of that book's atmosphere, with the 'Cyril' self of D.H.L.'s personality at hand.

Later in the week we go by train to Mablethorpe, where Muriel spent a summer holiday with David and his family some years ago...A small, red-brick town, scarcely more than a village, protected from the sea by its sand-dunes. We lie and talk or read in the hot, loose sand by day, and at evening walk bare-foot along the shore where still pools reflect the moonlight. We have, for other company, that old philosopher of Tennyson's in *Locksley Hall*.

The infinite variety of human-kind has hitherto appealed to me only as shown in the artist's mirror. Men and women I have seen 'as trees walking'. David spoke truly when he remarked 'The house of your soul has no reception rooms; you either admit a guest to intimacy or leave him standing on the doorstep.' But now I see David through Muriel and Muriel through David. I look on an image of each which is not of my making.

Once David makes directly the suggestion that we might marry, but so tentatively that his own words would seem to surprise him. I hear with a curious discomfort, a sense of the fantastic. I know that if David and I were locked within the inescapable intimacy that characterises the married state of the poor, we should kill in each other the very essential of creative living – we should become like dry sticks compelled by friction to smoulder until reduced to ash.

Muriel, I feel, has schooled herself to patience – has taught herself to believe that David, never losing consciousness of their complementary relationship, will ultimately come home to her. She is writing, in novel form, the story of their long friendship; it may be, I like to think, the counterpart of *Paul Morel*.

My brother Arthur, after five years of military service in China, has returned home. Disciplined life under good officers has transformed a weedy, irresolute and purposeless youth into a healthy, active and intelligent young man. He has gained promotion, has become used to issuing, as well as obeying orders; he is popular with officers and men. But for five years he has been relieved of all responsibility for the economic side of life. He is discharged from the army with a small gratuity and a reservist's pay of $2\frac{1}{2}d$ per day. With these assets he immediately marries. His wife is the daughter of a farm-worker, met during the days of his Sheerness training, to whom he had pledged himself before leaving England. Nance is big, simple, strong-willed, resourceful; on Arthur's departure she had contacted an agency for supplying wealthy American families with English domestic help, and secured entry to a family living on an extremely generous scale. Five years of life upon this standard is no preparation for marriage with a discharged soldier *sans* prospects. Within the year twin children have been born.

I plan to visit them during the summer holidays of this year. Muriel will accompany me. We book passage on a coastal boat plying between the London docks and Plymouth, but arrive at the dock on a day of broiling heat to find the gates picketed, and no boat leaving or likely to leave – the dockers are on strike. There is a stench of rotting meat and fruit. We travel to Plymouth by train, under threat of a general railway strike, timed to begin the following day. This is my introduction to a revolt of labour. Our stay in Plymouth is short; my brother, anticipating a complete break-down of the railway service, advises us to return home the following day.

Such movements in the outer world will henceforth find me aware, but not, for several years, personally concerned. My attention may be concentrated upon a group of stunted collier lads playing football on a corner of waste land, a porter carrying a load of luggage, fellow passengers in a railway carriage...An ambulance drives up to a house door, I am suddenly the driver, the mother, nurse, patient, in turn. There is a sort of centrifugal movement operating within my consciousness, and I have a novel satisfaction in the apprehension of an external world of folk to which I have hitherto been blind.

The struggle between capital and labour is a cogent reality to Muriel, who is in touch with industrial Nottingham through friends and pupils. She introduces me to active members of the local Labour Party and I.L.P. In the Midlands poverty is not a vague, inescapable condition, but has a well-defined cause – the greed of capitalists and their exploitation of the labouring classes. The Southerner still tends to see it as the state into which it has pleased God to call the majority, or as the outcome of individual misfortune or mismanagement. This has hitherto been my impression. But these Midlanders regard the capitalist as the common enemy, against whom the poor actively or passively unite.

A French correspondent of Muriel's, Marc Boutrit, comes to the farm for summer vacation. He is a village schoolmaster of peasant family from the Bordeaux district, thickset, with round, red face and heavy, clumsy gait, intelligent dark eyes and a fine, native courtesy. We hear that his teaching certificate – his *brevet supérieur* – entitles him to a salary much smaller than that of his English counterpart, and that his village school is a dilapidated building, rotten and rat-eaten. Marc B. accepts these conditions with a shrug of his shoulders or with a self-deprecatory laugh. What would you! they *are* so – it cannot be helped. Life is good, notwithstanding; one has one's family home, the land and the sun; one works, studies, dances. Especially it is good to dance...But a harder look comes upon his face when his liability to military service is mentioned. *That* is execrable; that one exerts one's ability and ingenuity to avoid!

You come to me directly from David; you step from the threshold of me into the presence-chamber of David – I wonder how it affects you, the swift transition from one individuality to the other.

So Muriel writes, in the September of this year.

How does it affect me? With Muriel I have always a sense of encompassing warmth. I am drawn into an atmosphere within which homely human life blossoms. I rest content in the present moment and scene, conscious of near and immediate beauty. (Yet later Muriel would write: 'I can only deck you with little flowers of humanness, that presently fade.') With David I never rest; we are always wandering, exploring, beating out tracks in a spiritual wilderness. Who is the leader, he or I? We urge one another on, we tire each other out, we get mutually weary – he sometimes angry. Out of a dark mood we may dig a sharp crystal of truth, out of a tortuous argument a clear psychological definition. He is still *Wunderkind* to me. But his tenderness, his rare penetrative sympathy come out to me no more. Always he is asking of me something not mine to give, asking, and knowing at the same time that he is crying for the moon or perhaps only the moon's reflection in water.

Occasionally, and cynically, he will refer to his engagement. I feel it utterly wrong that he, complementary to Muriel, should marry a girl whose quality of mind he appears to despise. He admits that he engaged himself in an overwrought moment, at the time when his mother's illness threatened his mental balance. I feel that he had better repudiate than redeem his promise. It is strange that he does not realise this – he, the creator of George Saxton.

207

Saxton, in *The White Peacock*, is the complete study of a life which never comes to fruition, because, through such a marriage, it denies itself the essentials of further growth. Is David just drifting? I think not; he seems deliberate. He sends me to the biography of Blake to find justification for his attitude. But, however he defends it, I cannot but see that he is wronging both himself and the girl.

There are some letters between us on the subject.

12 Colworth Road
Tuesday
[Undated, but written in late summer 1911]

Sometimes it strikes me one way – sometimes another – Sometimes I think it the beastliest selfishness – sometimes I think it is poltrooning – sometimes it seems to me perfectly natural – my way.

After all, Helene, what difference is there between your arrangement and mine? You say, let us be together, because it stimulates you. You know you would take my arm when we were alone; you know, when I was a bit tormented, you would put your arm round my neck. Now, if you can tell me any difference between this and the ultimate, I shall thank you. I tell you this because you are moved to irony against me. Might I not also turn round to you in irony, when you proffer your request.

If I became necessary to you, would it be because of the physical intimacy? Would there be no necessity developed from companionship as soul-intimate as ours is sure to be? We are always so intimate, vitally – that the other seems to me merely natural, like a phrase in the conversation. If it is not natural and good, God is an idiot. Between my proposal and yours, Helene, in the eyes of the seer, what difference is there? You ask me for my intimate company – I say, all right, so long as I need not keep a clutch on a discord.

Finally, to your heart of hearts I speak – and be truthful. *Could* we marry without making a horrible smash? 'We have broken down the bounds of the individual' – it is true – that's why it is perfectly honourable for you to take me: but with the bounds of the individual broken down there is too concentrated an intercourse not to be destructive. (Bad English – can you understand?)

You have this on your side: that I look on my life as moving on, phase by phase: you on yours unhappily, as being all one-coloured web. Then, if I want, you might be at a loss to find life. But, my dear, Siegmund went, and, inevitably, loving as you love, your lover must go – unless you love differently, lighter, more reservedly. You are passionate, ay, as passionate as I. But your passion smoulders and consumes your energy that way – I tend to blow your passion into flame – even then I cannot – it is a heavy, sullen smoulder – and mine is top-heavy with flame.

Do you remember Beatrice in *Tono-Bungay*? do you, do you? There! that is your way.

Look here, Helene – I genuinely believe I was *not* wrong in what I asked you.

And if you had not asked me for what I consider is all – you see it is, for the time, all, for me – and your reservation is as much as mine, only yours is in the past, mine in the future – I should not have asked the moiety extra. But you see, Helene, we could not go on as friends – we have known each other too well; you know what the end would be: then I should feel a coward.

You think of me what you like, and be as ironical as you like – I do not mind.

There, Helene – let's have done. It is sickening, this cats-pawing...I have begun *Paul Morel* again...glory, you should see it. The British public will stone me if ever it catches sight.

The publisher remains obstinately silent – offended by my cool cheek in asking for the *Saga* back. You shall have the MSS. if you like – when I get it. Though, you remember – you say it's not – not – anything of yours except in name, I suppose you mean.

Vale, Helene

DHL

The common, everyday, rather superficial man of me really loves Louie. Do you believe that? But do you not think the open-eyed, sad, deep-seeing man of me has not had to humble himself pretty sorely to accept the imposition of the masculine, stupid decree...We have to put up with it. There is a decree for each of us – thou shalt live alone. . .We may keep real company once in our lives – after that we touch, now and again – but do not repose.

A few of the ways – the ways which I used to puzzle over, I feel pretty certain of now. It doesn't much matter. The laws of life, even of nature, are made for the unseeing, unintelligent mass, and we have to submit also, *nous autres*. But *entre nous*, and *entre nous* alone – we can make our own laws. Step out of the common pale, and the old laws drop obsolete – you know that – and new laws suddenly reign. But you judge me by the old laws. The light has gone out – suddenly fallen.

Tenebres

DHL

I begin to feel that the subject must be avoided. . .I have an image of David that I cannot bear him to deface. The 'beastliest selfishness', the sacrifice of the 'deep-seeing' to the superficial man – if I dwell upon such aspects I shall be compelled to judge and condemn.

The matter of our own relationship is bound to recur, especially when David's communal self insists on fitting me into some localised department of society. Why cannot he accept me as myself, as individual? Why must he try to *classify* me?

Sometimes I spend an evening with Laura M. and her father in their little villa at Purley. Laura will arrange a musical evening to which David is also invited. Laura plays the piano with a childlike vivacity. A Grieg sonata, performed by the two of us, means nothing at all. David will sing Schubert songs with a queer abandon which accentuates the looseness of his thin limbs; and there may be another singer – a girl of the fluffy type, with fair hair and a good complexion, but frizzed and rouged. She and David flirt blatantly, to the great amusement of the hostess ...There is one other member of the household, an old aunt, a pathetically gross old woman, once, Laura tells me, a great beauty. To her David is gently and chivalrously attentive.

(A collection of D. H. Lawrence's short stories published after his death includes one entitled 'The Witch à la Mode', which recalls this evening. Reading it, I could understand much in his attitude and behaviour of the time then incomprehensible. The story itself is a skilful blend of fact and fiction, with an entirely imaginary *dénouement*.)

Muriel waits, believing that she has more to give David, more to share with him, than any other woman. He has, indeed, admitted as much. She assumes that time is on her side, and looks for the gradual passing of David's mother's adverse influence. Mine she does not fear, perhaps realising that I, who refuse to be bound, bind no one. I am content that she could turn to me with trust, and do not ask, at this stage, whether what she loves in me is intrinsic me, or the reflection she sees in me of David's personality.

About this time I meet with Edward Carpenter's book, *Love's Coming of Age*. It throws much light on my own problem. If I may accept the hypothesis (and it seems well substantiated) that sex presents a graded scale of values and attributes, and passes between opposite poles of absolute male and absolute female qualities, I can reject the idea of a supposititious abnormality. The statement 'Male and female created He them' becomes too simple to be comprehensive. We may think of sex in terms of the colour band of the spectrum, and see it passing from the masculine scarlet through all the intermediate tones to feminine violet.

Perhaps indeed I stand at the half-way house, looking both ways, partaking of both masculine and feminine sex values, and therefore without paramount urge towards either. Alone, because I have no complement; the woman in me impelled towards the man, but checked by strongly masculine intuitions; the male in me responding to the woman, but countered by those which are female. It may be so. Yet, as I see it, the position is not necessarily a disability, either to society or myself. If it sets me free from the biological necessity to reproduce, there is a reserve of human energy to be applied in the field of creative or constructive thought, and in other departments of human activity.

(I am glad that I was able to approach this subject by way of the sanity of Edward Carpenter. It prevented me from taking too seriously the primitive tribal attitude to the matter as preserved in legal form, and also much unbalanced treatment of it in literature, when I came to these later.)

There were blue and golden Saturdays during the September and October of 1911, when David and I resumed our rambles over the Surrey Downs. Taking the path from Riddlesdown to Sanderstead village we would pass through the larch wood on the northern slope, where, by the path at its emergence from the wood, stood a single, very ancient yew-tree. It indicated a resting place and we would sit beneath it, peering into the misty valley, listening to the voices of down and wood, while behind a near hedge rose the yellow plaque of the harvest moon. Formerly we both loved this place and felt its peace, but now, at twilight, David becomes restless and irritable.

Leith Hill, in autumn sunlight; the air scented with browning brake and ripe bramble. We rest on the grass after a steep climb. 'Here we are on a green hill', says David, 'and it's as good up here as on any other green hill in the world.' I think he is perhaps consoling himself for his failure, so far, to gain a wider range than the Surrey Downs...I have dreamt the same dream, but latterly the colours have faded...Freedom, achievement – they would seem to be a variously stamped coinage, and the coin for the moment desired must be bought in terms of other coins. Meanwhile, on Leith Hill the grasshoppers whirr and leap – one green spirit bounds on to my white dress and sits, tensed energy absorbing the sunlight.

Farthing Downs – it is as though we walk along the smooth, rounded back of a huge animal, in mutual isolation from humankind. Above, an immense pall of ruddy cloud, toning to a saffron fringe which drops to the valley on either side. I have a queer intuition that David and I are performing walking-on parts in some vast cosmic drama.

The high woods above Addington village, in after-sunset glow on Sunday evening. We come through the woods as the cracked bell of the village church is tolling for service. 'Shall we go to church?' says David. 'When I am middle-aged I shall probably be married and settled, and take my family to church every Sunday.' I realise, as he says this, something of the antagonism between his community self, which wishes to be absorbed in the clan, divested of responsibility – and David Lawrence the individual, who must stand alone, responsible to his observant, discriminating, critical ego.

We visit Chaldon church (Surrey) and stand silently before its famous Doom, which fortunately escaped the attentions of Cromwell's iconoclasts.

The Doom covers the western wall of the church. Centrally a ladder connects Heaven, Earth and Hell. Souls departing from Earth pass before St Michael, who weighs each in his scales. According to its worth the soul ascends or descends the ladder – upward to the light of Heaven, downward to the attentions of devils in charge of a boiling cauldron, into which the unworthy souls are pitch-forked. It was a parable in plain terms that the simplest mind of the twelfth century could understand and appreciate – but we have lost our simplicity, and we merely smile. Eight centuries of thought and argument divide the minds of Peter Abelard and David Lawrence.

In the late summer of this year David is introduced to the critic and writer Edward Garnett, and a friendship develops between them. Garnett is shown the *Saga of Siegmund* manuscript, which he approves and recommends to the firm of Duckworth. David, stung by Ford Madox Hueffer's ironic disapproval of the book's intensity, finds Garnett's attitude reassuring.

(When I learned the story of Hueffer's life, and of the long, futile conflict of his relationship with two strongly possessive women, it seemed to me that his dislike of the *Saga* was explained. For him there was no satisfaction in life until it had been translated in terms of art. The connoisseur savoured a work as he did a wine, and regarded intensity in writing as a fermentation of emotional experience. Too much of that draught had been drained – he now turned from it with loathing.)

On a wet evening in November David visits Garnett, walking the miles between Edenbridge station and the Cearne; he remains for hours in damp clothes. Pneumonia is the result. He is nursed in his Croydon lodging by his sister Ada.

Muriel is staying at my home during a part of the Christmas holidays; we visit him together. He is propped up in bed; his eyes burn blue from hollowed sockets, a tawny growth of beard adds to his age; his hands are wasted almost to transparency. Muriel speaks nervously, charged with love and pity she fears to show – I, in very reaction, am flippant. Ada Lawrence, a placid presence, like and yet so unlike her brother, sews in the background.

During January David writes asking my sanction for the publication of the *Saga*. The firm of Duckworth is prepared to take it. I cannot but consent. His new novel, *Paul Morel*, is still unfinished. It is unlikely that after convalescence he will be able to resume teaching; he must have money. He says he is completely revising the manuscript. I stipulate that I shall see the revision before it goes into print. I wish he had not thought complete revision necessary; written at white heat it should keep the mould into which it ran – that is its truest form. Something of the kind I write to him – he replies from Bournemouth:

I am not altering the substance of the *Saga*, so that, in spite of my present tone, you will not find it perverted from what original truth it had. I recast the paragraphs and attend to the style. As soon as I can, I will send you the MS., that you may satisfy yourself. But, as you remember saying yourself, the *Saga* is a work of fiction on a frame of actual experience. It is my presentation, and therefore necessarily false sometimes to your view. The necessity is not that our two views should coincide, but that the work should be a work of art. I am not flippant with the *Saga*. But you shall see for yourself.

(David did not keep this promise.) The letter is dated 1 February 1912. A few days later, on his return from Bournemouth, I meet him at Waterloo station, we cross London to Victoria station for the Surrey train. He is going to stay with Edward Garnett at Edenbridge. I travel with him as far as Woldingham; it is a fine, calm evening and the Downs are a glowing, emerald green under the flush of winter sunset. In the train we are peaceful, for the instant gay and content, and our talk is like that of people who have just escaped a mutual danger. David tells me that after the visit to Garnett he will go home to Eastwood and concentrate for a couple of months upon the writing of *Paul Morel*. At Woldingham station I say good-bye with no more finality than usual, except for a wave of the hand, and take a train back to the suburb and the work that he is leaving for all time.

Two days later a letter comes from Edenbridge.

Should you like a walk with me one evening before I go? Should you like to meet me on Limpsfield Common, just outside the school, as early as you can one evening? Then you could walk down here and see The Cearne (Garnett's house). Perhaps you might even stay the night, if you would consent. You would not mind Garnett. He is most beautifully free of the world's conventions.

There is no sound but the fluttering of the logs on the open hearth... I am uneasy tonight.

But no! it is too late. David's letter only makes more clear the division of our ways. I know the nature of his unease, and my incapacity to deal with it. I could enjoy a walk over the snow-covered common with David, but not a casual introduction by night to the house of the unconventional Garnett. Indeed, suddenly worldly-wise, it seems to me that David is politely observing certain conventions of a kind wholly unacceptable to me.

(Sixteen years later, in the 1928 edition of Lawrence's *Collected Poems*, I read for the first time the one entitled 'Passing Visit to Helen', which was probably written at this point. A bitter clever poem, reflecting the mortification of that 'common man' of whom David's finer self was ruefully cognisant.)

David Herbert Lawrence and I never meet again...He returns to Eastwood, to work at the novel *Paul Morel*, ultimately published as *Sons and Lovers*.[1] Early in May Muriel writes telling me briefly that he has gone abroad. Later in the month I hear from David in Bavaria:

[1] See Jessie Chambers' *Personal Memoir*, pp. 104–17.

Gasthaus zur Post
Beuerberg
bei München
28 May 1912

Ada has sent me a copy of The Trespasser, and says there are two more at home, so I thought you might like one from me. Some day I will inscribe it, if you wish.

I am here in Bavarian Tyrol, near the mountains. They stand up streaked with snow, so blue, across the valley. The Isar is a quick stream, all muddy with glacier water now. If ever you come to Germany, come down the Isar-Thal. The flowers are in masses, masses, enough to satisfy any heart alive, and so beautiful. And the clear, clean atmosphere, and the peasants barefooted, and the white cows with their cow-bells, it is all so delightful. Yesterday we were at a peasant play – you know this is the Ober Ammergau Country. It was an old Miracle play, with the Devil & Death, & Christ, and Maria – quaint and rather touching. You would like it very much. Some time, come to Bavaria. It is the Minnesinger Country. I have been in the Rhineland, and the Mosel land, but I like Bavaria best.

Your last letter to me[1] wasn't very nice, I thought. But there, I don't wonder. We leave here on Friday.

Regards to Mr & Mrs Corke.

D. H. Lawrence

When the book arrives I open it with mingled exaltation and dread. Why, if there has been no sacrifice of its essential truth to his Moloch of technique and form, did he not send me the revised manuscript as promised? But indeed the work remains substantially the same – the eroticism of one imaginary scene has been heightened; there are several interpolations of imaginary dialogue – and I miss a fine piece of symbolism – yet it is still the record, faithful enough, of Lawrence's exploration into the territory of H.B.M.'s experience.

The *Saga*, and David himself, have emerged into a wider world. I wonder what region of personality equates to this mountain land for David Lawrence; the letter gives no suggestion. But for him I am glad; he is evidently happy.

Through my classroom window at Dering Place School I see the cypresses in the deserted garden bending rugged

---

[1] My February letter addressed to him at Garnett's.

boughs to the wind. Before me the pens scratch, the children lean to their work. While they are busy I write on the blackboard an exercise designed to fix in their minds the specific use of 'their' and 'there'. A woman inspector of physical training now enters and announces that she will see me give a lesson. In the play-ground I put the class through a programme of exercises I have been teaching for two years; presently, back in the classroom, I receive her criticism and comments. When she leaves it is time for the free play interval – I turn to a pile of exercise books on the desk, and mark sums until interrupted by the Head, who wants to introduce an American writing specialist who is claiming that his system of penmanship drill increases the speed and legibility of pupils' writing by fifty per cent. Play-time is extended while the specialist gives a demonstration to the staff. He goes, the children return, and until noon are happily absorbed in reading *The Water Babies* – the cheap paper-covered Stead edition with which I supplement the official primers.

Afternoon – an hour of teaching grubby fingers with bitten and broken nails to sew and hem. Play-time – my colleague from the adjoining classroom comes, full of a grievance against the head assistant...The last school hour of the day, when the air of the classroom is palpably foul, is heavy with accumulated exhalation, and the morning's superficial appearance of personal cleanliness has quite departed, when the children are tired, restless and irritable. I turn the blackboard, and give them a new poem.[1]

> Where dips the rocky highland
> Of Sleuth Wood in the lake,
> There lies a leafy island
> Where flapping herons wake
> The drowsy water-rats;
> There we've hid our faery vats,
> Full of berries
> And of reddest stolen cherries.

[1] The first stanza of 'The Stolen Child' by W. B. Yeats.

They like Yeats's refrain – they chant it in unison:

> Come away, O human child!
> To the waters and the wild
> With a faery, hand in hand,
> For the world's more full of weeping than you
> can understand.

School is the machine, and there is always weaving upon that loom. But how empty, vacuous, are the evenings and week-ends of this spring of 1912; only after David's departure do I realise fully the potency of his presence. It has become difficult to accept isolation. Yet I know, as if by instinct, that this is an essential discipline…Afar off, though in the same small house, the even lives of my parents appear to move with a circumscribed monotony that makes me afraid. They are resigned to their narrow round – content. I fancy they feel that *I* should be content – they believe that in time I *shall* be. My mother, although she never mentions the subject, is disappointed that I shall not marry David – she had hoped against conviction that this would happen. But now she is consoling herself with the thought that she will not lose me – that I shall continue to live at home – always. In a mood of desperation I write the poem 'Prayer For The Dead'.

My life, nevertheless, moves towards its next stage. For two years it has been polarised between David and Muriel. Now the stresses change.

In her own book,[1] Jessie Chambers tells of her contacts with Lawrence during the March and April of 1912, when he was writing the final version of *Sons and Lovers*. With a childishly cruel simplicity he sent her his finished study of 'Miriam' – his acceptance, for purposes of the novel, of his mother's image of Jessie. It was the son's last submission to the judgment of his dominant mother. The man revealed in that autobiographical story, the man who was asking her

[1] *D. H. Lawrence: a Personal Record* by 'E.T.', published by Frank Cass, 2nd edition.

to confirm and approve a work which challenged the essentials of her personality, and eventually the man who repudiated what she regarded as moral law, could not be identified with the Lawrence of her earlier conception.

He had begged her not to tell me the facts relating to his departure from England; but I knew that the 'Miriam' presentation had wounded her – how bitterly I realised only after reading *Sons and Lovers* when the book was issued a year later.

During the summer of 1912 chance offers me a newspaper cutting advertising a Rhine trip for no more than £7. My salary is now £100 per annum – it can be done. Muriel rather languidly agrees to this plan for the summer holidays.

We cross to the Hook at night, on an old boat carrying decrepit horses. In the tiny, stuffy cabin I cannot sleep, but listen to the grinding of the screw, and the gnawing of a rat in the cabin partition behind my berth. I try to shut from my consciousness the sight of the sad horses, standing, knock-kneed and with drooping heads, on the wet deck in the cold wind. By early morning we are in Holland, steaming up the grey Maas, and I look out to see a ship of dream, a full-rigged ship of sail with seven masts, gliding slowly down.

Rotterdam – noisy wharves and acrid smells. We leave it on the Rhine steamer, and thereafter watch, for a long, sleepy day, lines of poplar and willow slipping back on either side. At seven in the evening the boat moors at Emmerich, quaint town on the Dutch–German border. Wandering in its narrow streets at twilight we disturb a hound lying in shadow by an inn door; it springs up, growling, menacing – Muriel, used to the management of the farm dogs, drives it off. We enter an ancient house open as a café, and I have the odd and inexplicable sensation of having been there in the remote past. We drink coffee, under a ceiling embossed with scenes from the life of Christ. At night, again on the moving boat, the lights from the long Rhine barges, and the luminous foam of the paddle-wheel shine into our sleep.

The next day gives us Düsseldorf – wide streets and long, formal picture galleries. At evening, Cologne.

A strangely *alone* experience – Muriel beside me, yet apart. Everything I have known of spiritual anchorage seems drifting from me with the backward-gliding Rhine banks. This is because Muriel, the warm, vivid Muriel of the past two years, is changing; her fire is sinking; she is like a jar I have seen glowing rose-red in a furnace, but which is now cooling, turning grey and rigid. At this moment I do not understand how I, to Muriel, have been simply a mirror reflecting the self of David which she loved, and now cannot even pretend exists.

The boat moors at Cologne for the night; we sit on deck talking only casually, while great Rhine flows serenely down, its waters patterned by a myriad of lights; the Cathedral spires point to the dimmed stars; eddies of music drift on the wind from pleasure steamers passing up and down...On the morrow, Mainz...the over-powering *weight* of that city! Then, in late afternoon, Wiesbaden – the Kursaal grounds illuminated, a large orchestra playing, at twilight, in the open air. My mind is curiously dazed – I feel that I might be slipping into fantasy, and I grip my consciousness with a sense of fear. The woman walking beside me is an unknown; the Kurhaus surroundings, in the half-dark, have no link with any past phase of experience.

At Mannheim the boat reverses its course; we are on our way home. Muriel, absent, continues to read the book which has occupied her during sunny hours on deck, Dostoievsky's *Brothers Karamazov*. As a rule, on journeys we share a book, but this one does not appeal to me at the moment; my single concern is the change in Muriel. I feel convinced that its cause is, intrinsically, David. Yet she never mentions him. The letter I received from him in May, announcing a copy of *The Trespasser*, came from Irschenhausen. Perhaps, if Muriel and he were to meet, there might be a change in what, to me, is the present intolerable situation...So, when we moor again at Cologne, I make this suggestion to Muriel.

The voice that replies is one I have never heard before. It wakes me, abruptly, from a silly dream of re-union. David, leaving England with another man's wife, has passed the point of return. It is a kind of death. We cannot go to him, and he will never return to us.

Back in Rotterdam we are met by a Dutch school-mistress – a chance acquaintance made in London some months previously. She is determined to show us historic Holland, and we pass a strenuous day of sight-seeing in Den Haag and Delft. At the end of it Muriel is exhausted, sick and faint during a sleepless night in the hotel; and I must concentrate on arranging for her the easiest possible journey home.

'Lead, kindly Light!' In her *Memoir* Jessie Chambers tells how, at this crisis in her life, she found illumination in the reading of Dostoievsky's *Brothers Karamazov*. Murky beams, at best. The light which flickered before me during the succeeding year came from Romain Rolland. *Jean Christophe*, beating his way indomitably through an incomprehensible world, appealed to me – a portent, a challenge – the reminder of H.B.M.'s injunction to persist, to continue in action, though action seem purposeless and vision be withdrawn.

In such mood I pass into my thirties.

APPENDIX

THE FRESHWATER DIARY[1]

I will not dress too early this morning altho' the sun and the dancing green boughs outside the open window invite me to get up. I will try and sleep again – there are seven long hours to wait.

It is now nearly half past ten – how to make the walk to Yarmouth – a little over three miles – last till three oclock. I consider – and start strolling slowly up the lane towards Farringford.

Where is Siegmund now? Perhaps he has reached Portsmouth:

I linger under the noble trees which shelter the home Tennyson loved – then on past farm and cottage till a stretch of sunlit baked road makes me long for shade. There is none and the road winds up and up.

At the top. I stand and look over valley and down – the Solent shines blue to the north. I am not yet in sight of Yarmouth – but I am more than half way there. It lies somewhere at the bottom of this winding hill road which is the next stage of the journey. There is a little brick chapel standing near and I listen to the congregation within singing the hymn 'O Paradise'. I hum the tune and laugh happily and think how supremely foolish of people to shut themselves up in an ugly little building to sing about a mythical heaven when here outside the Lord God has planted a garden of delight.

Downwards now. I arrive at a pleasant green, shaded by trees. I will rest and read. A clock in the cottage opposite

---

[1] I wrote this memoir in diary form in the autumn of 1909 and during the spring of 1910 Lawrence used it as the basis for his novel *The Trespasser*. The original MS. of this unrevised material is presently in the possession of the Humanities Research Center, The University of Texas, Austin, U.S.A.

strikes twelve. O Time – if I could only treat you in Wonderland fashion. Three more hours!

Half an hour passes. 'Romola' is hard reading today. I stroll on down the hill. A soldier on a bicycle sings out a cheery 'Good-morning', which I return.

I am at the bottom of the hill and the sea is close – but Yarmouth itself half a mile further on. Through a gate I pass down a path on to the shore. I sit down close to the water, but the sun is very hot and here there seems no breeze.

Well. I will reach Yarmouth – the half mile of road is not interesting. Half way along it I cross a bridge and an official comes forth from a cottage at the side and demands a toll. I pay and ask for information about a big liner at present passing noiselessly very close in shore.

Yarmouth – the place is in its Sunday sleep. I am tired, and the sky is getting overcast. It is only twenty minutes past one.

I will go on the jetty – at present deserted. At least there is a seat at the end, and I can read. I try to induce an automatic machine to surrender me some chocolate, but it obstinately refuses. Patience: Siegmund is waiting at Newport – only twelve miles away.

Grey sky. Chilly wind – even a spot of rain. Perhaps I had better find the station.

There is the train – going to Newport. The clock of that grey church has just struck two. The station is in view, it lies close to the marshes.

Two small boys clamber over a gate at the side and suggest to me a similar course. But the gate is higher than I anticipated, and so I cross the metals, and sit down in a corner of the shelter on the down side of the station. I *must* read, and I do, only disturbed by the screaming of the restless, wheeling swallows.

By three oclock I am feeling damp and chilly – the draught is laden with mist. But there is only ten minutes longer to wait. The station master, who is also signalman, booking clerk and porter, proceeds to signal the train through. I cross to the opposite side, get my ticket, and return.

The little train is in sight. I am shivering with cold, and a vague doubt as to whether, after all, Fate is going to let us –

'You *here*!' I am dragged into a carriage, shaking almost too much to answer that familiar voice, with an unfamiliar ring of gladness in it. But the train has started, and Siegmund's arms are round me, holding me close enough to hurt.

'Is it a dream *now*, dear?' he whispers.

Ah yes! it is all a dream – and bad dreams have clouded my brain since then. It is very dark, and I have lost my Siegmund. In this night I am afraid to walk alone, so I crouch down and wait. With the greyest dawn I will seek him. But I am very tired –

Aug. 1st
The foghorn warning comes to us, muffled by the mist. We are together on the cliffs for the first time. We have hardly a regret for the vanished beauty of the morning – and it matters not at all that we can scarcely see five yards before us. The sunlight of the inner vision is unclouded – after nearly six years of waiting Fate has granted us five days of each other. Of this eternity the unseen sea is singing below us. Wrap us closer – grey damp shroud of mist. White, singing sea, lure us closer. Take us by the steep cliff pathway into the dark – let our last consciousness be the tighter clasp of each other's arms. For Fate is already setting upon her favours a price to be paid in agony.

We stand at the cliff edge and see how the smooth white chalk slope vanishes beneath. 'Shall we go down here and end all our troubles?' says one. But there is no sincerity in the suggestion. It is too absurd in the face of that illimitable five days prospect.

The foghorn in F, or in F$^{\#}$ – we disagree about the pitch – still calls from westward. We wander on in that direction. The Mist Spirit who has her home above the Lethe stream has dropped a beautiful cloud round our souls. So kind is she. Neither past nor future have we, but an infinite content.

Suddenly and strangely rises in our path, and but a few steps before us, the great dim outline of a cross. The Mist Spirit has no veil thick enough to hide its form. It stands like a shadow of itself: a gigantic, menacing shadow. We turn back and presently descend the cliffs to the Bay. It is nearing sunset time, and breaking masses of fog flying from cliff to cliff, uncover a still sky of mottled gold. We will go eastward now.

Beyond the links lie green mounds and turfed banks of earth. I am tired, and choose the driest to rest against.

'Children,' says Apollo, 'I give you the beauty of peace. You are mine, and the day is mine. Look, and worship!'

The curtains of the Mist Spirit become but transparent golden films through which we gaze into the light which satisfies. The light which can only be seen by those into whose souls it has been born. Greatly blessed and greatly cursed are they, for seldom is the light unobscured – and the black shadows are terrible.

Siegmund asks what music holds the best interpretation of the sunset. I am silent, but he is thinking of a Beethoven symphony. Afterwards, for me it blends itself into the sustained harmonies of the strings in the Grail music from 'Lohengrin'.

The glory is very transient: the fog thickens again, and our visible world is limited to a small circular path of wet grass. We will go home.

I look out at eleven oclock. The moon is wading through shallows into a clear depth of blue. We walk down the white road to the Bay, and stand at the beginning of the Moonpath across the full tide.

Aug. 2nd Monday

The morning breeze is fresh, and the stems of the creeper outside my window wake me with imperative tapping. It will be a day of alternate cloud and sun – but with more sun than cloud.

At nine oclock it is good to lean over the low sea wall and spread one's fingers out upon the warm stones. There is much content, and satisfaction unspoiled by satiety in the curling of the deep blue water round the little rocks below. But soon the breeze from over the green hill calls us westward. Upon the highest point stands clearly out the Tennyson Cross. No mysticism wraps it this morning: it is just a shining white stone monument – an admirable landmark, and memorial to the poet whose name it bears. We regret that it should be necessary to surround the cross with an ugly iron railing painted red.

Westward still! We are nearing the Needles. How the gulls scream and moan. Hundreds live in these cliffs.

'Come back dear: Oh *don't* go so near the edge.' Siegmund pleads, when I creep close as possible to the beautiful birds. But I laugh and feel proud of my steady brain, just for a moment. Only play: a kind of play with the possibility of separation which makes the joy of the reality of possession more intense.

This is the mighty cliff which terminates the south-western corner of the island. A slippery path of dazzling chalk ends in a sheer descent of something like four hundred feet. West of this bends Alum Bay. We enquire the nearest way down, and the coast-guard directs us to the Path of the Hundred Steps. Siegmund counts the steps, being sceptical about the number and reduces it to sixty-eight.

The water laps quietly in upon the beach. We lie down to rest upon the sloping terrace of beach nearest it, and look out through half closed fingers. One or two lazy sailing ships idle down the Solent. Siegmund attempts to classify them, and I listen and laugh, not at all respectfully – for he probably knows rather less about them than his pupil.

Clouds and sun, but more sun than cloud. Yet of any cloud Siegmund is impatient. I am not, for I know the good north west wind controls those big black masses and that their day's journey is far.

We do not talk much, and our thoughts are heavy winged and have no desire to fly above the cliffs. I can hear the curling splash and retreat of sleepy little waves, and the strong beat of Siegmund's heart.

Later in the afternoon we decide to walk on to Colwell Bay. The way of the shore is strewn with crumbling cliffs. We climb heaps of slippery stone and jump running water; we scramble up half obliterated paths and creep round dangerous corners; we halt for breath upon reaching a grass crowned mound midway. Siegmund holds me tightly and breathes hard. I cannot speak. It is full tide.

We are alone upon the shore but for three children, who are searching for treasures. They are presently enriched by the gift of an electric light bulb which Siegmund finds. Curious that the frail thing of the city should lie there intact, where the sea has strewn wide the ruins of the land.

The way home lies across country. We pass a little Catholic church in the fields: a carved Christ looks down from his cross over the mounds of the dead. Our path, skirting the churchyard wall, leads through a fir copse, and down a very steep tree-shadowed hill. At the bottom of this, we have much argument as to the right direction – but presently find our way through a pasture bordered by great elms, out behind a poultry farm. Then we see the woodlands of Farringford. Somewhere in the distance a band is playing the 'Watch on the Rhine'.

As we pass under the beeches by the Tennyson bridge, I wonder, carelessly, what next Monday will bring for us. It hardly matters – being so immense a distance away. But Siegmund grips me as if parting were imminent, though his laugh is quite natural.

'Quick curtain!' he says joyously.

227

August 3rd Tuesday

The little waves run up the beach full and clear and foamless. I lie in the deliciously cool water and look lazily round the Bay, its rocks and cliffs, and out over the shining sea. It is seven in the morning. Existence is a calm perfection of delight.

We decide, an hour later, that today we will explore eastward in Eden.

The sand of Compton Bay is firm and white. A narrow strip is beyond high water mark. We descend by means of a gap in the high cliffs, where a landslip has crumbled them.

The breeze is left behind, up on the hills. Down here is glowing heat quivering from sand and stones. When my bare feet feel scorched I run into the water to cool them. We have no desire to walk further – but sit down upon the sand, leaning against a smooth, flat bar of glistening brown stone.

We are silent. Even thought fades in this compelling, enthralling sunshine.

So we lie for hours, and the sea creeps close up to us and sinks again: sinks till a boulder strewn way is opened for us, along the shore. Late in the afternoon a breeze finds its way down. I stand up and shake the sand out of my loose hair, and let the wind comb out its tangles, and feel a wonderful sense of harmony and happiness. Siegmund smiles up at me, then rouses himself to say 'You look now as if you belong to the sea'! 'I do, and someday I shall go back to it', is my instant answer.

Our progress among the rocks is slow. We have to climb them and it is easy to slip off into sand and water. We linger over lovely rocks pools, seaweed curtained and full of red anemones, and meanwhile the sun is slanting down beyond the Cross. At last Siegmund, looking doubtfully at two miles more of glistening sunlit boulders, suggests ascending the cliffs. I am in no hurry to put on stockings; and sit upon a rock looking at pink toes in a warm little pool.

'Come!' says Siegmund, holding out his arms. 'You are only six years old today.'

The sand is being invaded by way of the cliff path. A whole family, including the kitten, which the youngest child liberates upon the beach. Poor bewildered little atom: it scampers mewing after the dog.

We stand upon the edge of the cliff and see the two bays. On our left, blue water and the House of the Brown Stones. On our right a rippled, sun-gold sea, and Freshwater in partial shadow from the west cliff. Siegmund lingers over the view.

'I want to absorb it *all* into my memory', he says earnestly after a long silence.

Yes, we can retain the details of our vision – it may be an exquisite photograph – but what, for want of a clearer definition we call 'atmosphere' fades as quickly and surely as the scent of a dying rose.

The moon rises late this evening. We think to find our way through the lanes to Alum Bay, and eventually, keeping the Cross in sight, to return over the down, with the Moon-path before us.

The twilight dims more rapidly than we anticipate. The lane winds, and we have lost our landmark. By the time we reach the next sign post there is barely light enough to show its wording. The Down, its slope darkened by furze, is to the left.

We approach it by a path leading to a disused chalk pit and ascend till we reach the lower edge of the furze. Then Siegmund tries vainly to find a way through. It seems an impenetrable forest of black prickles.

He comes back to me at last. 'I'm afraid we must give it up tonight', he says. So we sit down on the sloping grass. Northward, over the trees below, we can see the little lights of the moving ships in the Solent, and the big fixed light on Lymington pier. After a little while, intense quiet is over everything, and the lamps are put out in the farmhouse which we passed on our way up.

We take a wrong turning, upon the way home. When the moon shines above the Down behind us, she is still struggling through cloud barriers. Being lost, we simply keep as directly as possible to the eastward, but the lanes wind. We walk on, thinking.

'We may be on the road to Newport', I say presently, as the country develops yet more unfamiliar features. 'And the distance is ten miles.'

I laugh, not caring in the least whether we are really going further astray. I am drunk with freedom. Let the lane turn about as it will, and let us wander on through scented fields and past sleeping farms till we are quite tired. There is no one to question us, even in look or thought. The Dreams only share with us this island of peace: the dreams of those in the locked and darkened cottages. So have we often sent our dreams forth, but all that their weak willing little hands gather to bring back for us they lose upon the way, and only the scent of Night's flowers still clings round them.

We cross a stile, and recognise, on the right of the path the graveyard of the Catholic chapel. The shrinking moon has slipped between the clouds, and shines upon the white stones. The carved Christ upon his cross hangs black against a silver grey sky. The path before us disappears into the pine copse.

We step softly into the darkness – intense darkness to our vision. Siegmund's arm is round me, but I cannot see him. No cathedral ever enshrined such a depth of silence.

'Are you quite sure that this is the right way?' Siegmund whispers.

I am quite sure – and presently we come out into the hazy moonlight, and stumble down the steep hill, and very cautiously cross the pasture and the poultry farm. A merry noise would there be should we wake all the fowls.

But this does not happen, and we are presently safe upon the Farringford road.

Aug. 4th Wednesday

The garden in front of our house is long and crooked with a sunken flagstone pavement running up to the door by the side of the lawn. The high fence screening the garden on either side is heavy with mingling clematis and honeysuckle. A bushy little laburnum shades the seat where I sit, tracing out the course of our wanderings upon the map.

Siegmund's hand upon the latch startles me. He is standing at the gate in the sunshine. We greet each other across the tall roses.

The people of the farm below the Down are busy dipping their sheep this morning. The process is quite primitive. In the middle of the yard is a big zinc bath, half full of a dirty yellow liquid. Two men seize a fat sheep from the little group penned in a corner, and with difficulty hold him more or less in the bath, while the third bales the yellow stuff over his back with an old tin bowl. The farmer's family stands ready to assist, if necessary.

We pass on to the slope of the Down, and directly in front is the path through the furze which last night we missed. The sun is hot and a stiff breeze is energetically chasing the few little white clouds. We climb slowly and gain the highest point near the Cross.

A green hollow, by the edge of the cliff, shall be our house today. I make a book-rest of Siegmund, and read, while he, with hands crossed behind his head looks lazily over the sparkling sea.

The sun scorches and the breeze and Siegmund drop asleep. I change my position and try to shade his head, which he *will* bare in defiance of the strongest sun. The veins in his wrists are blue and swollen with the heat.

There lies Freshwater, tucked down in the valley, and the little Bay below the hill, and green Farringford on the slope, all asleep too.

I long for shade.

'It is worth while to sleep, for the sake of a waking like this'; says Siegmund, when he rouses. 'I was dreaming of huge glittering ice-crystals.'

At the cliff's edge the wind comes fresh from the water, cool against my sunburnt face and arms. We can see the path from this point. An invalid's chair is being wheeled over the short grass, and its misshapen and helpless occupant turns pain-sunken eyes towards the sea. We look once only, and then leave him the quiet of our green hollow. Torn, shrivelled seaweed, beyond reach of the tide; the life-tide in which we exult, in whose infinity our selfconsciousness is lost.

The curtain of the Mist Spirit is thinning. Siegmund sees beyond it more clearly than I:

'Do you want anything better than this, dear,' he says, as we walk slowly home. 'Shall we come here next year, and stay for a whole month?'

I wonder if he himself feels the unreality of his apparently commonplace suggestion – whether his words are a protest against the conviction that has come to *me* with a strength forbidding question, and yet with a calm dispelling all fear. The conviction that the Fate who has been, since the beginning, resolving obvious discords gradually, by unfamiliar progressions, and out of original combinations weaving wondrous harmony with our lives, is too great an artist to suffer an anti-climax.

'If there be any next year', I say carelessly, and Siegmund needs no explanation for the reply.

But later, in the warm gloaming, when a dusky stillness is rising from the sea, and we are alone on the eastern downs, I feel myself slipping into an unforeseen valley of shadows. There is void and darkness around me, and out of it comes only the distant crying of many lives that have touched mine. These I know, but beyond them, low and plaintive, I hear the complaint of a little unknown voice. What have I done to hurt it so?

Siegmund, in an irresponsible mood, is whistling the 'Spring Song' from 'Die Walküre'. He is very far away from me – indeed, I half wonder if I have loved only a dream woven soul, and no reality. I call to him, despairingly – only he can silence with comfort those wailing voices. If my Siegmund exists, I must send him back into their darkness.

I cannot find him. I drag myself free from the passionate grip of his arms, and drop down sobbing, in the shelter of the tumuli – trying to shut out the unreasoning pleading of his voice.

He is beaten at last. There is quiet, and I become conscious that a stranger, passing along the cliff, is looking curiously towards us.

Thursday. Aug. 5th

The flowing tide trickles noiselessly among the rocks, widening and deepening insidiously the little pools. Only an occasional gurgle, at once subdued, tells of its return, as it takes possession of this dim, clammy cave I am exploring. From the shiny boulders upon the floor the seaweeds stretch down their fingers into the dark water. I climb and wade towards the ragged arch at the entrance, and so come again into the sunshine of the early morning.

Warm and sweet is the air of this lane, remote from the sea: the belt of dewy grass on either side is thick with little pink and white convolvuli. They have climbed half way up the dwarf fir trees in the hedge – the stiff old trees, keeping forever their winter mourning and winter thoughts. It is a perfect day to which these flower children have been born, and in sun-glow and wind-thrill its hours will pass uncounted by them. When it is over and the dainty cups curl sleepily, night will touch and seal them against the possible gloom of tomorrow.

'It is good when life holds no anti-climax,' I say softly to Siegmund.

He agrees, but fails to find the path of my thought. He cares nothing for the details of Nature's working. He stands

233

apart, in her holy places, till her soul bends to his blind worship. With spirit and sense he adores her and only through music does he seek to interpet her.

The lane leads upwards to the freedom of the eastern down. At the end of it stands a low bungalow, roofed with dusky red, in the midst of a large square of the coolest green lawn. The flowers and bushes in the border touching the lawn on all sides are sparkling with sunlit dew.

On a garden seat, with his face turned from the sun, sits the owner of the house, reading a paper. As we pass, he flings it irritably down, calls twice a name we do not catch, and hurries indoors.

'Isn't he in a bad temper!' says Siegmund, much amused. 'And all because breakfast is a little late. Look – here come his wife and daughter.'

They look flurried and anxious. They push open the gate, rush across the lawn and enter the house by the shady verandah. 'It's pitiful', says Siegmund, still smiling, but with much regret in his voice. 'Imagine the things he is saying – the life inside that house – even this morning.'

I feel as if a fussy cock and two hens had just scurried across my path.

Our little kingdom dreams on. There is no thought in its dream, but only the consciousness of all satisfying light and colour and heat. The mist curtain, thick and golden, wraps it heavily – so heavily that no wind from beyond can even sway its fringe.

In six hours we shall be exiles. We shall have passed the curtain. I can thin it with a wave of my hand. But the present is a warm drowsy calm. There is something of the quiet of exhaustion in it. We suffered so last night.

Sometimes a bee drones softly, aimlessly, over the scented grass. No ship sails the sea; the white light dances fitfully, leaping to and fro over the blue ripples.

Presently we climb down the cliff's edge and seek the House of the Three Brown Stones. At midday the sun

234

scorches very fiercely. I hide my smarting arms under Siegmund's coat. Something in his voice makes me cling to him half savagely when he says, looking wistfully away, 'I *think* I should be able to follow your moods, if – if only I could have you a little longer.'

I will have no mercy on those shadows, the next time they come between us. They may go back to hell.

An hour passes – fleeting before us in sea-woven blue and gold: or perhaps three sister hours, playing on the edge of the foam; or maybe none of these, but a Life, in sheen of countless softened hues. Our eyes are sun-dimmed, and we can scarcely trust our vision.

When the ebbing tide has left the rocks, and the sun has bleached them white, we turn at last from the lonely, lovely shore. Standing silently above, on the grass, we look hopelessly at our beautiful world, and hopelessly at each other.

'Addio!' says Siegmund presently.

Letter from D. H. Lawrence of 21 June 1910, continued from p. 186.

You see, when I am out with you for a day, and you practically ignore my presence all the time! perhaps it is my vanity: the second of your two conclusions 'the giftie'. But you have a wonderful blindness! I am exceedingly sensitive to other people, to their wants and their wishes: you hardly at all. You have a cruel blindness. It is not sexual: that is another mistake you make: it is very rarely sexual. With your spiritual eyes you fix me with a 'stony Britisher'!

I would yield to you if you could lead me deeper into the tanglewood of life, by any path. But you never lead: you hunt from behind, 'jagt man tiefer ins Leben!'[1]

Nay, how gladly will I bend and follow you if you will lead. But you will not. Nor will you walk with me en camerad. You hang away somewhere to the left.

I am wrong to be impatient and ironical; but surely for my impatience we are wiser.

I was thinking today, how can I blame the boys for breaches of discipline? Yet I must not only blame, I must punish. Once I said to myself 'how can I blame? why be angry', then there came a hideous state of affairs. Now I say 'When anger comes with bright eyes he may do his will. In me he will hardly shake off the hand of God. He is one of the archangels, with a fiery sword. God sent him; it is beyond my knowing.'

I ask you for nothing unnatural or forced. But a little thunder may bring rain, and sweet day, out of a stuffy torpor.

I will come and see you after a day or two. Gradually we shall exterminate the sexual part then there will be nothing, and we can part. Inevitably you must go on weed-killing – grass in the gravel path.

Muriel is not coming also this week, she says. I should like to go to 'Louise' on Saturday.

Addio,
D. H. Lawrence.

[1] Quotation from Hauptmann's play, *Elga*, which we had been reading together.